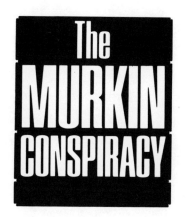

The MURKIN CONSPIRACY

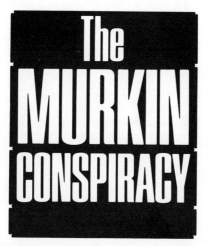

The MURKIN CONSPIRACY

An Investigation into the Assassination of
Dr. Martin Luther King, Jr.

Philip H. Melanson

PRAEGER

New York
Westport, Connecticut
London

Library of Congress Cataloging-in-Publication Data

Melanson, Philip H.
    The Murkin conspiracy.

    Bibliography: p.
    Includes index.
    1. King, Martin Luther, Jr., 1929–1968—Assassination.
    2. Conspiracies—United States. I. Title.
    E185.97.K5M39   1989   364.1′524′0924   88–15262
    ISBN 0–275–93029–7 (alk. paper)

Library of Congress Catalog Card Number: 88–15262
ISBN: 0–275–93029–7

First published in 1989

Praeger Publishers, One Madison Avenue, New York, NY 10010
A division of Greenwood Press, Inc.

Printed in the United States of America

∞

The paper used in this book complies with the
Permanent Paper Standard issued by the National
Information Standards Organization (Z39.48–1984).

10 9 8 7 6 5 4 3 2

The MURKIN* Conspiracy: An Investigation of the Assassination of Dr. Martin Luther King, Jr.

James R. Hoffa did not vanish after a rendezvous with a James Earl Ray "acting alone," loose nuts did not do in the Yablonskis, new editions of Lee Harvey Oswald or Sirhan Sirhan did not murder Sam Giancana in the basement of his home while he was under twenty-four-hour guard by the FBI. It is time to accept the fact that the question is not whether groups with such power exist, but how these groups use their power, who their allies are—in and out of government—and what if anything can be done to protect the democratic process against forces and alliances that operate out of sight and often beyond the limits set by the law.

Allard K. Lowenstein, 1977**

In view of the numerous communications in connection with the case involving the murder of Martin Luther King, Jr., in Memphis Tennessee, on 4/4/68, it is felt that the code name MURKIN should be utilized in order to more efficiently handle the mail. This code name has been checked through the indices and there is no prior record of it having been utilized as a code name.

April 6, 1968 FBI memo, A. Rosen
to Assistant Director De Loach

---

* The code name MURKIN is used to suggest a conspiracy manifesting a clandestine modus operandi and involving elements of American intelligence.

** "Suppressed Evidence of More Than One Assassin," *Saturday Review*, Feb. 19, 1977.

To Robert Emmet Hart

Contents

Photographs

Acknowledgments

The author gratefully acknowledges the numerous persons whose varied levels and types of assistance helped bring this five-year endeavor to fruition. My students at Southeastern Massachusetts University, in senior research seminars and in my course on Political Assassinations in America, have provided questions and insights that both stimulated and aided my research. My colleagues in the political science department have been very supportive. Funds from the university helped with the extensive travel required.

I thank those who, while not necessarily agreeing with my analysis or conclusions, read part or all of the manuscript and gave valuable feedback: especially Professor David Wrone, University of Wisconsin at Stevens Point and Sylvia Meagher. Also, Paul Hoch; Professor Lauriston R. King, Texas A & M University; and my departmental colleague John Carroll, who also took time to listen and advise.

Helpful expertise was provided by Ms. Helen Neer and her staff at the FBI reading room in Washington, D.C.; by Donald Swoger at the *Toronto Star* library; Attorney Dan Bernstein, who assisted with Freedom of Information Act requests, investigative journalists Tony Summers and Dan Moldea; Professor Peter Dale Scott, University of California, Berkeley; and Professor Gerald McKnight, Hood College, Frederick, Maryland. Liz Tucker, our departmental secretary, typed most of the voluminous correspondence. Alyson Wihry helped as my research assistant in 1987–88.

Valuable insights came from Bernard Fensterwald, Jr. (director of the Assassination Archives and Research Center in Washington, D.C.) and his colleague Attorney James H. Lesar. While often disagreeing with my hypotheses, Harold Weisberg gave generously of his vast knowledge of the case and of his files.

Without the strong support of family and friends too numerous to mention, this demanding project would never have been completed. My extended family was an important source of support and was always willing to listen. Of course, my Mom always knew this would be successful. My sons Brett and Jess have been understanding of my workload and of the import of the tasks.

I thank Floyd Nelson for his sustaining wisdom; Larry Schlossman for his sympathetic but hard-nosed counsel; and Paul Schrade for helping to sustain my morale.

My gratitude to those journalists, Canadian and American, who took the time to assist in pursuing the unanswered questions—Jay Walz, formerly of the *New York Times*; Cameron Smith, formerly of the *Toronto Globe and Mail*. Special acknowledgment is due Canadian journalists Earl McRae and Andy Salwyn. They vigorously investigated the Canadian dimension of this case in 1968—more so than some law-enforcement agencies—and they unselfishly shared with me their files and sources.

This book would not have been possible without the information obtained from law-enforcement personnel and citizens—Canadians (such as John Willard) and Americans. These persons were willing to speak, most often on-the-record, when many of their colleagues or contemporaries would not, often because of fears (some logical, some not so logical, some feigned). Eric Galt courageously cooperated in seeking the truth about his 1968 ordeal as an innocent man whose name was usurped by James Earl Ray, not knowing where the trail might lead or how the effort might affect him.

I thank those who came forward to offer material or who leaked it to me (intelligence and law-enforcement people). Though their agendas were usually quite different from mine, they made the work more interesting and my understanding richer.

Susan Pazourek, my editor at Praeger, advanced this book not only with her systematic guidance but with her belief in its potential contributions. Karen O'Brien, senior project editor, provided invaluable assistance.

My gratitude to my research colleague political scientist Greg Stone, who, although not a student of this case, has generously given of his time to proffer general advice and professional support.

By far my largest debt is to my wife Judith. Her skilled and extensive work on all phases of producing the manuscript was essential to its completion and markedly enhanced its quality. Even more important for my efforts on this long, and sometimes difficult enterprise was her support, understanding, patience, encouragement, and willingness to listen and advise—without which I could not have completed the work. For all this, I am extremely grateful.

Introduction

Writing in *Civil Liberties Review* in 1978, Frank Donner unleashed a scathing review of Mark Lane and Dick Gregory's *Code Name Zorro*, which contended that Dr. Martin Luther King, Jr., had been assassinated by a conspiracy involving the Federal Bureau of Investigation (FBI).[1] Donner's review was entitled "Why Isn't the Truth Bad Enough?," a reference to what he viewed as the inability or unwillingness of many Americans to accept the conclusion that deranged individuals acting alone can so profoundly alter our history and our political process. But the truth is only "bad enough" when we know what it is. Otherwise, as Santayana warned, we may be compelled to repeat those historical events that we do not understand.

There have been several versions which, at a given point in time, have passed for "the truth" about the King assassination. In 1968 the official truth was that a small-time criminal named James Earl Ray had acted alone in killing Dr. King, motivated by racism and by a desire for fame, spawned by his stunted self-image.

In the mid–1970s, culminating with the disclosures of the Senate Select Committee on Intelligence (generally known as the Church Committee), America learned the awful truth about Hoover's FBI. The Bureau had engaged in a protracted persecution of Dr. King; it had worked to discredit him, and even to destroy him, both personally and politically. The FBI's illegal vendetta smacked of police-state tactics.[2] Did this revelation change the official version of the truth concerning King's assassination? Was the FBI involved in a conspiracy?

In 1977, prompted by the disclosure of Hoover's war on King, the Carter Justice Department released and endorsed a review of the FBI's investigation of the assassination and of its possible complicity in the murder. The probe found no evidence of a conspiracy: James Earl Ray had acted alone.[3]

In 1978 the House Select Committee on Assassinations (HSCA) offered a radically different version of the truth: namely, that "on the basis of circumstantial evidence available to the committee, James Earl Ray assassinated Dr. Martin Luther King, Jr. as a result of a conspiracy."[4] Did the FBI conspire to assassinate King? No, said the committee. The conspirators who allegedly put a bounty on King were based in St. Louis and included a drug-dealing real estate developer and a wealthy, racist industrialist who was fond of dressing up in a Civil War uniform.[5]

In a way, there was something quite cathartic, even comforting, about the House Assassinations Committee's version of the truth. Hoover and his police-state apparat had not murdered America's greatest civil rights leader. It was instead a sleazy cabal of racist right-wingers who seemed to be behind Ray. King's martyrdom was enhanced by this latest version of the truth: a conspiracy of petty racists had slain the Nobel-prize winning black leader. King had been eliminated by the very same forces that he had fought to overcome on the long road of nonviolent struggle from Birmingham to Memphis.

The House Committee's truth provided a kind of cleansing of the body politic. It was a bad truth, but one that did not involve the federal government or sinister networks of American intelligence. And it did not raise questions about the basic structure of American democracy. Instead, it further exposed the same virulent racism that King himself had worked so hard to illuminate and eradicate.

Yet, the House Assassinations Committee's version of truth was highly speculative. It was supported by only the vaguest circumstantial evidence.

If we eschew both of the rigid mind-sets whose polemics and tunnel vision tend to dominate the analysis of American political assassinations—the first believes that every three coincidences prove a conspiracy; the second believes that every pervasive pattern of conspiratorial evidence can be explained away as coincidence—then we can proceed to another level of truth about the King case. This truth is more valid than those previously offered by official investigations. It is also a worse truth.

The freshest and best evidence precludes not only the possibility that James Earl Ray was a lone assassin but also that a crude and flamboyant conspiracy, allegedly hatched in St. Louis, propelled the assassination by putting up $50,000 to recruit a hit man. The truth of the King assassination is that it was a much more sophisticated conspiracy executed by persons possessing the kind of expertise generally found within intelligence circles.

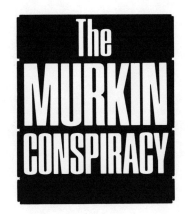

1   Murder In Memphis

" . . . the bullet had entered his right cheek and I patted his left cheek, consoled him, and got his attention by saying, 'This is Ralph, this is Ralph, don't be afraid.' "

Rev. Ralph Abernathy to Martin Luther King, Jr., on the balcony of the Lorraine Motel

Martin Luther King, Jr., had come to Memphis to support the city's 1,100 striking sanitation workers, 90 percent of whom were black.[1] The strikers were protesting for better job safety, working conditions, pay, and against racial discrimination; it was the latter issue that gradually emerged as the main focus. The National Association for the Advancement of Colored People (NAACP) took up the workers' cause. Newly elected Mayor Henry Loeb III refused to negotiate, calling the strike illegal.

On February 23, 1968, the strikers held their first protest march, after the Memphis City Council had refused to listen to their demands. Police handled the march with excessive force, using mace and nightsticks to disperse the crowd. The city went to court and obtained an injunction banning further marches.

King appeared in Memphis on March 18 and gave a speech in support of the strike to 17,000 people. He announced that there would be further action: On March 28 he would lead a citywide demonstration of sympathy for the workers.

But the event was curtailed by violence. As demonstrators marched through the city, rampaging black youths broke store windows and looting occurred. Police, clad in gas masks and riot gear, were poised for a head-bashing assault on the crowd.

Faced with the escalating violence and the prospect of a brutal police attack, King asked that the demonstration be called off. As the situation degenerated even further, his aides feared for his safety. They commandeered a private automobile and whisked King to a nearby Holiday Inn. Back at the scene of the aborted march, police moved on the crowd, wielding mace and nightsticks—and guns. A 16-year-old black youth was shot and killed; 60 persons were injured. King's nonviolent strategy had failed.

The Memphis strike was by no means atypical of King's involvements. The Nobel-prizewinning civil rights leader seemed to galvanize political passions wherever he appeared. The elements present in Memphis—a hostile white power structure, white hate groups, young black militants, and undercover infiltrators and surveillants from both local and federal agencies—were fairly constant in King's political activities.

King departed Memphis after the March 28 debacle. He was back on April 3, intending to conduct successfully a peaceful march. His lawyers went to court seeking to overturn the city's ban on public demonstrations.

The specter of assassination was all too familiar to King. FBI files catalogued no fewer than 50 threats against his life.[2] In addition to threats from white hate groups and violence-prone individuals, King was well aware that the FBI was, as he put it, "out to break me."[3]

In November 1964 the Bureau mailed King a tape recording containing "highlights" from FBI buggings of his hotel rooms.[4] The unsigned letter accompanying the tape implied that he should kill himself rather than face the public humiliation of having the tape exposed: "There is only one thing left for you to do. . . . You are done. There is but one way out for you. You better take it before your filthy, abnormal fraudulent self is bared to the nation."[5]

The night before his assassination, King delivered one of his most stirring speeches. Despite tornado warnings during the afternoon, followed by heavy rain in the evening, a crowd of 2,000 filled the Mason Temple Church to hear what would turn out to be his last speech. Andrew Young, who was then one of King's aides, recalled that the speech was "almost morbid."[6] It concluded with what seemed to be a reference to King's own death.

Well, I don't know what will happen now. We've got some difficult days ahead. But it really doesn't matter to me now, because I've been to the mountaintop. I won't mind.

Like anybody, I'd like to live a long life. Longevity has its place but I'm not concerned about that now. I just want to do God's will and He's allowed me to go up to the mountain. And I've looked over. And I've seen the Promise Land.

So I'm happy tonight. I'm not worried about anything. I'm not fearing any man.[7]

King spent the last day of his life (April 4, 1968) closeted inside the Lorraine Motel conferring with aides and planning strategy for the upcoming demonstration. He made plans to have dinner at the home of Rev. Samuel B. Kyles at six that evening. At 5:30 P.M. Kyles walked into King's motel room and announced, "O.K., Doc, it's time to go."[8]

Kyles noted that King seemed in good spirits as he dressed for dinner. King asked if his tie matched his suit. He teased Kyles about the dinner menu, saying that he had been to dinner at one preacher's home where he was served Kool Aid and cold ham. "I don't want to go to your house for cold food," King jested. (King had instructed Rev. Ralph Abernathy to call ahead and check out the menu, so he already knew that prime rib and hot soul food awaited).[9]

As King finished knotting his tie, he and Kyles stepped out onto the second-floor balcony overlooking the motel's courtyard. King exchanged greetings with several persons who mingled below waiting to join him for dinner. He leaned against the iron railing and instructed Chauncey Eskridge, Southern Christian Leadership Conference (SCLC) general counsel, to invite Jesse Jackson, then an SCLC staff member, to come to Kyles's house for dinner.

King's chauffeur, Solomon Jones, stood in the courtyard next to the funeral-home limousine that served as the civil rights leader's transportation. Nearly a dozen persons, mostly King's aides and associates, waited for his departure.

It was time. Rev. Ralph Abernathy was inside King's room splashing on a final dollop of after-shave lotion. Kyles left King and headed downstairs to get his car. King stood alone on the balcony.

It was 6:01. A single shot from a high-powered rifle cracked through the humid evening air. The bullet tore into the right side of King's face, tossing him violently backward.

Inside King's room Abernathy heard the sound—like a "firecracker"—as he gazed into the mirror. He rushed to the door and looked onto the balcony. Only King's feet were visible: the powerful impact had caused him to reel backward and fall diagonally. Abernathy rushed to King's side. Amid the screams and groans emanating from the courtyard he cried out: "Oh my God, Martin's been shot. . . . This is Ralph, this is Ralph, don't be afraid."[10]

SCLC attorney Chauncey Eskridge heard the "zing" and looked up at the balcony: King had already fallen and Abernathy was at his side.

King's chauffeur, Solomon Jones, was chatting with Andrew Young and James Bevel of the SCLC. At the sound of the shot, Young and Bevel shoved him to the ground. Jones glanced upward and saw King's prone body. Young and Bevel took cover behind the parked limousine. When they looked up, they saw King's feet protruding through the metal railing.

A young black man in the courtyard later testified that he had seen King standing alone, facing a row of rundown buildings on Mulberry Street.[11] As he turned away from King, he heard an explosive sound which he immediately recognized as a gunshot. Turning around, he saw King grab his throat and lurch backward. The young man instantly rushed to the balcony. Upon seeing the massive face wound, he grabbed a towel from a housekeeping tray and tried to stop the bleeding.

The man was Marrell McCullough. He was ostensibly a member of the Memphis Invaders, a militant black group that had helped to ignite the violence which caused the cancellation of the March 28 demonstration. Although it would not be revealed by official investigators in 1968, and although the House Assassinations Committee would conclude that McCullough had no direct relationship with federal intelligence agencies and no involvement in the crime, he was not a black militant at all. Marrell McCullough was an undercover Memphis police officer. His presence—along with other factors to be discussed later—would subsequently raise a series of complex questions concerning who knew what, when, and how about King's movements on the day of his assassination.

Andrew Young arrived at the side of his fallen mentor. He checked for a pulse. "Ralph," Young said to Abernathy, "it's all over."

"Don't say that! Don't say that!" blurted Abernathy.[12]

But it was over, King lay unconscious in an ever-widening pool of blood.

Rev. Samuel Kyles poignantly recalled for the author the horror of the scene, and his reaction to it. "So much blood," said Kyles, "that everyone who went near got it on their clothes. Someone scooped it up in a bucket, later."

In the shock of the moment, Kyles worried about retrieving the cigarette that had been in King's hand. "Martin never smoked in public."[13]

Several men on the balcony pointed to where the shot seemed to originate—the row of ramshackle buildings along Mulberry Street, including Bessie Brewer's rooming house. It was there that James Earl Ray had registered under the alias John Willard that very afternoon. It was there that, according to authorities, the assassin took aim on King, firing from a bathroom window located down the hall from Ray's room.

An ambulance arrived only five minutes after the shooting and sped the victim to St. Joseph's hospital. At 7:05 P.M. the 39-year-old King was pronounced dead. The search for his killer or killers began; 20 years later, it still goes on.

America's cities smoldered as widespread rioting erupted following the murder of the nation's preeminent black political leader. The largest manhunt in the history of law enforcement was launched—the search for the alleged assassin, "Eric S. Galt."

The day following the assassination, U.S. Attorney General Ramsey Clark called a press conference. He assured the country that, "We are getting close" [to an arrest], and stated that he was "extremely confident" of an arrest. He also asserted that the case was believed to involve only one man and that there was no evidence to indicate a conspiracy.[14]

Clark's optimism proved unfounded. An arrest was not made until June 8, more than two months after the assassination. Moreover, while there was only one gun and one bullet fired, there is now overwhelming evidence that the assassination of Dr. Martin Luther King, Jr., could not possibly have been the work of one man.

2   The Mystery of the Aliases

House Assassinations Committee Counsel: "It's just coincidence that there is an Eric Galt that lives near Sneyd, and Bridgeman?"

James Earl Ray: "That's right."

Long before he was charged with assassinating Martin Luther King, Jr., James Earl Ray led a life of crime. He served time for stealing a typewriter in Los Angeles in 1949, for holding up a Chicago cab in 1952, for stealing money orders in Hannibal, Missouri, and cashing them in to take a trip to Florida in 1955, and for a 1959 supermarket heist that netted him $120.[1] Ray made two unsuccessful attempts to break out of the Missouri State Penitentiary, in 1960 and in 1966. On April 23, 1967, a little less than a year before the assassination, he escaped from prison by concealing himself in the back of a bread truck. He would remain free, and a fugitive, until he was arrested in London for King's assassination on June 8, 1968.

Like many criminals, James Earl Ray used aliases to hide his identity from the law. In his criminal activities prior to the King assassination, he used the aliases James McBride, James Walton, W. C. Herron, and James O'Conner. After his escape from prison in April 1967, Ray lived and worked in the Chicago area under the name John Larry Raynes. "John Larry" is the name of one of his two brothers; "Raynes" was the original family name which his father changed to Ray.[2] According to Harold Weisberg, an assassination researcher who has worked on this case since its inception, Ray tended to select as aliases the names of persons known to him—prison associates, a brother, etc.[3] Ray confirmed this during our interview, asserting that he wanted names that were easy to remember.

In his role as either fall guy or hit man for the assassination conspiracy, Ray also used aliases. But there is a conspicuous difference: nearly every alias used by Ray in the nine months before the King assassination was the name of a real Canadian with whom Ray had no prior association or familiarity. As Weisberg puts it: "In every case it was someone he knew, except the Canadian ones. That's what makes them so interesting."[4]

During the nine-month period leading up to the assassination, Ray's use of aliases was as follows.[5] In July 1967, Ray went to Montreal, Canada, where he used the name Eric Starvo Galt. The Galt name was the main alias used by Ray for the next nine months. He established credentials for it—an Alabama driver's license, various letters and certificates.[6]

On March 29, 1968, Ray purchased a .243 caliber rifle and telescopic sight at the Aeromarine Supply Company in Birmingham, Alabama. The next day he returned it and replaced it with a more powerful rifle—the .30–06 Remington Gamesmaster that was found near the crime scene in Memphis. For these transactions, Ray used the name Harvey Lowmeyer. This was the only time Ray used the name, and he had no identification or credentials for this alias. It was the only alias used in the nine months prior to the assassination that was not the name of a real Canadian. Like the names used by Ray in his earlier criminal activities, Harvey Lohmeyer was an American known to Ray. Harvey Edward Lohmeyer had worked in a prison kitchen with Ray's brother John in Illinois during the late 1950s. Lohmeyer told the FBI that he had heard about James Earl Ray, but did not know him.[7]

Ray arrived in Memphis the day before the assassination. According to Ray, he was there to consummate a gunrunning deal. He checked into the New Rebel Motel using his primary alias—Eric S. Galt. Then, the day of the assassination, Ray checked into Bessie Brewer's boarding house across from the Lorraine Motel. At Brewer's he used the name John Willard. This is his only use of the Willard alias, for which Ray had no credentials or paper trail. Both Galt and Willard are real Canadians living near Toronto.

When he fled to Toronto in the wake of the assassination, Ray first used his old standby, the Galt alias. Then he took a room on Ossington Street under the name Paul E. Bridgeman. Later he took another room on Dundas Street under the name Ramon George Sneyd. Ray obtained a false Canadian passport in the name of Sneyd and took a plane to London, where he was arrested on June 8. The Bridgeman and Sneyd aliases were the names of individuals living near Toronto in 1968.

By all the available evidence and by his own account, Ray had never been to Toronto prior to his arrival on April 8, 1968, after fleeing the scene of the King assassination. Yet, four of the five aliases used by Ray in the nine months preceding the crime were real Canadians who lived in close proximity to each other. All four resided in Scarborough, a sprawling mix of suburban neighborhoods and industrial complexes bordering Toronto's eastern boundary. In 1968 the Toronto metropolitan area had 2.5 million inhabitants; Scarborough was approximately 60 square miles in area. Galt, Sneyd, and Bridgeman lived in a triangular cluster, approximately 1 3/4 miles from each other. Willard lived approximately 3 miles south of this triangle.[8]

The geographic proximity of the four aliases is dwarfed by the striking physical similarities shared by Ray and the Torontoans. Three of the aliases—Galt, Bridgeman, and Sneyd—very closely approximated Ray's general appearance (height, weight, hair color).[9] Willard was the least compatible of the four but still had ball-park compatibility on some basic characteristics. With the exception of Willard's being significantly shorter than Ray, the four aliases fail to manifest any of the salient discrepancies that might crop up in any random selection of names—corpulence, baldness, conspicuous youth or advanced age, color of complexion. In 1968 James Earl Ray was 40 years old, five feet ten inches tall, and weighed approximately 170 to 175 pounds.[10]

Paul Edward Bridgeman was 35 years old, six feet tall, and weighed approximately 170 pounds.[11] He worked for the Toronto Board of Education as the coordinator of the Language Studies Program for the primary schools. Bridgeman was also the epitome of the *good citizen*—married, father of two, and described by his supervisor, Donald Rutledge, as "Mr. Clean." "It's ironic," said Rutledge, "that he [Ray] would use Paul's name. If I would trust my life to anyone, it's Paul Bridgeman."[12]

Police showed Bridgeman a picture of Ray, which he did not recognize.[13] Since Ray adopted the Bridgeman alias after arriving in Toronto, police asked Bridgeman if his home had been broken into or if his IDs or mail or any of his possessions had been lost or stolen. The answer was negative: nothing unusual had occurred in Bridgeman's life prior to learning that his name had been usurped by an infamous fugitive. In fact, Bridgeman did not discover that his name had been used until after Canadian authorities had questioned him.[14] The Royal Canadian Mounted Police (RCMP) quizzed him and cautioned him not to discuss his questioning with anyone, but they did not tell him why he was being questioned. The day following his RCMP interview, Bridgeman went to his summer cottage and was aghast to hear his name broadcast on the radio in connection with Ray's arrest.[15]

The House of Representatives Select Committee on Assassinations

(HSCA) claimed that during its reinvestigation it could not find Paul Bridgeman. Through his former employer, the author did locate him. Bridgeman refused to respond to the author's attempts to discover how Ray obtained the Toronto aliases. As will become clear from the experiences of the other aliases—two of whom did cooperate—having one's name suddenly surface in connection with the world's most publicized fugitive is an ordeal that some persons would sooner not relive, even decades later.

This seems to have been the case with a second Toronto alias, Ramon George Sneyd. In 1968 Sneyd was a 35-year-old Toronto police officer. He has since retired. Sneyd refused to respond to my requests, even though a police colleague of Sneyd's, who was convinced of the historical import of the research, interceded on my behalf.

Several Toronto police officers with whom I discussed the case expressed outrage—still strong 16 years later—that one of their own would be victimized by an infamous American fugitive. "That poor fellow," says Deputy Chief Bernard Simmonds, referring to Sneyd. "The poor man is totally innocent!" he protests, as if Sneyd's innocence were somehow in doubt.[16]

One Toronto officer, who requests anonymity, insists that Sneyd was chosen as an alias precisely because he was a Toronto police officer, although the officer is not certain why. Perhaps, he speculates, Sneyd was selected in order to distract the police investigation. The use of Sneyd's name contributed to the suspicions of some Toronto law-enforcement personnel that the King assassination involved a complex, sophisticated plot.

The sense of outrage, and anxiety, felt by Ramon George Sneyd in 1968 must indeed have been strong. Like Bridgeman, Sneyd first heard his name surface on Saturday, June 8, when it was broadcast by the media. "I heard it on television while watching the Kennedy [Robert F. Kennedy] funeral," said Sneyd.[17]

The 14-year police veteran told reporters: "I never saw or knew of him [Ray]."[18] Sneyd had not been robbed nor had he lost any identification. "I have no idea where he got the information."[19]

Sneyd's status as a respected police officer did not protect him from being pressured by the press. At one point when he apologized to a reporter because he could not talk about the case per order of his superiors, he was misquoted as saying, "I hope I will be forgiven when it all comes out." Sneyd's apology to the reporter was misrepresented as an apology for his linkage to the assassination.[20]

Reporters called Sneyd late at night to expound their latest theories on how Ray might have obtained his name.[21] The gag order imposed by his superiors did not help his relations with reporters. "I can't talk now," Sneyd told them. "You will have to go to someone in authority to find out what you want to know." The *Toronto Telegram* huffed that Sneyd would not even admit that he was a policeman.[22]

Like Bridgeman, Sneyd closely approximated Ray's general appearance in height, weight, and hair color.[23]

James Earl Ray used John Willard's name only once—to rent a room in Bessie Brewer's boarding house across from the Lorraine Motel. Authorities deduced that the shot was fired from a bathroom down the hall from his room. In 1968 Willard was a 43-year-old insurance appraiser. Of the four Toronto aliases, he was the only one whose physical characteristics did not closely approximate Ray's. Willard did have dark hair, but he was five feet eight inches tall (Ray was five feet ten inches) and weighed 150 pounds (Ray weighed about 170).[24]

Of all of the Toronto men whose names Ray used, Willard was the least willing to talk to the press in 1968. To his surprise, the House Assassinations Committee did not interview him. HSCA claimed that it could not locate him.[25] In 1981 Willard was approached by the Canadian Broadcast Corporation, which was considering making a television documentary on the Toronto dimension of the King case. After thinking it over, he declined to be interviewed.

Unlike the House Assassinations Committee, I had little trouble in locating John Willard, but considerable trouble in getting him to talk.[26] The 1968 experience had been a traumatic one. The media hounded him unmercifully, day and night. Willard and his wife were scared and had a sick infant daughter to tend to. His refusal to talk precipitated such warnings from rejected reporters as "You better talk to us or you'll be in deep trouble with the police."[27]

My first contacts with Willard were not productive. When he received my letter, he turned it over to his daughters, then 14 and 16, thinking that they might respond since it "had to do with history." Willard recounted that his older daughter warned him that he didn't really know what it had to do with; the younger daughter had no idea what history was being referred to and had to be given a library book on the King assassination, in which her father's name appeared.[28] Mrs. Willard told me by phone that she was sure her husband would not want to talk about the matter. Despite my sympathetic assurances, she blurted: "It was totally innocent."[29]

After a series of telephone conversations culminating in our meeting in Toronto, the soft-spoken, reserved 58-year-old insurance adjuster became not only cooperative but enthusiastic about the process of historical reconstruction, after receiving a negative response to his question as to whether my work—and, implicitly, his participation in it—was dangerous.[30]

Like the other Toronto men, Willard had not been robbed, lost no

IDs, etc. I asked him if he had ever engaged in defense-related work (as had the real Eric S. Galt) or served in the military. He responded negatively.

Willard has never talked with any of the other three men whose names Ray used, although they live very near to him. But he has always been troubled by something he read in the papers in 1968—that James Earl Ray had a scar on his face, as did the real Eric Galt. During our interview Willard pointed to a clearly visible two-inch scar on the right side of his cheek just below his eye. He wondered whether it was coincidence: Galt and Ray have scars on the right side of their face but above the eyebrow.

John Willard had a theory about how Ray got his name. We drove to the older section of Toronto where Ray rented a room at 102 Ossington Street. Except for a few cosmetic changes, the neighborhood has remained basically as it was in 1968—a mix of three-story, Victorian-style houses and brick storefronts, with wide streets etched by trolley tracks and lined with shade trees.

Directly across the street from Ray's room at 102 Ossington Street is what was then Bart's Body Shop, an auto repair establishment. In 1968 Willard made frequent visits to Bart's, to appraise damaged automobiles and to keep tabs on the work being done for his insurance company. During the period from April 8 to April 21 when Ray was on Ossington Street, Willard estimates that he made five to six visits to Bart's. Each time, he parked his car in the lot adjacent to the body shop and carefully placed his business card in the windshield, as a way of legitimizing his parking there.

Willard pointed out that it would have been very easy for Ray to spot him entering Bart's, then get his name from the business card. He recalled that Bart, the proprietor, had told him that Ray wandered into the shop on several occasions and observed the work being done.

There is a basic problem with this explanation. Ray used Willard's name in Memphis *before* fleeing to Toronto. There is no evidence that Ray was ever in Toronto prior to the assassination. Willard seemed to find this chilling. We explored other possibilities.

"I've never been involved with the law," Willard asserted with pride. "I have no record." Upon lengthy debriefing, however, it turned out that Willard had been briefly involved with the law as the victim in an auto accident in the United States. In September 1964, while Ray languished in prison, Willard and his wife were driving just north of Atlanta when their car was rammed by a vehicle driven by an escaped convict. The accident was serious. Mrs. Willard was taken to a nearby hospital and X-rayed. Naturally, detailed police reports were generated.

Willard was a car-racing enthusiast who traveled to the U.S. almost every year during the mid to late 1960s—to Daytona, Indianapolis, the West Coast. In 1965 he had been through Tennessee, but not Memphis.

In 1967 he had driven to Florida. His travels in the U.S. and his inter-action with local law officers are similar to the experiences of Ray's primary alias—Eric S. Galt.

Unlike the other Toronto aliases, the Galt name was used consistently by Ray for nine months prior to the assassination, and it was substan-tively documented. The other Toronto men were shocked and embar-rassed by the usurpation of their names; but, for Galt, the risk went far beyond negative publicity. His name served as *the* cover identity for the alleged assassin. "Galt" was the subject of a worldwide manhunt. James Earl Ray had used the name to rent apartments, purchase the car alleged to have been the assassination get-away vehicle, obtain a driver's license, have plastic surgery, attend bartending school, take a locksmithing course, and rent a safe deposit box.[31] Most importantly, he had used it to rent a room in Memphis the day before King was shot, and he used it when he first fled to Toronto after the assassination.[32]

In 1968, Eric S. Galt was 54 years old; Ray was only 40. But Galt had a rugged, youthful appearance and looked to be in his forties.[33] Galt was five feet eleven inches tall and weighed 180 pounds.[34] He had dark brown hair. He also had two scars—one on the palm of his right hand, another on his forehead (just barely to the right of his nose). So did James Earl Ray.[35]

In Canadian and American newspaper accounts from 1968, there was never any mention of the color of Galt's eyes. Since the press was fo-cusing on similarities, I assumed this was because the color was in no way compatible with Ray's. Upon interviewing Galt, however, I dis-covered that his eyes were greenish-blue, not at all incompatible with Ray's "blue-eyed" fugitive description.

Up until 1966, Galt had a very distinctive way of signing his name. His middle name was St. Vincent. He abbreviated this to the initials "St. V." For the two periods he drew two zeroes. The result was a unique, difficult-to-read scrawl that, as the press noted in 1968, looked remark-ably like Starvo. The author has further discovered that when James Earl Ray first used the Galt alias, he used the name Eric Starvo Galt. Then he switched to simply Eric S. Galt. This is the same switch the real Galt made in 1966.

There are more intriguing facts about Galt. He was a crack rifle shot and secretary of the Viking Gun Club.[36] He worked as a warehouse supervisor at Union Carbide in Toronto, in an area where top-secret military work was performed. In 1968 he was the only Eric S. Galt in all of Canada.[37]

Galt's experience in 1968 was a difficult one. His first encounter with the name Eric Starvo Galt came approximately two weeks after the as-sassination when he saw it mentioned in a Toronto newspaper describ-ing the worldwide manhunt.[38] At first, Galt was not upset that a name so similar to his had gained such infamous status. But his ordeal had not yet begun. Subsequently, he was grilled by authorities about whether he had an alibi for the day of the assassination. He did: He was at work at Union Carbide. Then the crank phone calls began and continued day and night. His bosses at Carbide warned him that some "nut" might take a pot shot at him.[39] Jay Walz, who covered the alias story for the *New York Times* in 1968, told the author that Galt was "very reluctant" to be interviewed.[40] Who can blame him? Because Galt's name received worldwide notoriety, the problem did not end after the case had been closed. Galt recounted an experience he had in 1970 when he drove into a Chicago gas station. After Galt proferred his credit card, the attendant asked him how things were up in Scarborough. This surprised Galt since the name of his home town did not appear on the card. As Galt drove off, the attendant yelled, "I always thought they got the wrong man."

In 1968 Galt had been quoted as saying, "It seems like more than just a coincidence that he [Ray] used that name. There were so many similarities between Ray and myself."[41] In 1984, we were to discover more "similarities" between Ray and Galt—their travels, their use and abandonment of "Starvo," their trips to Ossington Street. In a process that began in March 1984 when I first contacted Galt, we have exchanged data, queries, and documents.

Despite the passage of 16 years, Galt was determined to find the truth. Motivated by a combination of indignation and intellectual curiosity, he worked enthusiastically to provide whatever information I requested. Comparing himself to the other Toronto aliases, he observed, "I'm the one whose real identity was used, not just a name."[42]

Galt had no theory, only his gut feeling that, "It was all too pat to be coincidence." He has never talked with any of the other aliases. Incredibly, the man whose identity was used by the convicted assassin of Martin Luther King, Jr., was never interviewed by the House Assassinations Committee.

In 1984 I interviewed Galt at his home—in the same house in Scarborough in which he lived in 1968—located in a quiet, treelined middle-class neighborhood. He was then 69 but appeared to be in his late fifties or early sixties. His hair was now gray; his scars, still visible. Galt proved to be an able source. He was energetic, mentally crisp, and thoughtful in his responses. His recall was excellent, aided by his longstanding hobbies. While many people would be hard-pressed to remember what they were doing in a given month 16 or 18 years ago, Galt's hobbies—collecting minerals, participating in the local gun club, scuba diving—provided a detailed record of his travels and whereabouts. Galt had gun-club records that he kept as secretary; he had mineral and coral samples tagged by date and place of collection—Miami, Georgia, Tennessee.

The House Assassinations Committee, which could not locate Willard and did not talk to Galt, claimed to have thoroughly investigated the possible similarities or linkages among the four Toronto men. HSCA's only discovery was that Bridgeman and Sneyd had the same doctor.[43] In actuality, Willard and Galt shared certain experiences that appear much more potentially relevant to the case than does having the same doctor. For two men who didn't know each other, Galt and Willard had a lot in common besides living in the same section of Scarborough.[44]

Galt, like Willard, traveled extensively throughout the U.S. on annual vacation trips during the 1960s. His scuba-diving club drove to Miami in the spring or summer of each year. On the way, he would pursue mineral samples in a variety of locations in the eastern and southeastern United States. Both Galt and Willard visited Miami—Galt in 1967, Willard in either 1966 or 1967 (he is not sure which).

While Ray was confined to prison, Galt and Willard traveled through southern locations that would later be visited by Ray while using the name Galt—Alabama, Georgia, Tennessee. Galt passed through Birmingham, Alabama, in 1966 and 1967; Willard motored through Georgia in 1965 and had his auto accident then; Galt visited Warm Springs, Georgia, in 1966. Willard passed through Tennessee in 1965, but not Memphis. Galt visited Memphis in 1966.

Like Willard, Eric S. Galt also left a paper trail within a local southern law-enforcement bureaucracy. In the summer of 1967 Galt's scuba club was using a Miami diving shop as its temporary home base. A thief entered the shop in broad daylight and walked out with some very expensive scuba gear. Galt saw the man leave but assumed that the equipment had been purchased. When he learned of the robbery, Galt called the Dade County police offering to identify the thief, and later did so at police headquarters. Galt's statement was a formal part of the case record.

Ray, Galt, and Willard seemed to gravitate toward the same Toronto neighborhood. Willard frequented Bart's Body Shop, directly across the street from Ray's apartment. Galt's scuba club met in a rented room only two blocks from Ray's room.

The aliases used by a criminal are typically viewed by investigators as providing some insight into the modus operandi of the crime and/or the psyche of the perpetrator. How did Ray obtain his Toronto aliases before he'd ever been to Toronto? Are the striking similarities simply a matter of coincidence, as Ray claims? The failure to produce any plausible explanation for the mystery of the aliases has flawed every official investigation, both American and Canadian.

3   The New, Official Six-Million-Dollar Truth

> But it [the House Assassinations Committee investigation of both the JFK and King cases] was intense and wide ranging. Trips were made to foreign countries, including Mexico, Canada, Portugal, England, and Cuba. In all, there were 562 trips to 1,463 points for over a total of 4,758 days in the field; 335 witnesses were heard . . . ; a total of more than 4,924 interviews were conducted; 524 subpoenas were issued; and immunity orders wee obtained for 165 witnesses.
>
> G. Robert Blakey, Chief Counsel, HSCA

> "REALITY IS IRRELEVANT"
> Inscription on the front of t-shirts made up by HSCA staff members disgruntled with aspects of the JFK investigation

The House Select Committee spent two and a half years and $6 million investigating the assassinations of President Kennedy and Dr. King. The committee concluded that James Earl Ray was the assassin, but that there was a "likelihood" that a St. Louis-based conspiracy had encouraged him.[1]

In March 1978 the FBI brought to the committee's attention a 1974 Bureau report in which Russell Byers, a St. Louis underworld figure, told an FBI informant that he had been offered money to assassinate King. Byers later told the committee that in late 1966 or early 1967, John Kaufman, a St. Louis criminal type who allegedly dealt drugs, approached him and asked if he would like to make $50,000. That very evening, Byers claimed, he and Kaufman went to the home of John Sutherland, a wealthy St. Louis patent attorney and right-winger.

Byers recounted how he and Kaufman went into Sutherland's study to find the host seated amidst a cache of Civil War memorabilia, complete with a large rug designed in the image of a Confederate flag. In keeping with this ambiance, Sutherland was decked out in a Confederate colonel's uniform, complete with hat. The host allegedly offered $50,000 to kill King, or to arrange to have him killed. Byers's story is that he told Sutherland he would think it over, then left; but nothing ever happened, to Byers's knowledge.

HSCA found Byers's story credible. The committee concluded:

Although the investigation was hampered by the death of many of the principals, the Committee uncovered enough evidence to be convinced that the Byers allegation was essentially truthful. There was in existence in 1966 or 1967, a St. Louis conspiracy actively soliciting the assassination of Dr. King.[2]

Sutherland's bona fides as a right-winger certainly seemed solid enough. An organizer of the local White Citizens Council and a member of the ultraconservative Southern States Industrial Council, he may have put out a "standing offer" to have King killed, as HSCA alleges. One cannot help but wonder how unique this St. Louis situation was, circa 1966–67—whether in 3 or 13 or 30 other cities in the U.S., cliques of right-wing racists, Minutemen, KKK'ers, or Nazis plotted the funding of King's murder. The real question is not whether there was motive and madness in St. Louis but whether anyone in this particular coterie had any actual role in King's assassination.

The House Committee satisfied itself that it had discovered enough possible linkages between Ray and the alleged Sutherland offer to conclude that Ray was probably responding to it.[3] One of Kaufman's friends was Dr. Hugh Maxey, who served as the prison doctor at Missouri State Penitentiary while Ray was serving time there. Moreover, John Paul Spika, Russell Byers's brother-in-law, was a fellow inmate of Ray's and worked as an orderly in the prison hospital under Dr. Maxey.

Another possible linkage between Ray and the Sutherland offer was the Grape Vine Tavern in St. Louis, owned by Ray's sister Carol and managed by his brother John. This rough-and-tumble bar, located in the seedy south side, served as a watering hole for underworld types and petty criminals, a place where people went to make criminal contacts. John Kaufman frequented the Grape Vine. Thus, HSCA concluded, James Earl Ray could have heard it through the grape vine.

According to HSCA, the Grape Vine Tavern was also a hotbed of right-wing politics. The local headquarters for George Wallace's American Independent Party was across the street. Wallace organizers and supporters dropped in for drinks. The wealthy Sutherland reportedly was a big Wallace backer, personally paying the $600-per-month salary of the state chairman of the American Independent Party.

Despite all of this sociometric data and the accompanying conspiratorial flow charts churned out by the committee, there is no firm evidence that a St. Louis conspiracy was ever operationalized. As HSCA admitted:

Ultimately, however, the Committee's investigation of the St. Louis conspiracy proved frustrating. . . . Direct evidence that would connect the conspiracy in St. Louis to [the] assassination was not obtained. . . . Nevertheless, in light of the several alternative routes established by the evidence which information of the offer could have reached James Earl Ray, the Committee concluded that it was likely that he was aware of the existence of the St. Louis offer.[4]

Such tenuous reasoning is hardly sufficient to warrant either historical or investigative closure on the case. Then Congressman and Committee member Christopher Dodd (Dem., Conn.) dissented from the committee's conclusion:

The evidence which the Committee musters may suggest the outlines of a conspiracy, but, in my opinion, it falls short. After reviewing the evidence I am unable to say with any degree of certainty who conspired with James Earl Ray or under what plan they were acting.[5]

The committee's second most important finding was that: "No federal, state, or local agency was involved in the assassination of Dr. King."[6] HSCA's primary—nearly exclusive—focus in this regard was the role of the FBI, because of Hoover's legendary vendetta against King. The Memphis Police Department was also scrutinized for possible conspiratorial involvement. None was found. That no federal agency was involved is a very broad conclusion, considering that only one federal agency was investigated. It apparently never occurred to the committee that Hoover's pathological hatred of King was by no means the only federal-level motive for wanting King dead. As will later become clear from the CIA's own documents, that agency, for one, had intelligence indicating that Martin Luther King, Jr., constituted a threat to national security—particularly to the Vietnam War effort. In the perception of American intelligence, King was surely the most dangerous man in America. His putative Communist ties and sexual activities, coupled with his awesome abilities at political mobilization, caused him to be viewed as a potential Communist weapon of the first magnitude: through blackmail or ideological sympathy, he could be used by the Communists to undermine America's Vietnam War policies. Even so, the House Committee did not investigate the possible involvement of CIA or military intelligence or of some quasi-federal intelligence apparat melding public and private intelligence operations.

HSCA's investigation of the FBI was seriously flawed. Having concluded, based on what Ray might have known, that there was probably a St. Louis-based conspiracy, the committee proceeded to absolve the FBI of any complicity based on what the Bureau might have behaved like if it had been involved. Employing logic so simplistic it might have been lifted from a primer issued by the Warren Commission, HSCA concluded that the proof that the FBI did not set King up for assassination lay in the fact that when Ray arrived in Memphis he did not immediately take a room near the Lorraine, where King was already staying. Ray first checked into a distant motel, then moved to the rooming house near the Lorraine, the day after he arrived.

HSCA reasoned that if the FBI had set up the assassination, it would have to have had control over Ray. HSCA further concluded that: "Ray's presence at the New Rebel Motel on April 3 was evidence that it [FBI] did not have such control."[7] Evidently it never occurred to the committee that in a well-planned assassination, the conspirators might elect to keep their trigger man away from the target area for as long as possible, to reduce the chances that he could be identified after the shooting. The committee never defended the logic that a hit man must be dispatched to the crime scene as soon as he arrives in town.

With similarly dubious reasoning, HSCA decided that the fact that the FBI continued its dirty tricks against King, right up to the time of the assassination, was exculpatory of the Bureau. After all, deduced the committee:

It would hardly have been necessary to continue a nationwide program of harassment against a man soon to be killed. In a review of all COINTELPRO files on Dr. King, the committee found substantive evidence that the harassment program showed no signs of abatement as the fateful day approached.[8]

HSCA did not recognize the possibility that the Bureau might be providing a cover for its complicity, or that the agents who ran COINTELPRO might not be the ones who plotted the assassination. Such simplistic thinking regarding the compartmentalized, convoluted turf of clandestine activities was manifested all too frequently in the committee's investigation.

By similar logic, there is a litmus test for determining Hoover's personal complicity. If at 5:30 P.M. on the day of the assassination J. Edgar took his usual corner table in the plush, dimly lit, warrenlike environs of Harvey's Restaurant, and if he lingered over his two pre-dinner martinis (as he did habitually), then the committee could argue, albeit unpersuasively, that Hoover was not involved. Since, in the committee's view, business-as-usual constituted an alibi, the committee would probably reason that if Hoover knew of King's impending murder, he would make sure he was near an FBI teletype and close to his phone, so he could monitor the murder of his arch enemy.

In a related matter, the committee went to great lengths to try to establish that Marrell McCullough, the undercover Memphis policeman who was at the Lorraine posing as a black militant, was not an FBI employee; and that, further, the Bureau wasn't aware that McCullough was a policeman.[9] This, the committee believed, was further evidence that the FBI was not involved. However, within the context of what the FBI could have known, the committee missed or totally neglected the presence of an FBI informant within King's SCLC, as revealed by David J. Garrow in his book on the FBI's surveillance of King.

The informant was in place from 1965 right up to the assassination. According to Garrow, this operative "soon eclipsed the wiretaps on the SCLC office as the Bureau's most valuable source of information on King."[10] The FBI's spy was with King in Memphis the day before the assassination, then departed for Atlanta.[11] While there is no evidence that the informant played any role in the assassination, the point is that the HSCA's attempt to absolve the FBI by analyzing the resources and information available to the Bureau was glaringly superficial.

So too was the HSCA's investigation of the crucial question of Ray's aliases. The matter of the aliases was described by committee staff as: "a matter of primary interest because of the almost unbelievable nature of the coincidences involved" and because of its "possible sinister implications."[12] Ultimately, HSCA's faith in the validity of coincidence as an explanatory variable remained resolute. The coincidences were described as "remarkable," as "almost" unbelievable, but the committee still perceived them as coincidences.[13]

Ray's eight interviews with HSCA produced no logical answer as to how he obtained his aliases. The committee staff described Ray's responses as "highly incredible."[14] Thus the committee had to find its own explanation.

Committee investigators claimed to have "carefully examined" the possible linkages among the four Toronto men whose names Ray used.[15] Yet they could not locate two of the four (Willard and Bridgeman),[16] nor did they bother to interview Galt.

HSCA's staff groped to explain the striking similarities among the aliases. It discovered that none had reported losing any identification, nor could it find any meaningful linkages among them. However, in touting the superiority of its investigative efforts, the committee staff offered the lame finding that whereas the FBI and RCMP could find no interconnections among any of these gentlemen, HSCA did find one: "Committee counsel and investigators learned from Mr. Sneyd that he and Mr. Bridgeman utilized the same Toronto doctor, Marvin Maxman."[17]

There was no suggestion that this had any relevance to the case, except to demonstrate how dogged the committee's investigation was. It is almost as if the committee had become so enamored with coincidences that it wanted to find more of them. Had it continued its dogged pursuit of such data, it might have discovered that all four men rooted for the Toronto Argonauts or drank Molson beer.

HSCA's investigative staff also floated the bald notion that, "It is possible that Ray traveled to these neighborhoods to check the appearance of the men whose names he was to adopt."[18] While it is remotely possible that this applies to Bridgeman and Sneyd—both men were listed in the 1968 Toronto phone book and a Toronto map left behind by Ray had marks near their addresses—this cannot apply to Galt and Willard. Ray used these aliases in the United States before he had been to Toronto.

Regarding the false Sneyd passport obtained by Ray in Canada, the committee was impressed when a knowledgeable RCMP officer reported that Ray could easily have purchased "a complete set of false identification in his own neighborhood for as little as $5."[19] This is what Committee Chief Counsel G. Robert Blakey meant when he told the author that Ray got his false passport "the hard way": Ray supposedly researched an alias then applied for a passport when, for five dollars, he could have simply purchased phony credentials.[20] To HSCA, this was persuasive evidence that Ray acted entirely alone with no outside help.

From another perspective, however, Ray's failure to avail himself of the local black market in IDs fits perfectly with the notion that he did have help. It is only if one believes Ray's conflicting and implausible stories (as examined in the next chapter) about how he got his aliases that his failure to purchase an instant ID means that he got them on his own, the hard way. If, as is highly probable, the conspirators provided Ray with his very compatible aliases, then he did not obtain them the hard way even though he had no need of the services of Toronto's criminal element.

Despite its attempts to dispense with the alias question by shrouding it under a cloak of coincidence and by offering up pseudo-explanations, HSCA finally admitted that "the alias question is still, regrettably, considered open."[21]

The committee did investigate the Toronto dimension of the case, beyond the alias question. It looked into Ray's possible contacts. As with its investigation of possible federal involvement, the Toronto probe was narrow and superficial. The committee believed that the most inhibiting factor in its work north of the border was that it was operating in a foreign country. In reality, it was HSCA's preconceived notions about the case and the way in which it posed the questions to be pursued that presented the most formidable barriers to progress.

Chief Counsel Blakey told the author: "You can't just march up to a foreign country and investigate."[22] After months of negotiations with the Canadian government, the committee finally sent a contingent to Ottawa to meet with the RCMP and the Canadian Department of Internal Affairs. The Canadians were not inclined to allow a freewheeling investigative foray by a foreign government, and certain restrictions were placed on the HSCA.[23]

The restrictions turned out to be somewhat inhibiting. Blakey indicated that the committee got everything it wanted by way of file material, "but in terms of talking to citizens, we did not."[24] Some potential witnesses refused to talk.

The HSCA's Canadian investigation focused on three areas: how Ray obtained his false Canadian passport, whether he had any "criminal associations" in Canada before or after the assassination, and his financial transactions.[25] There is considerable evidence that Ray had contacts in Canada and that he received help. There were phone calls to him, mysterious visitors, a drinking companion. As we shall see later, the available data strongly suggests that the so-called "fat man" who visited Ray at his rooming house was a courier, however unwitting, who delivered an envelope containing money for Ray's escape to London.

Still, the committee stated that it "did not find that Ray had any criminal associates, nor did he receive any financial assistance during his April 8 to May 6 stay in Canada."[26] Nowhere in its final report or in the 13 volumes of published material is there any indication of a serious investigative effort in this regard. The crucial "fat man" incident was completely neglected.

Blakey told the author:

We went up there [Canada] thinking that there might be something sinister and came away with the idea that there was nothing sinister. The Canadian dimension to what he [Ray] did was just not all that significant. The idea that he had help and, therefore, that there was a dimension of conspiracy was very popular at the time [1968]. But we found out that he could have done it [gotten a passport] easier had he had access to the criminal underworld. He did it by using newspapers.[27]

In 1968 Canadian authorities speculated that Ray had sophisticated help in obtaining a false passport.[28] It turned out that Canadian passport procedures were quite lax. As Blakey described, "We verified how easy it was to get a passport."[29] It could be gotten by looking up a birth notice, writing for a birth certificate under the name selected, then applying for a passport—all without any criminal or intelligence expertise. But Blakey and the committee confused the possibility that Ray could have gotten a passport without help with the certainty that he had no help of any kind. HSCA admitted: "Like the RCMP and the FBI, the Committee was unable to resolve the question of how Ray obtained the aliases he used."[30] Thus the finding that there is "no evidence that Ray used a passport ring" hardly constitutes proof that there was no conspiratorial assistance.

Whether in science or sleuthing, perspective is a crucial variable in determining what the investigator will find. G. Robert Blakey had spent most of his distinguished career researching and investigating organized crime—as chief counsel for the McClellan Committee in the U.S. Senate, as a special prosecutor in Robert F. Kennedy's Justice Department. Under Blakey's stewardship, HSCA seemed to be more attuned to underworld dimensions than to intelligence-related dimensions.[31] The committee searched for Ray's "criminal associates" rather than for his intelligence handlers or for couriers. It looked exclusively for a "passport ring," for "access to help from the criminal underworld," but it never looked for clandestine, intelligence-based sources of assistance.

Clandestine assassination conspiracies do not depend upon purchasing aliases or false IDs from "alias rings." Instead, they create their own covers for assassins or for patsies. Sometimes, as in the King case, they do so by using official files.

4   Who Didn't Know What, When, and How

House Assassinations Committee counsel: "How did it come about that you used the Galt name?"
James Earl Ray: "I have no idea."

The physical similarity and geographic proximity of Ray's aliases, along with the fact that he adopted the Galt and Willard aliases before he'd ever been to Toronto, have obvious conspiratorial implications. Discovering the origin of the aliases became one of the key questions in determining whether there was a conspiracy and, if so, who the conspirators were. Neither American nor Canadian authorities provided viable answers; nor has James Earl Ray.

At least Canadian authorities were open-minded about the case in 1968. Given Ray's Toronto aliases and the evidence of apparent contacts, a Royal Canadian Mounted Police (RCMP) spokesman told the press in June 1968 that Ray was part of a "huge conspiracy," that: "He didn't come into this city and make all his own arrangements. There was help of some kind."[1] Similarly, Toronto Police Officer Bernard Simmonds stated that Ray undoubtedly received support of some kind, and police believed that it was "organized" help.[2] While a conspiracy seemed very logical to Canadian authorities, U.S. authorities continued to insist that there was no conspiracy. This, even before Ray was captured and questioned, even when the FBI was mistakenly looking for Eric Starvo Galt.

It is as if there were two cases—American and Canadian—defined less by international boundaries than by psychological ones. To U.S. authorities, this was a manhunt for a lone assassin who had murdered for racist motives. To the Canadians, the case was so fraught with intrigue that it must have seemed at times to have sprung from the pages of a Le Carré novel: a nearly perfect cover identity, the mysterious "fat man," unexplained phone calls.

The author reasoned that Canadian authorities might prove to be a richer source of data, because they had been willing to consider seriously the possibility of a conspiracy; and, unlike their American counterparts, did not seem wedded to the mythology of the lone, deranged, apolitical assassin. Despite the attitude of Canadian authorities in 1968, their posture by 1984 was, for a variety of reasons, not much more forthcoming than that of U.S. authorities.

In response to my March 1984 inquiry for information, the Toronto office of the RCMP responded that it had no documents or data on the King case. I was referred to RCMP headquarters in Ottawa, where Public Affairs Officer John Lehman told me that if I would put my request in writing, RCMP would review its case file and I could obtain copies of documents which were not classified.[3] Two months after submitting my request, I was told that it had been forwarded to the RCMP's immigration and passport branch, because it was that office that had done most of the work on the case. I was assured that this constituted neither buck-passing nor resistance but was simply a matter of getting the request to the correct office.[4]

One week later, however, I received a surprisingly negative response from RCMP's Privacy and Access to Information Coordinator, P. E. J. Banning. The letter, and a follow-up call, made it clear that the promised disclosure had, for whatever reason, been squelched by rigid secrecy: All data on the King case was inaccessible.[5]

Banning's first response was that only Canadian citizens could have access to government records. Fair enough. This presented no problem since I had contacts in the Toronto press who had offered to help. The real problem was the way in which Banning's office interpreted the Canadian privacy act. He stated that under Canadian law, any material even distantly relevant to an individual was considered to be part of the individual's personal file and could only be accessed by the person in question. Therefore, Banning asserted, RCMP files on the case were dispersed within the personal files of individuals, and the residual material was negligible. As Banning described it: "Ninety-nine percent of a file of this kind is personal. All that would be releasable are newspaper clippings."[6]

Banning's interpretation might be subject to challenge in the Canadian courts, by a Canadian citizen acting on my behalf, but this would be an expensive lengthy process. I consulted Professor Peter Dale Scott, a former Canadian diplomat and respected assassinologist who has considerable expertise in the area of governmental secrecy. Scott was not at all surprised by RCMP's response, observing that the Canadian government in general and RCMP in particular are not accustomed to public disclosure. Scott views Canadian freedom of information policy as being narrower and more rigid than in the United States but more open than in Great Britain, where the Official Secrets Act has drastically curtailed public disclosure.

I retreated to simply trying to discover if the Ray/King case was still open; or, if not, on what date RCMP had officially closed it. I put the question in writing. Banning responded that RCMP refused to confirm "whether or not any investigations we may have regarding Mr. Ray are active or closed."[7]

Eric Galt indicated that his last interview with RCMP concerning the King case was in October 1981. He had the definite impression that the Mounties were still very actively interested in the case in general and in the question of the aliases in particular.[8]

In discussing the King/Ray files with another RCMP officer, Inspector George Timko, I learned that there was another dimension to RCMP secrecy, which Banning had not discussed.[9] Timko referred to RCMP's policy of withholding information at the request of federal agencies in the United States. He perused one file relating to the King case and observed that there was "quite a bit of correspondence between RCMP and FBI," which fell into this category of withholding. I inquired as to whether FBI or CIA requests to withhold information applied only to documents originating with these agencies or could also apply to investigative material generated by RCMP itself. Timko replied: "Oh, both kinds of data, yes." The long arm of federal intelligence reached all the way to Ottawa in continuing to withhold vital information about the King case.

I telephoned P. E. J. Banning and inquired as to how much RCMP file material was being withheld at the request of U.S. agencies.[10] Banning was surprised by the question. "Did I say that in my letter?" he asked. Responding negatively, I pressed for an answer. "Well," Banning replied, "the majority of stuff in files is FBI supplied and covers their investigation."

I decided to try the Toronto Metropolitan Police Department and contacted Bernard Simmonds, the officer who in 1968 told the press that Ray definitely had "organized help." Simmonds still harbors profound suspicions about the case. He characterized the Toronto police and RCMP investigations as "not very conclusive."[11]

"We tried hard to find out certain things," said Simmonds, "but we didn't. They [the homicide division] didn't have a helluva lot, didn't get much information. RCMP did most of the investigation, but they didn't find out much either."[12] Unlike the vast majority of U.S. law enforcement officers who worked on the case, Simmonds likens it to the most complex and puzzling unsolved cases that he dealt with over the years.

He opines darkly: "It was very deep rooted, I believe. I'm sure there was more behind him [Ray] politically than we know. He was much more than just an ordinary person."

Simmonds expressed a willingness to help, but was unable to provide any new data about the key facets of the case (fat man, the aliases). Simmonds, who had risen to deputy chief before retiring, expressed the opinion that RCMP "should have some releasable files." He also stated that the Toronto police homicide division possessed relevant files and he referred me to his former colleague, Staff Inspector Walter M. Tyrell, assuring me that Tyrell would be very helpful.

The bad news was that Tyrell claimed to have no files: they had all been given to RCMP in Ottawa; catch–22, Canadian style.[13]

I decided to try to glean some data from the fourth estate. In 1968 the *New York Times* had extensive coverage of the Toronto angle. One correspondent in particular, Jay Walz, had a series of bylines that seemed to focus on the key aspects: "Police in Canada Investigate Whether Ray Had Assistance," "Real Galt Calm about Publicity over Ray's Use of His Name," "Three Men Whose Names Ray Used Resemble Him." Walz had since retired, but I located him at his home in western Massachusetts.

He expressed a willingness to help with my research.[14] I hoped that he might have some notes, file material, or insights beyond what had appeared in the *Times*. He did not.

"I've been racking my brain," said Walz. "But I know nothing more. Sorry. I did interview Galt. He was very reluctant. I know nothing about his background."[15]

I had imagined that reporters would have been assigned to keep digging to find the origin of the aliases. Not so. As Walz explained: "I was on this for only three to four days. Then it [the King case] switched elsewhere. I kept no notes and there was no occasion to follow up. . . . But you may be sure I tried hard to learn what your investigative reporting is now trying to find out. It is an intriguing and difficult project."[16]

In June 1968, at the height of speculation concerning the aliases and Ray's Canadian contacts, he was arrested in London. The focus of the story immediately shifted to Ray himself and then to his trial. The alias question was old news, and was abandoned.

The Toronto press had devoted extensive coverage to what was, for them, a local angle. Reporters did much more investigative work on Ray's contacts and on the alias question—especially Cameron Smith of the *Globe and Mail* and Earl McRae and Andy Salwyn of the *Toronto Star*, all of whom I contacted.[17]

Although the Toronto press had pursued the local conspiratorial angles longer and harder than the U.S. press and had generated some of the most important data on the case, the local hook was still insufficient to sustain a prolonged interest in the case. Earl McRae, whose energetic investigating of Ray's mysterious Toronto contacts will be discussed later, eventually suffered the same journalistic fate as Walz. McRae recalled: "Shortly after [at the end of June], I was taken off that and put on something else."[18]

One possible source for explaining the origin of the aliases, although not necessarily the best source, is James Earl Ray himself. He must have some idea where they came from, even if they were handed to him by an anonymous courier or were retrieved from a blind drop.

Assassinologist Harold Weisberg has had extensive access to Ray. Weisberg served as an investigator for James H. Lesar, a Washington, D.C. attorney, when Lesar represented Ray for a period in the 1970s. During their association, Weisberg talked with the prisoner for hours at a time with no prepared agenda. He believes Ray is innocent—a patsy for a sophisticated conspiracy. He also believes that Ray's responses to his questions have been generally credible and truthful.[19]

Even so, as we sat in Weisberg's rural Maryland home, which hosts more file cabinets than the FBI reading room in Washington, D.C., he had a profoundly different feeling about Ray's responses to questions about the aliases. Weisberg grimaced and asserted: "Every time the aliases came up, Jimmy either lied or changed the subject."

To see what Weisberg meant, one need only examine Ray's responses to HSCA. During 1977–78, he was interviewed on eight separate occasions. The committee got no closer to discovering the truth than did official investigators or the media in 1968.

Regarding the Galt alias, Ray's nonexplanations ranged from evasion to absurdity. Then HSCA Chief Counsel Richard Sprague quizzed him as to how he first came to use the Galt name (in 1967 in Montreal).[20]

Sprague: How did it come about that you used the Galt name?

Ray: I have no idea. I just, just a name. I might have seen it in the phone book or something.

Sprague: Where were you when you saw this name in the phone book?

Ray: I don't know if I saw it in a phone book. I just, I'm just trying to explain to you where I could have gotten these various names from.

Ray claimed that he was looking for an alias that "was something that you can remember like Smith would be hard to remember, whereas Galt or something, it is easy to get accustomed to."

Sprague: What was the full name you used?

Ray: I think it was Eric S. Galt.

Sprague: Now, do you have any idea how you happened to pick that name?

Ray: I could have gotten it out of a phone book, or anything. It's something that I'd remember and it could have been, the names could have been from several different sources. I can't specifically say.

Sprague: Well, did anybody ever give you that name?

Ray: No, I don't . . . No one give [sic] it to me.

During one interview, Ray opined that he may have gotten the Galt name from a Chicago or Birmingham, Alabama, telephone book.[21] But in a subsequent interview, he recanted.[22]

Q. Do you now recall how you got the Galt name?

A. No, now I don't recall how I got the Galt name.

Q. Did you get it out of the phone book?

A. I, I can't recall that.

Q. You told us earlier in these interviews that you got the name out of a Chicago phone directory, do you have recollection about that?

A. No. I said that's a possibility. I don't know, I, the only reason, only, the only time I ever remember looking in a phone book for the Galt name was in Birmingham and I didn't want to have someone's name just like mine. It was one Galt in the Birmingham phone directory, but—

Q. Was it Eric Galt?

A. I don't believe it was, I probably—

Q. Did you check the Toronto and environs phone book to see if there was an Eric Galt?*

A. No, I didn't check on that.

Q. You don't know if there is one or not?

A. I seen in the book, I don't know, there might be a, there's an Eric St. something Galt but I don't know, I have no knowledge of it.

Q. You didn't know about it until after you were arrested?

A. No, I had no knowledge of it.

Ray claimed that he decided not to use Smith or Jones not only because such a name "sounds bogus" but also because they were so common that they might "create a conflict" with a real individual.[23] The real Eric S. Galt finds this ironic.

During Ray's eighth and final interview with HSCA, he was asked about the Galt alias one last time:[24]

---

*Ray had never been to Toronto when he first used the Galt alias. The 1967 and 1968 Toronto telephone books listed the real Galt as Eric Galt (no middle initial).

Where. . . . Where as you best recollect now, will you give us some alternatives, as you said sometimes you are not 100 percent sure and you have alternatives, what are alternatives that you think could possibly be the truth as to how you got the Galt name?

His final response was, if anything, more nebulous than ever:

It, I apparently seen it written down somewhere, but where I seen it written down I don't know. Because that's the only way you could get a name is, you know, to see it written down somewhere, or some former associate maybe. . . .

Ray consistently avoids or denies the most logical possibility: that the name was provided to him. As to where he got the singular middle name "Starvo" he replied: "I couldn't say."[25]

Not only did Ray seem to have amnesia regarding the origin of his main alias, but he came close to lying in his attempt to downplay the similarities between himself and the real Galt. Ray was questioned about his scars during an HSCA interview. The reader will recall that Ray had two scars matching those of the real Galt (on the right hand and the forehead). Ray seems to deny that he has any scars at all.[26]

Q. Did you have any scars on your person at that time when you were in Canada?

A. Scars?

Q. Yes.

A. Visible or?

Q. Well, we'll start with visible.

A. None that I know of.

Q. Do you have any that are not visible?

A. Well, I have the gun shot wound in the foot. No, that's the only one, I never had any operations or anything.

Q. Do you have any scars on either of your hands?

A. Well, I had one. I had one, you can't see it, it's a lawn mower scar, it's really thin.

Q. Can I see it?

A. I think it's gone now. I believe it's, I think it's gone away.

Q. You are pointing to an area in your right palm, is that right?

A. Yes.

Q. Do you have any scars on your head?

A. Let's see, yes, I think I have a . . . Yes, I jumped through a window one time and got one right here.

Regardless of whether the scar on his palm had faded by 1977, it was part of the FBI's fugitive description of Ray in 1968. Moreover, the woman who handled Ray's passport application in Toronto, Miss Lillian Spencer, noticed the scar on Ray's face.[27]

Then there is the John Willard alias, used by Ray only once (to rent a room opposite the Lorraine Motel). Whether Ray is guilty or not, his presence in the rooming house at the crime scene is a fateful occurrence in his life. Yet his recall about his alias is exceedingly vague.[28]

HSCA: What name did you use when you rented the rooming house room?

Ray: The Memphis one?

HSCA: Yes.

Ray: That's Willard. I had a recollection one time of using that name, but I can't think of any place I ever used that name.

HSCA: You don't recall where you got the name John Willard?

Ray: Someone else might, no. I don't recall it.

In a subsequent interview, Ray was again asked about the Willard alias. His response tortured both syntax and logic:

Uh, now I have some recollection of that name somewhere but I don't know where I got it. But it must have been some kind of criminal associate because most of my names were, not most of, but some of them comes [sic] from some type of indirect criminal associate. In other words, maybe somebody, someone else used that name for an alias and I heard about it or something and. . . .[29]

Ray told HSCA interviewers that upon arriving in Toronto, he searched a graveyard looking for tombstones which might provide a name with which to obtain a passport. He claimed that he continued his search for an appropriate alias by going to a Toronto newspaper— he couldn't remember which one—and researching old birth announce- ments. (In his first version of this story, Ray told HSCA that he went to a library rather than a newspaper.)[30] This, Ray asserted, is how he came up with the names Bridgeman and Sneyd. It is true that birth announcements for Paul E. Bridgeman and Ramon George Sneyd ap- peared in two Toronto newspapers.[31]

The coincidence of it all! From thousands of birth announcements, Ray claims to have picked out two men who still lived in Toronto, who lived near Galt and Willard, and who fit his general physical description.

HSCA: How did . . . How did it come off that you happened to bear a strong physical resemblance to both Bridgeman and Sneyd?

Ray: I don't if I . . . I don't know if I bear a strong physical resemblance to them. Uh, uh, most these in Eng——, in Canada I don't know about now, but I don't think that'd be really something extraordinary, because most of them are the same nationality to me, English or Irish. I don't think you'd have too much problem having two features, you know. You might, I mean, there wouldn't be no radical—radical difference in appearance, Chinese or something like that.

HSCA: Well, how did you know their height and weight?

Ray: I had no idea their height and weight. I didn't know if it was similar to mine or not.[32]

Ray told the HSCA that he came up with the Sneyd and Bridgeman names by checking back birth certificates "near to my own age."[33] But Sneyd and Bridgeman were born in 1932; Ray, in 1928. This seems a strange way to proceed. Why should Ray select the names of men who were four years younger?

HSCA: Why did you pick that year, 1932?

Ray: Well, I thought that, I thought I looked closer to that age than the other age.

HSCA: You thought you looked young for your age?

Ray: Yes, well I had . . . that was one reason yes, and I suppose there may have been other reasons.

HSCA: What were the other reasons?

Ray: Well, I can't recall any specific ones right now, but there is certain advantages of being a certain age. . . .[34]

As implausible as Ray's responses are, official investigators have never posed any credible, alternative explanation.

5   The Galt File

It's a fat file. And it has everything—my background, my picture,
even my scars. They have it there on the desk when they talk to
me, and they pull things out of it.

Eric S. Galt, 1984

Was the use of Galt's name the most striking and elaborate of coincidences? Was it really blind luck, as Ray implies? And what of the St.
Louis cabal alleged by HSCA to be lurking in the shadows behind Ray?
Did these men carefully select Ray's aliases for him, seeing to it that
everything was well synchronized? It seems very unlikely: allegedly,
Sutherland merely offered a $50,000 bounty and had no idea who the
hit man would turn out to be or what modus operandi he would use.

The answer to one of the most crucial unanswered questions in this
case—the origin of the Galt alias—lies in the background of the real Galt.
Eric St. Vincent Galt was not just any Canadian: He was one who worked
on a top secret project intimately linked to American weapons research
and development. Because of this work, Galt was the subject of a very
detailed dossier. Whoever had access to it had all the information needed
to use Galt's identity as a cover, to match Galt to Ray.

From interviews with Galt and from information gathered from U.S.
military and defense agencies, the author has pieced together this national security dimension of Galt's background. In 1968 he worked for
Union Carbide of Canada Ltd., as he had since the early 1950s. Throughout much of his career, Galt worked in a department within Carbide

that had a very special assignment—one so secret that, as Galt described it, "A lot of people had no idea what was going on."[1] Canadian and U.S. newspapers described Galt as a "warehouse foreman," which was true. From the late 1950s to the early 1960s, however, Galt performed his foreman's duties in a very special context: the ongoing research and development for a device called the "proximity fuse."

During World War II, the Japanese had developed a prototype of this device which greatly increased their success in downing U.S. fighter planes. From the end of the war until well into the 1960s, the U.S. government worked energetically and continuously to improve this crucial technology. The proximity fuse was used in antiaircraft shells. It could sense when the shell was approaching the target and would automatically ignite. Its tactical advantage was that it could bring down an enemy aircraft without achieving a direct hit.[2] The more sensitive the fuse, the better able it was to explode the shell at exactly the right moment. Thus the impetus for constant technological improvement. Proximity fuses were being tested well into the early 1960s.[3]

Needless to say, the work done on this device was highly secret. In response to a 1984 inquiry made by the author to the office of the U.S. Secretary of Defense, Edith W. Martin, Under Secretary of Defense for Research and Advanced Technology, described proximity-fuse research and development as having a high degree of "security sensitivity" due to the "extremely advanced technology" involved.[4]

All employees who labored on the project at Carbide's Toronto plant underwent intensive and periodic security checks conducted by the RCMP. Galt's last security clearance check was in 1961, seven years before the assassination.[5] He describes his RCMP file as extensive, containing background information as well as physical characteristics.[6]

The Americanization of Eric Galt began long before his name became a household word in the United States as the subject of the greatest manhunt in history, and long before he drove to Tennessee in search of rock formations or to Miami in search of coral reefs. Like the fuse he worked on, Galt had a proximity to the U.S. defense establishment. To begin with, the company he worked for—Union Carbide of Canada Ltd.—was 75 percent American owned. Though its corporate officers are wont to assert that, in terms of personnel and policy, their company has real autonomy from its American parent,[7] all indications are that proximity-fuse R&D was primarily a U.S. enterprise in terms of technological expertise.

The work was apparently complex and multifaceted. Most of it was done in-house by the U.S. military because the technology was considered so secretive and advanced.[8] For example, the Naval Surface Weapons Center and the U.S. Army Electronics Research and Development

Command (ERADCOM) each worked on different facets of the project at various times.[9] Carbide's Bennington, Vermont, plant developed a "reserve battery power supply" for the fuse.[10]

That the Union Carbide Corporation was intimately enmeshed in U.S. weapons research and development of the most sensitive kind is further demonstrated by the fact that from 1948 until 1984, Carbide's nuclear division operated the Oak Ridge National Laboratory in Oak Ridge, Tennessee.[11] Carbide's facility was originally part of the Manhattan Project (the development of the first atomic bomb). In 1968 Oak Ridge was working on the development of the Poseidon missile for nuclear submarines and the Sentinel antiballistic missile system.

It was the impression of Galt and his coworkers that the proximity fuse was basically an American invention, the product of American technology.[12] This was confirmed by a source in the U.S. military, an air force colonel who requested anonymity (primarily because it was not clear how much information about the fuse was supposed to be classified, even after more than 20 years). The colonel served as commander of a U.S. Air Defense Group in the late 1960s and, up until the mid 1960s, was involved in the management of research and development projects.

He asserted with confidence that any work on the proximity fuse, even if done in Toronto, would involve—or be intimately linked to—American technology and expertise, because of what he described as the U.S. defense establishment's proprietary interest in the device. He also noted, with undisguised disdain, what he perceived to be the retrograde level of Canadian weapons' research and development in the 1950s and 1960s. He offered this as further reason for a strong U.S. presence. "The U.S. was up to its ass in proximity fuse R and D," the colonel observed, "and we were involved with them [the Canadians] but it was our show."

Ray's use of the Galt alias seemed, at points, to reflect the data in Galt's file. For example, in seeking to establish credentials in the name of Galt while he was in Montreal in 1967, Ray wrote the Canadian Department of Veterans Affairs using Galt's name. When asked by a House Assassinations Committee interviewer why he had written the letter, Ray responded: "Well, I didn't . . . it was something insignificant. I was just trying to get an answer from them so I would have the Galt on the identification in case I had to. . . ."[13]

Unfortunately, Ray did not finish his answer and the subject was dropped. Ray could have written the letter without knowing anything about the real Galt; he could have been hoping that he would get lucky and hit upon some credentials with Galt's name on it. If the Department of Veterans Affairs had responded, "We have no record under your name," then the fact that such a negative response was addressed to Eric S. Galt would hardly be helpful in terms of establishing credentials.

Neither Ray's letter nor the response from Veterans Affairs—if any— are known, despite the author's attempts to retrieve the letter(s) from the Canadian bureaucracy by having the real Galt request them. Ray's letter would be particularly interesting: Did he write a very vague, generic request under Galt's name, fishing for a response; or did his letter contain some reference to Galt's interaction with the military bureaucracy during World War II? For although Galt was not a veteran, he did have a military paper trail.

Early in the war, he applied to the Canadian Air Force for enlistment. In addition to patriotism, he believed that he had a good chance to become an officer and the pay and benefits were attractive.[14] Union Carbide was not at all pleased when it discovered his plan to enlist. The company claimed that he was critically needed for defense work and could not be spared. Corporate personnel officials contacted the military and requested that Galt be given a civilian deferment.[15] He remained a civilian, but his application to enlist and the intercession of his employer generated a paper trail that created a new Galt file (with the air force) and augmented the old one at Carbide, which was eventually incorporated into his RCMP security file.[16] Whoever had the latter file would know that the military bureaucracy had information pertaining to Galt.

His security file contained information on his family background. Galt's father had been a prominent private detective in South Africa and had emigrated to Canada before Galt was born. The FBI's 1968 evidence index includes a letter allegedly written by Ray using the Galt alias, described as "letter from Galt to South African Council."[17] It concerned immigrating to Rhodesia. (The implications of this letter are discussed in Chapter 12.)

Then there is the middle name of Ray's alias—Eric "Starvo" Galt. The first known instance in which Ray used the Galt alias was in Montreal in July 1967. He rented an apartment under the name Eric Starvo Galt.[18] The reader will recall that the real Galt, whole middle name was St. Vincent, signed his name by abbreviating the middle name to St. V. and did so by placing oversized periods after the St. and after the V. The scrawled abbreviation looked remarkably like "Starvo," as the press noted in 1968. This was Ray's only known use of the name "Starvo." Subsequently, he shortened the Galt alias to simply "Eric S. Galt."[19] (Galt was listed in the 1967 and 1968 Toronto telephone directory as Eric Galt, with no middle initial. Galt told me that he never listed himself in any telephone book as Eric S. Galt, only as Eric Galt.)

HSCA asked Ray: "When did you first start using Starvo as the middle name?" Ray replied: "I think I used that in Canada [Montreal, 1967]. I used this stuff, I just signed an S. but I think I used the full name when I rented the lease in Canada."[20]

This fact, and its significance, have been obscured by inaccurate reports, by HSCA and by the press in 1968, concerning Ray's use of Starvo. HSCA stated: "When he rented an apartment or a room, bought a car, secured a driver's license . . . he did so as Eric Starvo Galt."[21] In fact, Ray's Alabama license, car registration, signature at the New Rebel Motel in Memphis, and assorted forms, letters, and coupons were all "Eric S. Galt."

The confusion originated in 1968. On April 9, authorities first discovered the Eric S. Galt name at the New Rebel Motel. Sometime between April 10 and 13, the FBI found a Galt letter from Montreal[22] and thus traced it back to the Starvo. On April 12, the press first reported the Galt name: the main suspect was Eric Starvo Galt.[23] Florida police had issued a bulletin on Eric Starvo Galt, which is where the press got the name. The Bureau was maintaining strict secrecy. In subsequent press coverage, April 13 to 18, the suspect's name and the unfolding discoveries about his activities were attributed to Starvo even though it was actually "S". FBI and CIA documents during that same period also refer to the suspect as Starvo.

The significance of Ray's change from Starvo to S is that this is exactly what the real Galt had done. Throughout most of his adult life, Galt had been using the St. V. abbreviation that looked like Starvo.[24] In a transition period spanning several months during 1966, he began to sign his name with a simple S. The motivation for jettisoning the St. V. was twofold. First, Galt liked the simplicity of the new signature; in part, because it helped forestall the usual jokes by his peers about his fitness for canonization. Second, Union Carbide's computer system preferred the simplicity of using only a middle initial.

This is indeed an intriguing parallel. And, unless one is willing to view coincidence as the dominant dynamic of the universe, it has a profound implication for the case. For one thing, this allows us to dispense with the lame explanation that Ray somehow caught sight of a motel register, or some other source with Galt's signature on it, and misread it as Eric Starvo Galt. Ray would have to have done so prior to 1966, before the real Galt changed to S, and Ray was then in prison.

Why would Ray change from Starvo to S? By his own admission, he was attempting to establish documentation for the Galt alias—a process that would dictate as little deviation as possible from the selected alias. Did Ray himself discover that the real Galt had made a change? Ray had never been to Toronto at this point.

This again leads back to Galt's security file. Galt's last security check took place in 1961. At that time, he was signing his middle name in a manner that, to the reader of his signature, would look like Starvo. Even though his file was rich enough to clearly establish that his name was Eric St. Vincent Galt, anyone using Galt's identity as a cover would want to imitate his signature. If the source for the cover was Galt's security file, the signature would have appeared to be Starvo.

Perhaps the conspirators did not discover until after the initial selection of Galt that the real Galt had changed his signature, and they then had to correct Ray's usage of the alias. Perhaps, since Galt's new signature was established in 1966 and was well known to his employer, Ray's switch from Starvo to S was not the result of faulty or incomplete data on Galt but was done so that Ray's cover would seem all the more like the real Galt: Ray, like the real Galt, stopped using Starvo, switched to S, and never went back to Starvo.

Since Canadian intelligence presumably had no interest in knowingly providing a cover to be used in the assassination of Martin Luther King, Jr., the question arises as to how U.S. conspirators with intelligence credentials or connections might have usurped Galt's security file. There are several possibilities. One is through American interface with the security arrangements for work done on the proximity fuse. It is conceivable that, although plant security was provided by Carbide itself,[25] the use of top-secret U.S. technology or expertise might have given U.S. intelligence some behind-the-scenes security role or security entre, in order to insure that U.S. military secrets would be safe in Toronto.

Another possibility is that, through some pretext request or some trading of dossiers whose ostensible purpose was unrelated to the assassination, the CIA or some other U.S. intelligence agency obtained Galt's dossier from RCMP. It should be noted that RCMP not only performed internal security functions like those performed by the FBI but was also Canada's premier spy agency—a combination FBI and CIA. In the 1960s RCMP had a close working relationship with CIA. The two agencies cooperated in attempts to destroy KGB spy networks in North America.[26]

One illustration of the intimacy of this relationship is provided by a case involving an RCMP internal investigation into the loyalty of its own counterintelligence chief, Leslie "Jim" Bennett.[27] During the 1960s, Bennett had worked closely with his American counterpart, the legendary James Jesus Angleton. The two spook catchers had cooperated in some of Canada's most famous spy cases, rooting out KGB penetrations into the Canadian bureaucracy. When, in 1972, Angleton discovered that Bennett was being investigated by RCMP as a possible double agent, he was outraged that he had not been informed and injected himself into the case, providing sources to help the RCMP investigation and reviewing and analyzing RCMP's findings.

A third possible avenue for obtaining Galt's file was through some quasi-official, highly secretive intelligence network in which a group of public agencies had private agreements to share data. One example of such an organization was LEIU (Law Enforcement Intelligence Unit), a private association of police intelligence squads formed in 1956. According to one police officer who worked as an undercover investigator for the organization, it was "so secret that even its very existence was denied."[28] By the mid 1970s LEIU boasted a membership that included 225 North American police departments.[29] The organization served as a clearinghouse for intelligence data; it exchanged, and sometimes generated, reports and dossiers on known criminals, private citizens, and political figures.

According to former CIA computer expert and Branch Chief George O'Toole, LEIU linked "intelligence squads of almost every major police force in the United States and Canada."[30] Still, it was a private organization, beyond public accountability (even though it received financial aid from federal and state governments in the United States).[31] Behind their fraternal cloak of secrecy, member agencies of LEIU exchanged dossiers at will, without regard for guidelines that sought to protect rights of privacy by placing restraints on the gathering and dissemination of information. It is quite clear that one of the primary motivations for establishing LEIU was to circumvent the usual restrictions which were perceived as hampering the abilities of public agencies to trade data.

LEIU membership also included an unspecified number of "penal authorities." Private corporations sometimes sent representatives to the group's regional meetings.[32] LEIU, or some similar entity, could have been the source for matching Ray (through his prison file) with Galt (through his security file), and might also have provided data on Willard, Bridgeman, and Sneyd.

6   James Earl Ray, The "Loner"

> Many blacks believe that Ray had powerful help. I understand their torment and sympathize with it as a human matter. But I had a duty to make an independent, rational judgement based on all the evidence—and from the very beginning, the evidence indicated only one person acting. In practically everything he did—robberies, travel, everything—he was a loner, a man who didn't plan and carry out things with other people.
>
> former Attorney General Ramsey Clark, 1986[1]

The mythology of American political assassinations tells us that all assassins and would-be assassins—from Oswald to John W. Hinckley, Jr.—were "loners." With rare exceptions, this has been the conclusion of law-enforcement agencies investigating various cases, of psychiatric experts who consult for the U.S. Secret Service, and of panels (such as the Kerner Commission) which have studied the problem of political violence in America.[2] Having labeled American assassins as loners, most analysts, agencies, and commissions proceed to argue against—or dismiss outright—the possibility of conspiracy.

Elsewhere, the author has criticized this line of argument as analytically flawed.[3] The "loner" label is not a clinically valid concept derived from psychological data. Rather, it is an analgesic for the body politic. Experts will often assert that European societies spawn conspiratorially involved assassins who kill for political goals while America produces only crazed isolates who kill for muddled personal reasons.[4] In other words, "It can't happen here"—conspiracies are confined to such hotbeds of political intrigue as Europe, or the Philippines, or to Communist plots against the Pope.[5] Here in America, we have nothing but lone nuts. Their murderous assaults have little, if any, political implication for American democracy, any more than being stricken with leukemia reflects on a person's probity.

Just what is a loner? If it means that most alleged assassins, including Ray, are not particularly gregarious, don't have an extensive social calendar, and don't interact well by upper middle-class standards, then, yes, they are loners. But this has little to do with conspiratorial potential, unless the allegation is that the conspiracy was hatched at a country club. If being a loner requires that an assassin have no friends or associates at all, then most American assassins, including Ray, are not loners. An individual may have only one associate; but if the associate is a KGB agent, or a CIA agent, or a mafioso, the potential for conspiracy is manifest.[6]

James Earl Ray was indeed a "loner" in the sense that he kept to himself, did not have many associates, and did not seem to forge lasting relationships with either sex. But this has nothing to do with his possible participation in a conspiracy. There is considerable evidence that Ray had contacts and help, however shadowy, in contexts relating directly and indirectly to the assassination.

In one instance, someone other than Ray obtained a duplicate driver's license in the name of Eric S. Galt.[7] In March 1967 Ray was in Los Angeles preparing to leave for Georgia. He was using the Galt alias. On March 1, someone claiming to be Eric Galt telephoned the Alabama highway patrol in Montgomery and requested a duplicate driver's license. (Ray had obtained a license in September 1968 under the name Eric S. Galt.) The caller asked that the duplicate be mailed to a Birmingham, Alabama address—a rooming house on 2608 South Highland Street. This was the flophouse where Ray had stayed before departing Birmingham for Los Angeles.

It is possible that Ray could have made the call himself, long distance from Los Angeles. But there is no indication that he needed a duplicate.[8] When queried about this by HSCA, Ray responded that he had the Galt license with him when he was on the West Coast and that he never lost his wallet.[9]

While Ray was still out west, someone in Birmingham received the license and forwarded the twenty-five cent fee to Montgomery, as requested by the bill accompanying the duplicate. Ray never did return to the South Highland Street flophouse, but he did return to Birmingham—to purchase the rifle found near the scene of King's assassination.[10]

Who did obtain the Eric S. Galt driver's license, and why? These questions remain unanswered. The second license never surfaced. Bernard Fensterwald, Jr., who served as Ray's legal counsel for a period in the early 1970s, told the author that he had "tried like hell" to resolve the matter, without success. Fensterwald termed the incident "very suspicious."[11]

After the assassination Ray fled the United States and went to Toronto, then London. In both cities there were mysterious phone calls. In Toronto Ray rented a room at 102 Ossington Street from Mrs. Fella Szpakowski. She recalled that during his 11 days as a tenant, he made two phone calls and received one.

Ray was out when the incoming call came. Lidia Szpakowski, the landlady's eight-year-old daughter, answered. She remembered nothing about the substance of the call, except that it was for Bridgeman (the alias Ray used at the time) and there was no announcement of it being a long-distance call.[12]

Another call for Ray came on April 27 at his second address, 962 Dundas Street, where he was registered under the alias Ramon George Sneyd. Ray's landlady, Mrs. Yee Sun Loo, answered the phone: A male voice said, "Call Sneyd."[13]

The caller's words are interesting. He did not say: "Is Mr. Sneyd there?" or "Is this the residence of Ramon George Sneyd?" or "May I speak with Mr. Sneyd?" Did the caller's phrase indicate that he knew that Ray/Sneyd lived in a rooming house and had to be called to the phone from his second-floor room? We will never know, unless Ray tells us. Mrs. Loo went upstairs to fetch "Sneyd" and found that he was out. The caller hung up and left no message.[14]

In London, where Ray flew on May 6 when he departed Toronto, there were more phone calls. At the inexpensive bed-and-breakfast hotel where Ray stayed, Arma Thomas, the proprietor, remembered Ray's strange behavior: He rarely left his room and refused to take any of the four phone calls that came for him.[15]

Scotland Yard determined that two of the calls were from British Overseas Airways and apparently related to Ray's attempts to book a flight to Brussels.[16] Despite the Yard's best efforts, the other two callers remain unidentified. Mrs. Thomas, who took the calls, remembered that one was male; the other, female. Thomas also remembered that the woman caller had a pronounced American "twang."[17]

Jane Nassau, the desk clerk at Ray's other London hotel, told reporters that when Ray/Sneyd checked in on May 28, he was accompanied by a man who appeared to be a "friend." The second man did not check into the hotel and Miss Nassau never saw him again.[18] Her account could not be corroborated because there were no other witnesses to Ray's check-in.

In Toronto Ray frequented a sleazy bar called the Silver Dollar Tavern, located two blocks from his room on Dundas Street. According to those who remembered him, Ray went there two or three consecutive nights between April 30 and May 3.[19] Two waiters recalled Ray as the man who sat at a front-row table just below the go-go dancers, ordering Molson's beer and paying with American $20 bills.

Patti Stanford, a young black woman who worked as a topless dancer, remembered Ray vividly: "He looked at me. It wasn't the way a man looks at a girl. It was the way a white man looks at a colored girl dancing. Sort of like he didn't approve. He looked kind of disgusted."[20] She also noticed something that was corroborated by other witnesses in the bar: Ray had a companion each night he was there.[21] The man was described as fair haired, fair complexioned, husky, and quiet.[22] He wore a tight-fitting, yellow Banlon t-shirt. His identity is unknown, as is his relationship to Ray.

Of all of Ray's putative, shadowy contacts, the most famous and most debated is a man whom Ray claimed to know only as Raoul. Raoul is the key to Ray's continuing assertions of innocence. Ray claims that during the nine months prior to the assassination, he met with Raoul 12 to 15 times—in Birmingham, Mexico, New Orleans, and in Memphis on April 3 and April 4. Ray contends that Raoul directed his every incriminating move in connection with the assassination: the rifle purchase (Raoul allegedly told Ray that the rifle was a demo model to show gunrunning clients); the rental of a room near the Lorraine Motel (to negotiate a gunrunning deal); the purchase of binoculars in Memphis.[23] Ray says that he first me Raoul in July 1967 in the Neptune Bar in Montreal. It was at this time that Ray first used the Galt alias.

HSCA is not alone in its belief that Raoul does not exist. The committee pointed to the fact that, despite a dozen or more alleged meetings, there is not a single known witness who saw Ray and Raoul together. The committee also found Ray's Raoul story "inconsistent on details as important as Raoul's physical description."[24] In a 1968 article by William Bradford Huie, Ray was quoted as saying that Raoul was a "blond Latin." In Huie's book *He Slew the Dreamer*, supposedly based on correspondence from Ray, Raoul is described as a "red-haired French-Canadian." According to HSCA, Ray told the committee that Huie's first description was incorrect: the second was correct. In an interview with Dan Rather of CBS news, Raoul was described as an auburn-haired "Latin Spanish." In a *Playboy* interview Ray was quoted as saying that Raoul was a "sandy-haired Latin." Ray told HSCA that *Playboy* misquoted him. After what the House Committee described as "an extensive investigation," it turned up no evidence to corroborate Ray's Raoul story.

In a segment of its final report, HSCA employed an appalling mixture of supposition, vague circumstantial evidence, and leaps of logic in an attempt to implicate Ray's two brothers John and Jerry in the assassination.[25] The committee asserted that "the tale of Raoul was fabricated to conceal contacts with one or both brothers."[26] Instead of Raoul giving money to Ray during the period between his escape from prison and assassination, HSCA asserted that Jerry Ray periodically distributed money to James—money from a bank robbery committed by John and James in Alton, Illinois in July 1967.

HSCA's case that the Ray brothers committed the Alton heist is exceedingly weak: James grew up in Alton; he was in St. Louis (only 20 miles away) near the date of the crime; eyewitnesses gave "imprecise" descriptions of the ski-masked bandits, but the descriptions did not "eliminate the Ray brothers as suspects"; a discarded shotgun and clothing were found on a dead-end street in the vicinity of where Ray's relatives lived.[27]

HSCA made much of the fact that six separate witnesses stated that James had referred to visiting or meeting or getting money from his "brother," at times which overlapped with Ray's alleged meetings with Raoul.

There were no reports that Ray mentioned a brother by name. Ray's brothers told HSCA that "brother" was James's euphemism for Raoul. HSCA rejected this explanation as "worthless," since it found no evidence to substantiate Raoul's existence. One wonders if HSCA would have viewed Ray's story as more credible had he told each of the six witnesses, "I'm off to meet the nefarious, shadowy Raoul, to engage in criminal enterprises."

Despite the absence of any meaningful evidence, HSCA's fervor to implicate Ray's brothers resulted in the pronouncement that John and Jerry manifested a general attitude of racial bias and a willingness to commit crimes for money—attitudes "consistent with their participation in the assassination of Dr. King."[28] By this standard, a great many of James's peers and associates could be linked to the assassination, however spuriously.

When Ray exchanged the rifle for a more powerful model, he allegedly mentioned his "brother." This was HSCA's point of departure for attempting to link the brothers to the rifle purchase; but the committee came close to clearing the brothers of involvement. There was no evidence of their presence at the Birmingham Travel Lodge where James stayed; the committee's investigation found no evidence to refute their claims that they were elsewhere during the purchase. Any attempt to further evaluate HSCA's investigation of this topic is hampered by an absence of source notes.[29]

Those who reject the Raoul story usually leap to the conclusion that Ray was not aided or manipulated, that he was a lone assassin. But it is also possible that Ray was handled not by one operative but by a series of cutout figures, about whom he knew little or nothing. If so, the activities Ray attributes to Raoul may be true, but "Raoul" may be a composite entity invented by Ray (perhaps to make himself appear less culpable and more like a patsy). That Raoul is a composite is consistent with what we know about the post-assassination fugitive phase, during which a series of mystery figures cropped up—the fat man, the slight man, (discussed in the next chapter) the man in the bar.

Harold Weisberg believes that someone like Raoul did exist and did set Ray up as a patsy.[30] Nor is Weisberg surprised that Ray cannot produce proof of Raoul. In Weisberg's view, a skillful cutout or handler would employ every trick of tradecraft to hide his identity.

At least one credible investigator turned up some information which, although tentative in nature, convinced him that there was indeed a Raoul-like character in Ray's life. Andy Salwyn, now a correspondent for CBC radio in Canada, was the Montreal bureau chief for the *Toronto Star* in 1968. Salwyn and his colleague Earl McRae were assigned to investigate the two biggest conspiracy angles of the King case—Raoul and the fat man.

In 1968 Salwyn searched the neighborhood near the Neptune Bar in Montreal where Ray had reportedly met Raoul in July 1967.[31] He could not turn up any witnesses who saw Ray together with anyone who might have been Raoul, but he did find evidence of a mysterious character who seemed to manifest Raoul-like characteristics and who, according to Salwyn's data, was in the right neighborhood at the right time. The man turned out to be Jules Ricco Kimble.

Five blocks from the Neptune Bar, Salwyn found a rooming house where the landlady remembered a mysterious American who spoke little French and was known as "Rolland" or "Rollie." A janitor in the building remembered that Rollie dated a nurse from a nearby hospital. Salwyn tracked her down and interviewed her, although he found that Maryanne Levesque (a pseudonym created by the author) was very reluctant to talk and very frightened.

Miss Levesque knew the man only as "Rollie." She told Salwyn three things about him: he had a police-band radio in his car and was always asking her to translate police broadcasts, he had guns in the trunk of his car, he made a number of phone calls from her apartment. She saved her phone bill in hopes of collecting from him, but he disappeared. She had given the phone numbers to RCMP investigators and no longer had them.

According to Salwyn, he approached the RCMP and offered to trade information: he turned over whatever data he had in return for the phone numbers. Salwyn telexed the five phone numbers back to the *Star* in Toronto. There, his colleague Earl McRae called each one—five bars in Texas and New Orleans (Ray had been in New Orleans in December of 1968 and claimed to have met Raoul in a bar there). McRae did not obtain any information on "Raoul," Rollie," or Ray, but made only one pretext call to each number.

Incredibly, the numbers were lost. According to McRae and Salwyn, *Star* editor Martin Goodman, now deceased, initiated the unprecedented step of having the newspaper's attorneys review material relating to articles on the King case, mostly because of the political pressure from police as a result of the *Star*'s breaking the fat man story and the police's short-lived but severe embarrassment at not being able to find the fat man, suspected of delivering money to Ray.[32]

To the chagrin of the two reporters and their editor, a legal secretary for one of the *Star* lawyers lost Salwyn's data while it was under review—including the phone numbers. The two reporters remain convinced that this was entirely accidental, but the loss of the data killed their story. Worse, from an investigative viewpoint, Salwyn had hurriedly telexed the numbers from Montreal to Toronto so that they could be checked out, and he did not retain a copy of them. McRae, working at the *Star*, telephoned each of the numbers then passed them on for review. He too had no copy.

There were two good possibilities for obtaining data on the mysterious American. The author was not successful at either, but both still exist. The first was to locate and interview Maryanne Levesque (efforts to locate her were unsuccessful). The second was to obtain the RCMP's investigative file.

I contacted RCMP Sgt. Mike Power, the man with whom Salwyn claimed to have traded data in Montreal in 1968. Power had no trouble in instantly and vividly recognizing Salwyn's name. "That son of a gun," Power chuckled. "Is he still alive? No one's shot him yet?"[33] When I broached the subject of the "Raoul" investigation and the phone numbers, Power lapsed into total amnesia followed by something bordering on hostility. He quizzed me sharply about my work, then referred me to Inspector George Timko. According to Power, Timko would be able to compensate for Power's complete lack of recall by providing "archival" material on the case.

I reached Timko by phone.[34] I explained who I was and the nature of my research. It was not necessary to do so: Timko, like two other RCMP officers whom I dealt with—all of whom worked in different "branches" or offices—had all my letters to RCMP at-the-ready. (Part of the reason for this notoriety was that, according to RCMP's chief information officer P. E. J. Banning, I was the only individual, Canadian or American, who had ever requested data on the King case.) Timko stiffly asserted that no information could be released.

In 1978 Andy Salwyn had voluntarily flown to Washington, D.C., at HSCA expense, to provide as much data as possible about his 1968 investigation. His experience was not pleasant. It was his impression that because he had to work from recall and because he had failed to find a witness who placed Ray and Kimble together, the House Committee was not seriously interested in his findings. After flying him to Washington, the committee staff questioned him in closed session for less than ten minutes. Salwyn, who considered himself a resource-witness if not an investigative colleague, told the author that the staff grilled him sharply about his own data, almost as if he were a hostile witness, using a file that it had in its possession. By the nature of the questions asked, Salwyn believed that the committee had RCMP's investigative file. HSCA's final report, which Salwyn had not seen until I showed it to him, did contain citations of the RCMP file in question.

I telephoned HSCA Chief Counsel G. Robert Blakey, now a professor at Notre Dame.[35] Blakey did not remember Salwyn or anything about his data. He could not even confirm that Salwyn had testified before the committee because, as he put it: "No list of witnesses who testified in closed session is available in the public domain." This is a euphemistic reference to the fact that the committee succeeded in locking up all unpublished records, data, testimony, and documents for a period of 50 years. Unlike Sergeant Power of RCMP, Blakey's lack of recall did not prevent him from fully discussing the substance of the matter at hand.

Whatever Salwyn's data was, opined the Notre Dame professor, it was "bullshit." The very subject of Raoul seemed to spark Blakey's ire. There appears to be mutual antipathy between Blakey and Ray. In a letter to the author, Ray said of Blakey: "As an ex-prosecutor I'm sure he thinks everything I say is a fabrication. Usually the same type thinks everything an informant says is true." Blakey claimed that the committee had spent far more of the taxpayers' money than it should have in checking out Ray's Raoul story. Said Blakey: "I'm as sure Ray killed Martin Luther King as I am of my birthday." Ray opined: "He [Blakey] is extremely hostile and I suspect it has nothing to do with whether or not he thinks I'm responsible for the MLK incident. Instead he thinks I didn't 'cooperate' with him to make him look good."[36]

Even so, "Raoul" has potential relevance to the case which extends beyond Ray's unverified assertions of innocence. Ray could indeed be guilty and still could have been managed by shadowy cutouts like "Raoul."

HSCA's treatment of the Kimble matter was both perfunctory and misleading. Within a section of its final report composed of a laundry list of conspiracy allegations, most of which are unsubstantiated rumors or uncorroborated reports of plots to kill King, the committee devoted two pages to "Jules Ricco Kimble." Salwyn's data was generally dismissed as irrelevant, and the conclusion was: "The Committee found

no evidence to support a Ray-Kimble connection or to indicate that
Kimble was involved in any plot to kill Dr. King."[37] HSCA interviewed
Kimble. It asserted that he had "apparently" been in Montreal only after
Ray had departed. There are strong indications, however, that these
conclusions were reached without benefit of a thorough investigation
of the available data.

HSCA's two-page analysis of Kimble is replete with gaps, inaccuracies,
and distortions. The report refers to what Salwyn "wrote" about Kimble
in the *Toronto Star*. In fact, there was no article because the data was
lost and the story killed. The author's independent check of the *Star*
library confirms what Salwyn and McRae said: no story on the Montreal
angle ever appeared.

The report states that Salwyn "wrote that a person whose name was
actually Raoul drove a white Mustang. . . . " In three separate interviews
with the author over the space of a year, Salwyn was consistent and
clear about his findings: Kimble was known to his girlfriend and landlord
not as Raoul but as "Rollie" or "Rolland," and he reportedly drove a
pink Camaro.

In an apparent attempt to debunk Salwyn's data, the report claims
that he "wrote" that Kimble was "a member of the right-wing Minutemen." It then states that a review of Kimble's files found no links with
that organization, only with the Ku Klux Klan. Had the committee discovered that Kimble was affiliated with the NAACP, this might have
been a distinction worth trumpeting; although Salwyn never did write
anything and, during his interviews with the author, never mentioned
a Minuteman connection.

The report informs the reader that "RCMP files indicated that this
person, named Kimble, made daily calls to New Orleans, listened to
police broadcasts, carried guns and made racist comments." But it fails
to point out how corroborative this is concerning Salwyn's findings.

As for the "Raoul" angle, the HSCA concluded: "There is no indication, however, that Kimble was involved in narcotics smuggling and
gunrunning, the criminal activities that James Earl Ray attributed to his
contact, Raoul." While Kimble's arrest record does not reflect these two
crimes per se, there is indication that he engaged in activities involving
guns and drugs. Kimble's Montreal girlfriend told Salwyn that Kimble
carried guns in his trunk. In a footnote to the HSCA report, we learn
that in 1967 he was arrested in Louisiana for illegal weapons possession
and that he allegedly used phony medical degrees in order to work at
a hospital where he could "secure controlled drugs."[38]

Regarding Kimble's possible connectives to Ray, the committee added
a new dimension beyond Montreal, beyond Salwyn's data. Based on
interviews with Kimble's wife and with New Orleans investigator Joseph
Oster, who had an extensive file on Kimble, HSCA concluded that Kim-

ble was in New Orleans in December 1967 when Ray drove there from Los Angeles.[39] Ray claims he met Raoul there and received money from him.

The committee also concluded that Kimble "apparently did not visit Montreal until after Ray had left that city in August 1967." Kimble was described by the committee as "generally uncooperative" during his interview, but he "confirmed that he did not go to Canada until September." As one would expect, he denied ever meeting Ray.

The question of timing is, of course, crucial. One witness who could shed light on whether or not Ray and Kimble were in Montreal simultaneously is Maryanne Levesque. HSCA's final report makes no mention of her, or of anyone who knew Kimble in Montreal. Salwyn claims that he was told by an HSCA investigator that Ms. Levesque refused to be interviewed, shielding herself with her Canadian citizenship.[40]

Salwyn is adamant that Kimble's stay in Montreal overlapped with Ray's, based on what Levesque told him. He insists that her phone records proved this. "I can tell you," said Salwyn, his professional pride piqued by my question, "that if I had any evidence he wasn't there when Ray was I would not have bothered."[41]

A footnote to HSCA's Kimble section cites the files of Joseph Oster and an interview with Kimble's wife as the sources for Kimble "apparently" not being in Montreal in July or August when Ray was there.[42] Was Kimble in jail or otherwise accounted for during Ray's tenure in Montreal? "Apparent" is quite tentative for such a crucial point. Since the committee's files are sealed until the year 2028, the only avenue left was to pursue the Oster file.

I located Joseph Oster in 1985 in Louisiana, where he runs a private investigative firm and heads the state Polygraph Board. His foot-thick file, compiled when he investigated Kimble for the Louisiana Labor-Management Commission of Inquiry in 1967, had been subpoenaed by Congress. It was returned to Oster several years later, at his request. With access to Oster's data, which was HSCA's primary source for tracking Kimble, it was possible to assess the validity of the committee's conclusions.[43] The file presents a quite different picture of Jules Kimble than HSCA's brief, selective references to its contents: It indicates that Kimble's possible contribution to what is most likely Ray's "Raoul" composite cannot be ruled out without further explanation.

Oster tracked Jules Kimble, to the extent possible, from July through October of 1967; because, according to Oster, Kimble was a suspect in the bombing of a prominent Louisiana union official and was also suspected of involvement in other incidents of labor-related violence that had plagued the state from 1966–67. Oster succeeded in arresting Kimble in September 1967, when the suspect was lured down from Montreal to meet his wife in Miami. Angelina Lorio, Kimble's wife in 1967, was interviewed by HSCA. She cooperated with Oster in 1967 and was one of the main sources of his data. Her information as to her husband's whereabouts is all in Oster's file, and, according to Oster, she has no independent information that would account for her husband's movements any better than does the file.

Oster stated that Kimble had friends in Montreal, and that there is no doubt that he was there during most of September. Oster's file contains reports from Montreal police and from Mrs. Kimble, as well as informant reports, confirming his presence. While there is no data to establish that he was in Montreal in July or August when Ray was there, the possibility is in no way precluded. "He [Kimble] was in Canada in September," said Oster. "He also could have been there another time." Oster's file manifests gaps in Kimble's known whereabouts for parts of July and August, when he disappeared for days at a time.

One blank spot is from July 18 until Kimble was again spotted "sometime after July 21" (the specific date is not pinned down in the report). Ray is thought to have arrived in Montreal on July 18.[44] In August Kimble was "in and out of Louisiana," said Oster, and the destinations were not always discovered by Louisiana law-enforcement investigators. In December 1967 Kimble was in New Orleans at the same time as Ray, but Oster's file indicates that Kimble disappeared toward the end of that month.

HSCA states baldly that Kimble was arrested July 26, 1967.[45] This would appear to reduce his latitude for traveling to Montreal during the relevant period (there would seem to be no other reason for citing the date of the arrest, and it is the only specific date provided by HSCA concerning Kimble's criminal activities). What HSCA did not tell the readers of its report is that, according to Oster, Kimble posted a $500 bond and was on the street by 8:00 P.M., only hours after his arrest.[46]

With Salwyn's data placing Kimble in Montreal while Ray was there and with Oster's data easily allowing for that possibility, the committee still decided to opt for the notion that since Oster's files placed Kimble there in September, that is "apparently" when he first arrived there.

HSCA also chose to downplay some of the more provocative information about Kimble. It blandly mentions his "associations in 1967 with the Ku Klux Klan." According to Oster, his file reflects that on July 18, 1967, Kimble met with four Grand Dragons of the KKK, before he disappeared for several days. Kimble's wife reported to Oster that she saw guns and explosives in the trunk of his car on that same day (Andy Salwyn was told by Kimble's Montreal girlfriend that he carried guns in his trunk). Oster also alleges that Kimble had meetings with Klan leaders in February and March of 1967.[47]

Oster believes that even his detailed file does not give a full account of Kimble's political and criminal activities, or of his associations. (In his criminal activities Kimble was known to have used the alias "Max Lind-say" and the embellishment Jules Ricco Von Kimble.) Oster was familiar with Kimble's FBI file but was surprised to learn from the author that HSCA had made reference to a CIA file as well. While the Agency did target domestic political groups during the 1960s, usually illegally, its surveillance was largely confined to radical-leftist, antiwar, and civil rights groups. It would be interesting to know the substance and depth of CIA interest in Jules Kimble. As for HSCA's investigation of Kimble, Oster opined that it "left a lot of doors closed."

It would seem important to establish Kimble's precise whereabouts in March and April of 1968. It is possible that his FBI file or CIA file has him accounted for during this period. These were not available to the author but were available to HSCA. It is also possible that Kimble's activities and whereabouts remain unknown.

Ray has always claimed that he contacted "Raoul" through a series of telephone numbers that Raoul provided. If Ray has one or more such numbers, as yet undisclosed, he might get a lucky bingo that could provide strong corroboration for his story. That is, if Ray were to produce a number that matched a Kimble-related number, this would be evidence that there was in fact someone like Raoul in Ray's life at the time and place he described.

Some analysts of the King case believe that if Ray had any such phone number, or any corroborating data whatsoever, he would have revealed it long ago, in order to help his case. But this assumption is unwarranted. There appear to be powerful motivations for Ray not to talk: fear of reprisal from conspirators, fear of getting himself in deeper (appearing more guilty or betraying his actual guilt instead of exculpating himself).

Harold Weisberg, who believes Ray was a patsy, also believes that Ray is holding back at least one crucial telephone number, and probably more.[48] Weisberg claims that he pressed Ray to give him the numbers and Ray promised to do so, "and then wouldn't. Not even when it might have been useful in his own defense."[49]

During my interview with Ray, he asserted that he used "a lot" of numbers to get in touch with Raoul and, furthermore, that he still has these numbers in his possession or at his recall.[50] Ray would give me only one alleged Raoul contact number, appearing on a photocopy of a receipt given to him by the Shelby County Jail, dated December 23, 1968. He claims to have scribbled the last four digits (3757) of a Raoul contact number in New Orleans, which he "backwards" on the receipt for pur-poses of security.[51] (I was by no means the only person to be given this number. Ray had given it to his then lawyer James Lesar several years ago.)

With regard to other numbers that might be cross-checked in this manner, Ray claims to have completely forgotten one which seems to the author to be potentially very promising.

In a letter to the author Ray asserted: "I was initially given a ph. number in Canada [Montreal, 1967] to use in calling Raoul in New Orleans. I don't recall anything about the first number."[52]

If Ray's story is correct, then Raoul gave him this number at the same approximate time that the Salwyn-RCMP mystery man was calling New Orleans numbers from Montreal. Thus the number would seem to be a good candidate for a match with one of the RCMP numbers from Ms. Levesque's apartment. If Ray has not really forgotten it, it could be the contact number that some believe Ray is withholding.

Apart from Ray's ability or inability to produce a phone number that matches one of the RCMP numbers, these numbers could well provide valuable avenues of investigation which have yet to be thoroughly explored by Canadian or American authorities. I failed in my attempt to obtain the RCMP phone numbers. On page 762 of HSCA's *Report*, a citation refers to "RCMP reports supplied by Shelby County district attorney's office, August 31, 1978, pp. 2305–2310." Since committee documents are sealed, I requested permission to review the document in Tennessee. Shelby County District Attorney General Hugh W. Stanton, Jr., who had worked in the public defender's office and helped his father defend Ray in 1968, refused to release anything unless subpoenaed.

Not only was Ray's post-assassination fugitive odyssey replete with mysterious contacts but there is a crucial gap in his known whereabouts. No one can say whether James Earl Ray was alone or in the company of others soon after the April 4 assassination, because no one knows for sure where he was from April 6 to April 8.

He has always asserted that he checked into a Toronto rooming house on April 6, two days after the assassination. According to Ray: He drove from Memphis to Atlanta, where he abandoned his car; took a bus to Detroit; then a bus to Windsor, Ontario; and, finally, rode a cab to Toronto on the afternoon of April 6.[53] However, staff researchers for the HSCA determined that Ray's account was at odds with the 1968 bus schedule along his supposed route of travel.[54] The landlady at Ray's rooming house, Mrs. Fella Szpakowski, insisted that Ray did not rent a room from her until April 8.[55] The committee concluded: "Thus it is possible that he could have visited associates in other cities between April 6 and April 8, though the investigation could find no evidence of such meetings."[56]

In the string of unidentified phone calls, companions, or visitors that seemed to crop up in various phases of Ray's relationship to the King assassination—from the Galt driver's license in Alabama to a caller with an American twang in London—none received as much attention as the so called "fat man." For a time, investigators were convinced that finding the fat man would lead to the conspirators behind Ray.

7   In Search of the Fat Man

Who's the Fat Man?

Toronto Star, June 10, 1968

Mounties Hunt "Fat Man" in Ray Case

New York Times, June 10, 1968

The "fat man" incident was by far the most provocative episode in the fugitive phase of the King case. Its conspiratorial implications generated considerable interest within the American media and a frenzied level of activity in Canada, where reporters and Mounties alike thought that finding the fat man might break open the conspiracy.

Ray had already been arrested in London when the fat man story broke. Ray's landlady on Dundas Street reported to police that on May 2 a corpulent stranger had come to the door asking for Sneyd (Ray's alias at the time) and had handed Ray an envelope. That very day, Ray paid up his rent and purchased an airplane ticket to London, where he flew four days later. The ticket cost $345; Ray paid in Canadian cash. Speculation quickly arose that the fat man was a coconspirator or, at minimum, a courier delivering get-away money.

The hunt for the fat man was on. But in less than a week it was over. On June 12 Toronto police made a dramatic announcement. The fat man had been found, and he was completely innocent of any involvement in the King case. It was simply that the so-called fat man was a Good Samaritan who was returning a misplaced letter to Sneyd/Ray. A man claiming to be the fat man had come forward to police and volunteered the story about the lost letter. The man's identity was kept secret by police, at his request.

Had the authorities found the real fat man, or was the man who came forward so conveniently some sort of disinformation agent? Was the Good Samaritan story credible or was it more likely that Ray's escape money was in the envelope? We shall examine this key event by detailing the landlady's account, then analyzing the explanation of the incident given by Toronto police in 1968. These will then be related to Ray's behavior and, finally, to what the fat man had to say 16 years later.

The report of the incident came from Mrs. Yee Sun Loo, the 32-year-old mother of three who rented a room in her Dundas Street home to Ray.[1] Ray stayed 16 days in the second-floor room of the three-story, Victorian-style, red brick dwelling. It was located in what was then an ethnically mixed, older neighborhood on the fringes of Toronto's red-light district. During his stay, Ray had but one visitor. Mrs. Loo described Ray as very quiet. He would come into her kitchen, pay his rent, then "disappear"; he "never said anything."[2]

It was Thursday, May 2. James Earl Ray was the only boarder still in his room, the others had gone to work. According to Mrs. Loo, the events occurred as follows. She had just finished putting a diaper on her baby and had placed the child in his high chair. She glanced at the clock. It was noon.

She heard three raps at her front door and went to answer. Through her screen door she saw a man standing on the wooden porch.

"Yes?" she inquired.

"Is Mr. Sneyd in?" asked the visitor. He held a white, letter-sized envelope with a typewritten name on it.

"I will get him," said Mrs. Loo.

She went upstairs to Ray's room and informed him: "Mr. Sneyd, there is a man with a letter for you." Ray emerged wearing a dark suit and sunglasses. He nodded and descended the stairs.

Mrs. Loo observed as Ray went to the front door. She could not hear what was said but saw the visitor nod to Ray and hand him the envelope. They exchanged a few words. Ray put the envelope in the inside pocket of his suit jacket, turned and went upstairs. The visitor left.

Mrs. Loo described Ray's visitor as "tall" and "fat." He was Caucasian and appeared to be about 40 years old, with dark hair brushed back. He wore a white, short-sleeved t-shirt tucked inside his black trousers.

The hunt was on. Earl McRae, who now writes for a Toronto magazine, covered the story for the *Toronto Star* and obtained an exclusive interview with Mrs. Loo. He recalled for the author the excitement generated by the search for the fat man:

We worked round-the-clock to find him. Everyone thought: "This is it—the payoff was in the envelope. This is the conspiracy." The police felt particularly dumb because here was the key to the King case right in their backyard and they couldn't find the fat man.[3]

Each of Toronto's three newspapers—the *Star, Globe and Mail,* and *Telegram*—tried to find the fat man before its competitors did. The constant drumfire of publicity was an embarrassment to Toronto police, whose efforts to identify and locate the suspect were unsuccessful.

One lead came from a cab driver who had been dispatched to pick up two men across the street from Ray's rooming house at 12:18 P.M., shortly after the fat man's noontime visit. The driver described his two fares as being white males "forty to fifty years old," and one was "big and fat."[4] The two men were waiting on the sidewalk when the driver arrived. He took them to the Toronto Dominion Bank a few blocks west.

Records of the Diamond Taxi Company revealed that on three occasions on May 2, including the one just described, someone called for a cab to be sent to 955 Dundas Street West, a house directly across the street from Mrs. Loo's. No one at 955 Dundas called a cab that day, according to Anthony Szezepina, whose family occupied the dwelling.[5]

Police showed the cab driver pictures of Ray and two other men, none of whom the cabbie recognized. The driver did not recognize Ray as the man with the alleged fat man, but did recognize Ray as the fare he had picked up on May 1, four doors down from Mrs.Loo's. The cabbie's May 2 pickup seemed to be the police's best lead, but it was at a dead end at the Toronto Dominion Bank.

Then, on June 12, only four days after the incident had been reported, Toronto police held a press conference and made a dramatic announcement: They had found the so-called fat man and the matter had been resolved. He was described by police as middle-aged and not fat at all, simply "big." His story was as follows.[6]

He was working in the neighborhood where Ray's rooming house was located. He went to make a phone call in a telephone booth—there was, in fact, a phone booth located only a few yards from Mrs. Loo's door—and found an unsealed letter, apparently left by someone. He opened the envelope and read the letter, which had something to do with a job application. He could not remember much about the letter's contents beyond its general nature, nor could he recall to whom it was addressed. The man decided to return the letter to its owner and walked to the address of the sender and asked for Mr. Sneyd.

Police stated that the man did not know Ray and had no criminal connection with the King case. They checked out his story and they were satisfied. So far as the police and RCMP were concerned, the search for the fat man was over. Needless to say, there was a good deal of suspicion among the local press that the police were so anxious to settle the matter, and thus prevent further questioning of their competence, that they would grasp at any "solution" regardless of how tenuous, or even contrived, it might be. Earl McRae, for one, continued to pursue the fat man for two weeks, until his editors diverted him to other assignments. His main goal was to discover the identity of the self-announced fat man, and then check the validity of his story, but he was unable to do so. If we compare the version of the story accepted by police with Mrs. Loo's account and also with Ray's behavior, a string of problems arises concerning the validity of the Good Samaritan version.

The *Toronto Telegram* brought up two points which, when taken out of context or left unexplained as they were in the *Telegram*, implicitly cast doubt on Mrs. Loo's credibility.[7] First, the *Telegram* described Mrs. Loo as "near hysterics" when its reporters interviewed her. Second, the newspaper claimed that she had meant to tell police that the visitor was tall and big but because of a language barrier, police thought she meant to describe him as fat.

If Mrs. Loo was "near hysterics" by the time the *Telegram* talked to her on the evening of the day the story broke, it was probably because of the traumatic experience she had undergone during the day. Mrs. Loo was a Chinese immigrant living in one of the seedier sections of the city. It is likely that she regarded the white authority structure with considerable trepidation if not outright suspicion. Being grilled by Toronto police and then besieged by reporters must have been emotionally unsettling.

Earl McRae, who obtained an exclusive interview with Mrs. Loo before she was hounded by hordes of his colleagues in the Toronto press, told the author that he had no problems whatsoever in communicating with her. He found her to be a credible witness whose recall of the incident seemed both clear and detailed.[8]

Regarding the second point, police were wont to point out that the man who came forward with the Good Samaritan story was not fat, only tall and big. The police gleefully reiterated this point as a way of implying that the whole incident was blown out of proportion; that, implicitly, Mrs. Loo was either prone to exaggerate or could not accurately communicate the details of the event.

In fairness to Mrs. Loo's powers of perception and communication, it should be noted that to a slender Oriental woman, a tall, robust Caucasian man (whose girth may well have been accentuated by his tucked-in t-shirt) might appear to be fat, even though police officers would not choose to describe him as such.

There is no doubt, however, that the attention suddenly focused on Mrs. Loo was a difficult experience for her. When I contacted her she refused to talk about the incident. "Oh, no, no," she protested. Her son told me that she consistently refused to talk about the matter.[9]

There are formidable problems with the police's explanation of the fat man incident. First of all, there is the claim that the letter found in the phone booth was related to Ray's seeking employment. Within hours of the incident, Ray purchased a $345 airplane ticket and paid cash. Either he already had the necessary get-away money in his possession or it was delivered to him in the envelope. In either case, job hunting would have made little sense: The money to escape to London was in hand or on the way. Job hunting abroad would make no sense either. Presumably Ray knew nothing about London and had no idea where he would be staying. There was no suggestion by Toronto police that the letter was headed abroad.

Moreover, when we consider the circumstances and the time frame surrounding Ray's purchase of the ticket, it appears all the more likely that the fat man delivered money. It was on April 16 that Ray went to the Kennedy Travel Agency in Toronto and ordered a ticket to London and a passport under the name of Sneyd (the travel agency handled the passport application for its customer).[10] Ray was informed that it would take between one and two weeks for his application to be processed by the bureaucracy in Ottawa and mailed to the travel agency. He left his Dundas Street address and Mrs. Loo's phone number with the agency.[11]

Ten days later, on April 26, the "Sneyd" passport arrived. Ray had booked an excursion flight that departed Toronto on May 6. One would think that the world's number one fugitive would be anxious to pick up his passport and ticket as soon as possible, to have them in his possession in case he had to leave that section of the city or had to change addresses again—in case the law began to close in on him. There would be an advantage to having his get-away credentials in hand, even if it were not possible for him to arrange to leave sooner than May 6.

Yet, whatever the potential benefits, Ray was in no position to retrieve his ticket unless he could come up with the money. It might have seemed odd, and thereby called attention to himself, if he had picked up his passport but left his ticket there until later, clearly signaling that he did not yet have the necessary funds. The appearance of normalcy in this transaction was important to Ray. He told Mrs. Lillian Spencer, the travel agent, that he was a used-car salesman from a small town in Canada who had recently moved to Toronto. This was Ray's way of explaining why he had no one in Toronto who could vouch for his Canadian citizenship. And, as Ray described to HSCA, he purposely ordered a round-trip ticket because: "I figured that would be less suspicious than getting one way."[12]

Despite the obvious utility of getting his ticket and passport as soon as possible, they languished at the travel agency until May 2—the day of the fat man's visit. It will also be recalled that the visit took place at noon. Ray had all morning to go to the travel agency and retrieve his traveling papers if he had the money to do so. But he waited until afternoon.

Mrs. Loo glimpsed the envelope. It was white and had only a type-written name on the front.[13] She could not make out the name but believed that it was a name. Ray did not own a typewriter nor did he have access to one, so far as we know. Moreover, the envelope could hardly have contained a job query which was intended for mailing, not with only a name and no address. If—as seems likely, given the incident of the "slight man" which will be described shortly—the typed name on the envelope was Ramon Sneyd, then the envelope was to Ray.

Mrs. Loo recalled that when the fat man came to her door he asked: "Is Mr. Sneyd in?"[14] Mrs. Loo's house was not so large as to look like a hotel. One might have expected that, upon seeing a Chinese woman come to the door, the fat man might first want to confirm that Sneyd lived there—"Does Mr. Sneyd live here?" If he was confident of the address or willing to assume that Sneyd lived there, he might have simply slipped the envelope through the mail slot or under the door. After all, the fat man had supposedly opened and read the letter and knew that the envelope did not contain anything financially valuable or of an emergency nature. Yet, he was evidently such a thorough Good Samaritan that he was willing to spend part of his lunch hour waiting for Sneyd to come to the door and receive the envelope rather than just dropping it off and hurrying away. Although it was supposedly a routine letter whose substance was quite forgettable, returning it to the right address was not enough to satisfy the fat man: He felt compelled to hand it to the man who had penned it.

The key to the fat man incident is James Earl Ray's behavior. Ray was not known to hang around his room during the day. His Ossington Street landlady, Mrs. Fella Szpakowski, told police that he left every morning at 8:30 and returned just after supper.[15] During the week preceding the fat man's visit, Mrs. Loo saw almost nothing of Ray. His bed was always loosely made when she would check the room during the day, and Ray was always gone. She wasn't even sure that he was occupying his room, except that he did pay his rent for that week (April 26 to May 3).[16] It was during this same week that Ray was seen on at least two occasions in the Silver Dollar Tavern drinking with another man. It will also be recalled that on April 27, five days before the fat man incident, Mrs. Loo took a call for Ray in which the caller said "Get Sneyd." Ray was out at the time. But on Thursday, May 2, Ray had reappeared and was in his room when the fat man came.

Ray was a fugitive and, by all accounts, an extremely nervous one. Mrs. Szpakowski remembered his as appearing "so worried all the time."[17] One of his London landladies, Mrs. Thomas, described him as "very, very nervous." She recalled that Ray was so reclusive he refused to open the door to get his breakfast tray.[18] Instead, he asked Mrs. Thomas to leave it outside the door. Nor would he open the door to receive telephone messages: Mrs. Thomas had to slip them under the door, even though Ray was in his room at the time. Ray's behavior is easy to understand. He was, after all, the most sought after criminal in the Western world.

In contrast, when Mrs. Loo went up to Ray's room and told him "Mr. Sneyd, there is man with a letter for you," she recalled that Ray nodded and came downstairs.[19] Not only did Ray come downstairs directly, without hesitation, but he went straight to the door and began talking with the visitor.

Shouldn't Ray have been very suspicious of the caller, or, at minimum, hesitant to come downstairs? How did he know that it was not the police? Didn't he want to try to check out the supposed stranger before greeting him, perhaps by trying to catch a glimpse of him? Didn't Ray want to check out the situation—to see if there were cars outside or to make sure that there was only one person rather than a bevy of plain-clothes detectives?

If Ray would not open his London door to receive food or messages, why should he immediately make himself available to receive "a letter"? Didn't he want to ask "What kind of letter?" Ray could easily have told Mrs. Loo to get the letter for him and slip it under his door; he could have instructed her to tell the man to leave the letter. Are we to believe that, within the context of the police's version, Ray remembered he had lost a job-application letter somewhere and was hoping, or expecting, that some Good Samaritan would return it? Ray's behavior, as well as his very presence in his room, are much more logically explained by the idea that he was waiting for a delivery of money, that he knew full well what the envelope contained.

The press and official investigators from 1968 to the present have failed to perceive the relevance of another occurrence which bears upon the fat man incident. Ray's first Toronto landlady, Mrs. Szpakowski, reported that on April 25 a visitor came to see Ray at the Ossington Street address where he was registered as Paul Bridgeman.[20] Mrs. Szpakowski vaguely remembered that the visitor who knocked on her front door may have proffered some identification, but she could not recall what it was.[21] The visitor was "short, slight" had blond hair, and wore a suit and tie. He held up a white envelope with the name Bridgeman typed on the front.[22] When she informed him that "Bridgeman" had moved on and that she did not have a forwarding address, the visitor left.

What the press and official investigator's have missed is how closely this parallels Mrs. Loo's account of the fat man incident. She recalled that the fat man had given Ray an envelope with a name typed on it (although she did not see the name). The fact that the slight man had an envelope with Ray's alias typed on the front increases the likelihood that the fat man's envelope had "Ramon Sneyd" typed on it, and that it was to Ray. An FBI teletype from headquarters to Memphis on June 12 states that the letter "was to Sneyd at Dundas Address."

Canadian and U.S. authorities had kept secret the identity of the man who came forward. Released documents deleted his identity. But one document obtained by the author had failed to delete the name: William Bolton (a pseudonym created by the author).

I located William Bolton in 1984, expecting that his very appearance might preclude his having been the fat man. In 1968 Mrs. Loo had described the man as tall, "fat," with dark hair, and appearing to be about 40 years old. The man who did not answer his front doorbell, but whom I confronted near his car when he emerged from his back door, appeared to be in his mid fifties. He had dark hair, was about six feet three inches tall, appeared to weigh around 180 pounds, and was powerfully built. He also had a significant paunch. Even if the paunch was only in its embryonic stages 16 years ago, this was definitely a man who, when wearing a t-shirt tucked into his trousers, could easily have impressed a small Oriental woman as being not only tall but "fat."

I delivered a carefully rehearsed opening line, the logical response to which—for anyone other than the fat man—would be something like: "What are you talking about?" or "You must have the wrong address." The line was: "I'm a professor of political science and I'm interviewing a number of persons like yourself who had interesting encounters sixteen years ago."

Bolton stared silently at my rented car parked on the street. His face provided the answer to his identity long before he spoke. A hard, yet anguished expression swept his visage. His racing thoughts were almost palpable. Finally, he looked directly at the interviewer. "How did you find me?" he asked.[23]

The encounter was tense. Bolton's initial shock at being discovered after 16 years gave way to panic. "What's going on with this case?" he asked. "Is this a new investigation?" He demanded to know my identity and carefully wrote the name on a card in his wallet. Apparently somewhat relieved that the interviewer's affiliation was academic rather than investigative, he argued for continued anonymity. As I broached the substance of the incident, he became visibly agitated. "Nothing to it. I told them all I know."

Even so, Bolton went on to claim that he feared for his life. "They [the FBI] wanted me to be a witness [in 1968]. I refused. Why go [to Memphis] and get a bullet in my head?" He referred to the deaths of assassination witnesses in the John F. Kennedy case.

Bolton's sense of fear seemed genuine. But as he elaborated his story, it was clear that either it was not genuine—perhaps it was his way of lobbying for continued anonymity—or the police's Good Samaritan story was a cover for something much more provocative.

"Why would anyone kill you?" I asked. "Your only involvement in the case was as an innocent bystander trying to do a good deed. Substantively, there's no real involvement in the case."

Bolton was now anxious, even angry; but both emotions were controlled. "Ray and those people are gangsters," he asserted. "They'll kill anyone."

"Why would such gangsters want to kill a man whose only connection with the case was to find a letter about a job?" I asked.

He snorted and shook his head. "I've never told. . . . It was a job, all right." He talked softly and in ominous tones. "It was a job in Portugal and it [the letter] showed that he had help." Bolton asserted that there was "big money" behind Ray.

He went on to claim that it was the Portugal-related substance of the letter that led authorities to Ray. Thus Bolton contended that he was responsible for Ray's arrest.

I asked to whom the letter was addressed and whether it mentioned mercenaries. (Ray was, in fact, attempting to make contact with mercenaries in Portugal.) Bolton responded that he did not remember. I asked what he meant when he said the letter showed that Ray had "help." He replied darkly: "That's all I'll say."

In 1968 there was never so much as a hint that the substance of the letter had anything directly to do with the case, except that it was penned by Ray. It is true that Ray was headed for Portugal when arrested in London on June 8, but it is clearly not true that what Bolton told the police led to Ray's arrest: The fat man incident did not surface until after Ray's arrest, and neither did the self-announced fat man.

That Bolton could have been confused about the sequence of events leading to Ray's arrest, that he might have genuinely believed that it was his information that got Ray arrested, is highly improbable. Bolton seemed sharp. There was nothing slow about his intellectual processes. The very newspapers in which he supposedly first read about the fat man incident not only contained headlines and articles dealing with Ray's capture (on the same pages as the fat man stories) but most of the articles about the fat man contained references to Ray's arrest. Ray was arrested June 8. For the next five days, Toronto newspapers gave extensive coverage to his arrest, his extradition, and to the police work that led to his capture. The fat man articles appeared June 10 and 11, at the peak of coverage concerning Ray's capture. It strains credulity to believe that someone could be cognizant of the fat man story and avoid knowing that Ray was already behind bars.

The story that Bolton gave to the author was more substantively detailed, and more credible, in dimensions which did not relate directly to the letter. He accurately described the Dundas Street neighborhood and the house where Mrs. Loo lived. He recounted how the police checked out his story, taking him to the Dundas Street area and requiring that he lead them to the phone booth where the letter was allegedly found. He told how police dismantled the public telephone and checked the phone booth from top to bottom, how a frightened Mrs. Loo identified him for police.

Then I asked one of the most crucial and sensitive questions of all: What was Ray's demeanor? Bolton laughed (a forced, nervous laugh).

"He [Ray] was nervous, scared—turned his face from me and grabbed the envelope." Bolton mimed Ray's alleged actions. " 'Thanks,' he says to me."

Not only does this conflict with Mrs. Loo's description of the exchange between the two men; but if Ray was truly scared about the encounter, he would have had no reason to come down and meet the stranger.

There were always three possible scenarios for the fat man incident:

1. The man who came forward with the Good Samaritan story was not the real fat man, but concocted his story at the behest of others who needed to resolve the matter or who wanted to dead-end a lead to the conspiracy.

2. The man who came forward was the real fat man and the Good Samaritan story was true.

3. The man who came forward before he was discovered was, in fact, the fat man but he was a courier who delivered funds to Ray, even though he may not have known what was in the envelope, who "Sneyd" really was, or on whose behalf the delivery was made.

It is yet another indication of the HSCA's lack of initiative, or its myopia, that it did not find Bolton and thoroughly investigate the incident. On the basis of the data gathered here, the matter remains as intriguing as it was in 1968. Available evidence suggests that option 1 is not likely: William Bolton fits the description of the fat man and demonstrates a credible familiarity with the scene of the incident. In the author's opinion, William Bolton is the fat man. Yet, the Good Samaritan story remains as shaky now as it was in 1968, especially when considered within the context of Ray's behavior, Mrs. Loo's description, and the striking similarity of the "slight man" incident.

As for William Bolton, the interviewer was impressed with the credibility of one facet of his story: He seemed genuinely afraid for his personal safety. His primary reaction to being rediscovered after 16 years was not bemusement, annoyance, or apprehension about publicity. It was more like the kind of fear one might expect from someone whose cover identity under the federal witness-protection program had just been blown.

Perhaps the most important question is *who* or *what* Bolton was afraid of. If he feared what he referred to as the "gangsters" or the "big money" behind Ray, then it was not because he provided police with the lead that resulted in Ray's arrest. If William Bolton feared the men behind James Earl Ray, it was for another reason, as yet undisclosed.

8   The Window of Vulnerability

Here you have a situation where you have the major civil rights
leader in the country in your city, you have a riot situation looking
you in the face, security guards are removed, tactical forces are
removed, surveillance is removed, and there is a failure to issue an
all points bulletin after a description is made available . . . [1]
Congressman Christopher Dodd, HSCA, to Memphis Public Safety
Director Frank Holloman

The pattern had become legend in the King case—the melting away of
protection and pursuit forces within hours of the assassination, the failure to issue an APB until it was too late to catch the suspect, the presence
of a police undercover agent in the parking lot of the Lorraine at the
time of the shooting. Is the pattern conspiratorial or coincidental? Which
of its components are real; which, mythical? Certainly, petty criminal
James Earl Ray possessed no capacity to manipulate law-enforcement.
Nor did the alleged St. Louis conspiracy, whose only putative relationship to the crime was to offer a bounty on King. Any such manipulations
would require a sophisticated conspiracy with access to intelligence and
law-enforcement networks.

So conspicuous was the collapse of police presence at the crime scene
that even Memphis police officers voiced suspicions that the fix was in. [2]
HSCA implied that the failures were due to a combination of incompetence and latent racism rather than conspiratorial intrigue. After ex-
amining the possibility of a sinister FBI influence concerning the poor
performance of the Memphis Police Department (MPD) the committee

broadly asserted: "No federal, state or local government agency was involved in the assassination of Dr. King."[3] A careful analysis of each incident reveals that HSCA was, at best, premature in its conclusion: The possibility of federal intelligence-related manipulation is indeed very real in some instances, although the precise agency or network cannot be identified.

THE FAILURES TO COMMUNICATE

Word of the shooting reached the police communication system within minutes, from two different sources. MPD had a chance to catch any fleeing suspects by issuing radio commands for appropriate action. But this did not happen until it was too late. Ray's seemingly miraculous escape, during which he fled the boarding house and eluded onrushing officers by only a few seconds, continued as the law-enforcement nets that might have trapped him in the city and the state closed just after he slipped through.

Within a minute after King was shot, Police Officer W. B. Richmond rushed to a telephone inside the firehouse and reported to Memphis police intelligence headquarters.[4] From a patrol car parked near the firehouse, an officer from tactical unit number ten (TACT 10) radioed the police dispatcher. This occurred at 6:03—two minutes after the shooting.[5]

Data continued to flow from the crime scene to police headquarters, via TACT 10.[6] At 6:07 the dispatcher was advised that a weapon had been recovered and that a suspect had been seen running south on Main Street. At 6:08 there was a description of the suspect: a young, well-dressed white male. (The description from TACT 10 also included a reference to "dark colored [inaudible]," probably dark-colored clothing or a suit. The dispatcher failed to repeat this or to ask for clarification. There was no reference to clothing in his broadcast to police units.)[7] At 6:10 the getaway vehicle was described: the suspect had escaped "possibly in a late [model] white Mustang, went north on Main Street."[8]

MPD's standard operating procedure called for two responses in situations of this type. One was for the dispatcher to use a "signal Y," a code indicating that certain units were to proceed immediately to prearranged locations blocking all main exits from Memphis.[9] No signal Y was broadcast. The second response was to issue an All Points Bulletin (APB) describing the suspect. This was not done, neither for Memphis nor for the neighboring states of Arkansas, Mississippi, and Alabama. These three failures of communication allowed the assassin(s) to escape cleanly.

Among the standard and appropriate actions taken by MPD were: broadcasting a "signal Q," ordering all units to maintain radio silence and await information and instructions; ordering all downtown traffic lights switched to red, to facilitate emergency traffic; informing the Shelby County Sheriff's Office and the Tennessee Highway Patrol that King had been shot.[10]

The more important actions—those that might have caught the suspect(s)—were taken too late or not at all. The two-block area around the Lorraine was not sealed off until 6:06. The dispatcher's order came three minutes after the shooting was reported.[11] According to Memphis Public Safety Director Frank Holloman, MPD procedures gave the dispatcher "broad authority and responsibility" to deal with situations without waiting for orders from anyone else.[12] Holloman told HSCA that, based on his 25 years of police experience, the suspect description relayed to the dispatcher at 6:08 contained sufficient information to issue an APB and to seal off the city.[13]

HSCA grilled Holloman as to why these standard actions were not taken. The committee noted, with particular ire, that the dispatcher was not reprimanded much less demoted or fired.[14] As cathartic as this may have been for the Congressmen, they might have learned more by directly questioning Lt. Frank Kallaher, the "shift commander of communications," and the dispatcher, instead of taking affidavits. Top-administrator Holloman had no operational responsibility for communications on April 4, 1968.

Lt. Kallaher's affidavit did not provide a sufficient basis for resolving the failures. He assured the committee that:

I was never instructed by anyone not to direct a broadcast of "Signal Y" or not to communicate an "All Points Bulletin" to neighboring jurisdictions. My failure is attributable to the massive confusion and huge volume of radio traffic which erupted immediately following the assassination of Dr. King and which caused me to overlook the function of these duties.[15]

This may be so, but absent a more thorough probe of the workings of the communications center, this explanation seems inadequate, for several reasons.

If there was "massive confusion" it is not reflected in the transcript of police communications. The dispatcher's transmissions seem unfrenzied and logical. For example, at 6:07 the dispatcher is told that a rifle has been found. He reminds the TACT 10 officers: "not to touch the weapon. The weapon is not to be touched. Any physical description on the subject?"[16]

As for the huge volume of radio traffic, it did not prevent the issuing of a signal Q (all quiet); but a signal Y (seal off the city) was not issued. Nor did it prevent MPD from informing the Sheriff's office and the state police, from ordering the traffic lights turned to red, or from sealing off the Lorraine at 6:06.

As to why neighboring states were not alerted after the fugitive had escaped Memphis, Kallaher asserted: "It was not my normal practice [to issue an APB to Mississippi]due to a past history of noncooperation from that state."[17] What about Alabama and Arkansas? Kallaher does not explain why these states were not worthy of contacting. If there was a problem with Mississippi, Public Safety Director Holloman was apparently not aware of it. He told HSCA that issuing an APB to neighboring states "would have been proper procedure."[18]

Kallaher also offered a second explanation: "It was my belief that in a case of a fugitive escaped over the Tennessee state line, it was the Federal Bureau of Investigation's responsibility to disseminate fugitive data."[19] Such a preeminent federal role was never mentioned by Holloman, a 25-year FBI veteran. How would the Bureau obtain fugitive data if not from the Memphis police. Kallaher communicated with the sheriff's office and the state police but not the FBI.

Neither Kallaher's inadequate explanations nor HSCA's flogging of Holloman provided an acceptable resolution of the communications failures.

WITHDRAWAL OF SECURITY

The necessity of police protection for King did not derive solely from his public prominence and from MPD's recognition of that prominence. This was a public figure whose life was in constant danger. A post-assassination review of King's FBI file, conducted by the Bureau in order to identify potential suspects, revealed no fewer than 50 threats against his life.[20] One came only three days before the assassination. An "urgent" FBI radiogram from the Bureau's Memphis office relayed a threat received by American Airlines in Memphis on April 1. The menacing call stated: "Your airlines brought Martin Luther King, Jr.,to Memphis and when he comes in again, a bomb will go off and he will be assassinated."[21] The FBI passed this information to military intelligence, the Secret Service, the Federal Aviation Administration, and the Memphis police. Information about another alleged assassination plot against King was received by MPD on April 2.[22]

MPD's sudden and unexplained withdrawal of King's security spawned a great deal of speculation concerning conspiracy. On April 3 King arrived at the Memphis airport at 10:30 A.M. and was greeted by a four-man police security detail.[23] The unit was apparently assigned because of the violence that had erupted during King's previous visit to Memphis.

King had not requested security. In fact, the police presence made King's entourage uneasy. MPD was perceived as an instrument of force wielded by a hostile white power structure.[24] Police were viewed as having been overzealous in using force to break up King's attempted nonviolent march in support of the striking sanitation workers. It is not surprising that the security unit got an icy response. According to Inspector Donald Smith, who headed the detail, information about King's agenda was not provided. Rev. James Lawson, the Memphis minister who had invited King, told Smith that King had not yet made up his mind about the itinerary. Mrs. Tarlese Mathews, another member of King's party, allegedly told Smith that King had not requested security.[25]

Nevertheless, the security detail followed King from the airport to the Lorraine. It also accompanied him to an appearance at a local church, where police secured the front and rear exits. On the return trip to the Lorraine, King's party allegedly took side streets without signaling. Inspector Smith claims that he thought King was trying to lose the police. Smith got tired of "tagging along" without knowing where he and his men were headed.

At 5:00 P.M. on April 3, Smith telephoned Chief of Detectives W. P. Houston and asked permission to withdraw the detail because of lack of cooperation. Smith's version is that Houston quickly conferred with "someone," then granted permission to withdraw. (Unknown to Smith, the "someone" may have been Police Chief James McDonald, according to MPD's Henry Lux. McDonald told HSCA he had no recollection of the removal.)[26]

Twenty-five hours before the assassination, King was stripped of police security: the detail departed shortly after the 5:00 P.M. phone call, never to return. While this sequence of events is often perceived as conspiratorial (in part because of the false allegations of Detective Edward Reddit which will be discussed shortly) the weight of the evidence suggests otherwise.

That there would be antipathy between King's party and a police security detail is understandable. Police regarded King as the supreme outside agitator. They were not disposed to do him any favors. In addition to King's distrust of MPD, it was not in keeping with his image as a people's champion of nonviolent struggle to be surrounded by armed, uniformed guards.

The presence of the security detail could not have prevented the assassination, because it offered no protection against a long-range sniper. This was not a Secret Service-type unit that would constantly surround the protectee, search tall buildings for snipers, check each entrance and exit in advance, and whisk the protectee from doorway to limousine as quickly as possible.[27] The unit was comprised of regular policemen who had no special training in protective methods and whose idea of security was to stand near a doorway and keep the crowd back. The only pro-

tection this provided was against an assault of the kind perpetrated on
Governor George Wallace or President Reagan, an assault in which the
would-be assassin attacks from close in.

Even so, the withdrawal of King's security was unjustified. The inconsistent nature of the decision is attested to by the fact that despite
the alleged rejections by King's party, the detail remained on duty for
six and a half hours; and its size was actually increased from four to
seven officers.[28] Then, instead of being decreased, it was summarily
withdrawn in toto. King was neither consulted nor informed.

Tensions between King and the police notwithstanding, there was a
precedent for his accepting police help in a difficult situation. A week
earlier, during the ill-fated march, King's party had asked for police help
in escaping the violence. Police cleared the way for King's vehicle to
depart. One officer was asked to escort King to his hotel, and did so.[29]

The inappropriateness of MPD's withdrawal becomes vividly clear
when we consider that it provided special protection to one of its own
(who did not want it) because of what turned out to be a false threat,
while stripping King of security even though the FBI had reported an
assassination threat against him and MPD itself had learned of a second
threat.

THE THREAT AGAINST DETECTIVE REDDIT

Over the years, the Reddit allegation has been a central element in
many conspiracy theories. Edward Reddit, a black Memphis police officer, appeared on TV with various authors, recounting how King's
security had been purposely stripped away in order to assure a successful
assassination.[30] Reddit claimed that he was removed from security duty
under the pretext of a false threat against his life.

HSCA's probe of the matter clearly established that Reddit's allegation
was false. On April 4, 1968, he was actually working for MPD's intelligence squad: His job was not to protect King but to surveil him.[31]
Reddit was stationed inside the firehouse, across from the Lorraine,
with the police spy team. Even if he had not been removed from duty,
he could not have prevented the shooting. All he could have done was
to give chase to fleeing suspects, as numerous other officers attempted
to do.[32]

Under sharp questioning by HSCA, Reddit admitted that the notion
of his providing security was "absolutely false."[33] Despite his apology
for any misinterpretations created by his past statements, the committee
asserted that he had "knowingly" allowed such misinterpretations to
be "exploited by advocates of conspiracy theories," which HSCA labeled
"reprehensible."[34] Having discredited Reddit's story, the committee concluded that his removal from duty "was not part of any plot to facilitate

the assassination of Dr. King."[35] If the incident under scrutiny is narrowly defined, this is true—that since Reddit was in no way involved in security, his physical removal from the crime scene was not germane to any plot.

As is all too typical of HSCA's handling of the case, it focused narrowly on Reddit's allegation rather than on the Reddit affair. The false death threat could have been designed to distract key elements of MPD in order to facilitate a successful assassination. Consider the potentially disruptive consequences and mysterious, federal origin of the false threat.

On the day of the assassination, top MPD officials spent considerable energy dealing with this problem. At police headquarters there was an afternoon meeting attended by Chief McDonald, Inspector Graydon Tines, and Public Safety Director Holloman. (There is some difference of opinion as to the participants: Chief McDonald does not recall Tines being present; Tines claims he was.)[36] Reddit was informed that there was a contract out on his life and that he and his family were to be placed under police protection. Holloman proposed that Reddit hide out in a hotel using an alias.[37] Reddit rejected the idea of protection, but he was sent home under police guard anyway.[38]

The meeting took place between 4:00 and 5:00 P.M. Across town at the Lorraine, at approximately the same time, King's security detail was withdrawn without informing him.

The officer who protected Reddit was E. H. Arkin, head of MPD's intelligence unit. He drove Reddit home. The two men were sitting in a cruiser in front of Reddit's house when news of the assassination crackled over the police radio.[39] Arkin, whose surveillance team was ensconced in the firehouse, was removed from both the firehouse and police headquarters at the time of the shooting; baby-sitting the reluctant Reddit in response to a false threat.

Whether the Reddit affair negatively affected police performance in any direct way is problematic. However, if conspirators wanted to divert the attention of key administrative and intelligence personnel during the crucial two hours before King's murder, they could not have done better than to inject into federal channels a false assassination plot designed to distract police from the real one. (A police memo dated April 4 refers to the threat as an assassination plot: "Information Concerning Assassination Plot of Possibly Det. Reddit.")[40]

The origins of the threat lie not in Memphis but in Washington, D.C., in the murky labyrinth of the federal law-enforcement bureaucracy. Memphis Public Safety Director Holloman recalled that news of the threat was relayed to MPD by the U.S. Secret Service. But HSCA's check with the Service negated this possibility. Instead, the source seems to have been federal informants.[41]

An April 4 police memo states that at 3:00 P.M. MPD "received word from Washington" that a "reliable informer" had advised "of a plan of the Mississippi Freedom Democratic Party, MFDP, to kill a negro Lt. here in Memphis. It is believed that they are referring to Det. Reddit." The memo warns that the plan had "already been set in motion." It advises that "the names of those involved in the plot," and "all the particulars," will "possibly be relayed to us later tonight."[42]

Police seemed to regard this information as both reliable and verifiable, but it turned out to be neither. The threat was actually directed at a black police sergeant in Knoxville, not a black lieutenant in Memphis.[43] This correction was later relayed to MPD by the Memphis FBI office.

There is a second MPD memo dated April 4, from Arkin to his boss Inspector Tines. It asserts that at 4:15 P.M. the FBI telephoned and made a correction concerning the target of the threat.[44] Either the stated time is grossly in error or MPD behaved very strangely after receiving the correct information.

The meeting at police headquarters, during which the threat was discussed, took place sometime after four o'clock. According to Holloman, it broke up around five.[45] There is no indication that the group knew that the original information was wrong. For one hour, beginning 45 minutes after the time stated on the memo (4:15), Arkin was baby-sitting Reddit.

Inspector Tines, to whom this memo was written, told HSCA: "We had not received this information at that time undoubtedly. I think if this information right here had been available at the time, I think the decision would have been different all the way around with everybody."[46] Tines speculated that the time stated on the memo could have been in error.[47] Holloman told HSCA that he had no recollection of seeing this memo.

I attempted to interview Arkin. At first, the ex-intelligence officer was extremely wary about discussing the case. He cited a variety of reasons for not talking: unfamiliarity with my bona fides, lack of knowledge concerning the assassination, the possibility of a federal gag order. Finally, after four phone calls and one no-show appointment, I met him at a hotel on the outskirts of Memphis.[48] Now retired from MPD, he is director of security for a local corporation. Arkin is tall, powerfully built, and distinguished looking; he appeared to be in his late forties.

As to how the information about the Reddit threat reached MPD, there is much confusion. Arkin said he did not receive the data directly: It was phoned from Washington to someone in MPD, but Arkin does not know who. Arkin believed there may have been a memo from Washington as well. His immediate superior, Inspector Graydon Tines, told HSCA that it was Arkin who first informed him of the threat. Arkin told HSCA that he was called into Tines's office and told of the threat.[49]

HSCA was mainly interested in Reddit's role. Despite the falsehood of Reddit's original allegation, this convoluted affair remains unsolved.

THE RETREAT OF THE TACTICAL UNITS

While the committee gave considerable attention to the Reddit affair, it relegated to footnote status an equally disturbing matter. Because of the violence that had erupted during King's previous visit, MPD formed six TACT (for tactical) units on March 28. Each consisted of three vehicles and twelve officers.[50] According to Public Safety Director Holloman, such units did not operate on a regular basis but only in "emergency or riot situations."[51]

Holloman stated that three to four units were patrolling the five to six block area "immediately surrounding" the Lorraine.[52] On the morning of the day of the assassination the units were pulled back from the Lorraine—where they had patrolled since King's arrival on April 3—to a distance of five blocks away.[53]

While the removal of King's security detail was not essential to a well-planned assassination, the withdrawal of the TACT units would have been much more important. Had the TACT vehicles remained in place, swarming around the Lorraine, it would have been extremely difficult for anyone to escape the crime scene. The question of why the units were removed is central to any probe of possible conspiratorial manipulation.

MPD's explanation seems at first glance to be well-grounded in the department's chain of command. William O. Crumby, who oversaw the TACT squads, provided an affidavit to HSCA stating that the units:

were ordered, beginning on the morning of April 4, to remain in the general vicinity of the motel, but not within visual distance. This order was promulgated by an instruction from an unidentified member of Dr. King's entourage to Inspector Sam Evans, who was the street commander of the TACT unit.

This request was relayed by Inspector Evans to myself and in turn by me to Chief J. C. McDonald and to the Director of Police and Fire Safety Frank Holloman. As a result, the decision was made to honor the request beginning on the morning of April 4, 1968.[54]

Holloman directly disputed Crumby's affidavit, denying any participation in such a decision: "I have absolutely no recollection whatsoever of what has been said there, and I would have doubted that he would have reported to me and to Chief McDonald."[55]

In its final report, HSCA has a brief footnote explaining the withdrawal of the TACT units as stemming from "a request from someone in Dr. King's party." Crumby's affidavit is cited as the source for this conclusion. Evidently, HSCA did not recognize the basic improbability of Crumby's explanation, an improbability that becomes clear when one understands the mission of the TACT units and their relationship to King's presence in Memphis.

Unlike the police security detail, these units were not there to protect King but to protect the city of Memphis from King.[56] As TACT Officer Crumby described them, their mission was "to quell uprisings, unruly gatherings and riots."[57] King was viewed by police as an outside agitator whose previous visit had resulted in violence.

I interviewed Rev. Samuel Kyles, at the same Baptist church in Memphis where he served as pastor in 1968. Kyles, who was only 23 years old when he helped organize the March 28 demonstration, describes the TACT squads as "ruthless." He views them as having spearheaded what he describes as a "police riot" on March 28. According to Kyles, police did not seek out the youths who were breaking windows but waded into the crowd clubbing and macing peaceful demonstrators, including women and children.

It would not be surprising if, upon returning to Memphis, King's people wanted the TACT squads kept at a distance. But it is highly improbable that MPD would comply. The TACT units zeroed in on the Lorraine because, in the police's perception, King's presence there made it the vortex of potential civil disorder. It would be one thing for police to withdraw security at King's request (though there is no evidence of such a request); but to remove riot-control forces to a distance of five blocks from the group viewed as the source of the trouble is an entirely different matter. The notion put forth in Crumby's affidavit, that the removal was "prompted by an *instruction*" (emphasis added) from a member of King's entourage, is ludicrous. If anything, such an "instruction" might lead police to suspect that King's group was up to something and thereby strengthen police resolve to remain in close proximity; or the police might remain highly visible simply out of spite.

If, as Officer Crumby suggested, the pullback was in response to a request that the cruisers not be visible, then MPD would seem to have accommodated in the extreme. The Lorraine Motel is only two stories. There are taller buildings across Mulberry Street that block any extended view. A pullback of two or three blocks should have satisfied the alleged request, unless the King people were perched on the roof of the Lorraine scanning a five to six block area in search of police cars. A lesser pullback would not have sacrificed as much riot control capability. Prior to the withdrawal, there were three to four units (9 to 12 vehicles) within the five to six blocks surrounding the Lorraine.[58] That is a very large force to remove in its entirety to a five block distance.

The illogic of the police retreat makes it all the more troubling that the putative "instruction" came from an "unidentified" member of King's party. Instead of relying on Crumby's second-hand description, the author interviewed Sam Evans, the now retired Memphis police officer who was Crumby's superior and who was described in Crumby's affidavit as the original source of the pullback order. I asked Evans if the "unidentified" King person described in the affidavit was known to him.[59] He reiterated that the pullback had definitely been ordered by a member of King's party.

"Who was it?" I asked.

Without hesitation Evans responded: "I'm pretty sure it was Reverend Kyles, probably him . . . Yes, Reverend Kyles."

"Kyles asked that the TACT units be pulled back? Did you know Kyles by sight?"

Evans laughed. "I knew all of 'em."

(Memphis Fire Fighter George W. Leonneke, who was in the firehouse when King was shot, told the author in a May 15, 1985, telephone interview that the police intelligence unit operating inside the firehouse "had pictures under plastic of all the people who came in and out [of the Lorraine]," indicating that MPD was very concerned about identifying those associated with King.)

Rev. Kyles told the author that he does not deny the possibility that someone in King's party may have made such a request, because the police presence was generally unwelcome. However, although he did know Evans, Kyles is emphatic that *he* did not make any such request.

In light of these conflicting accounts, the matter of the Tact pullback is unresolved. HSCA embraced an explanation that is superficial and illogical.

There is a related incident regarding the position of one of the TACT squads. Unit number 10 was not in compliance with the order to remain five or six blocks from the Lorraine. Instead, it came within one block only minutes before the shooting. The officers of TACT 10 were inside the firehouse on a rest break. They rushed outside after the shot, narrowly missing any escaping assassin(s) by a few seconds. It has been implied by some researchers that the timing of the rest break may have been by conspiratorial design.[60]

The evidence suggests that this event was an innocent coincidence. TACT 10 had simply decided that it was time for an early-evening break after patrolling for several hours, and the firehouse was the only logical site.[61] As TACT 10 Officer Barney G. Wright explained to the author: "In a TACT squad there's three to four vehicles and four men each. You couldn't get sixteen men in a coffee shop. The firehouse was the only real place."[62] Wright said that the firehouse offered coffee, rest rooms, and a pay phone from which officers could call their families. This was confirmed by Fire Fighter George W. Leonneke, who told the author that police officers were relaxing, drinking coffee, and playing ping pong when the shooting occurred.[63]

THE LONG ARM OF FEDERAL INTELLIGENCE

HSCA concluded that the presence of federal intelligence at the assassination scene was minimal and nonconspiratorial.[64] But the committee failed to perceive the scope of federal intelligence networks operating at the time. Furthermore, it focused exclusively on the FBI without considering the CIA or military intelligence.

As HSCA's own data showed, MPD had extensive, if not unique, ties to the FBI. Public Safety Director Frank Holloman was a retired FBI agent whose 25 years with the Bureau included a stint as head of the Memphis field office (1959–64). He also served as Hoover's appointments secretary and was in charge of personnel in the director's office.[65] No wonder MPD's relationship with the Bureau was described by Holloman as "very cordial and cooperative," with a flow of information that was "a two-way street."[66] When Holloman became public safety director in 1968, he was dealing with many of his former colleagues in the FBI field office.

The author's interview with E. H. Arkin provides new insights into the richness of federal-local intelligence links. Arkin, who claimed he had received training in Washington from at least two federal agencies (FBI and Secret Service), proudly recounts how he founded MPD's intelligence unit in 1967, under the tutelage of FBI Agent William Lawrence. To this day, Arkin reveres Lawrence as the man who taught him "everything about intelligence work."

Arkin boasts that he was the only police officer in the country who could walk into an FBI field office and have access to the files whenever he wanted. "And," he said, "Mr. Hoover knew it and he approved, 'cause he knew I was good." Arkin also claims to have helped federal agents conduct intelligence-gathering activities in Memphis.

In return for this favored status, he generously shared intelligence data with the Bureau. A 13-page FBI memo on events before, during, and after King's March 28 demonstration contains information provided mainly by Arkin, and it shows that he maintained frequent contact with the FBI during this period.[67] Within minutes after King was shot, Arkin heard the news on his police radio. His first action was not to call police headquarters or to contact any of his intelligence units but to rush to a telephone and call William Lawrence at the FBI field office—at 6:05 P.M.[68]

There are other indications of federal presence. Arkin says that during the March 28 violence, Army intelligence agents made a nuisance of themselves by hanging around his office and reporting "half conversations" back to Washington, to the point where he had to "kick them out." When I asked about a CIA presence, he went on to another subject.

An April 3 intelligence report from Arkin's surveillance team inside the firehouse states: "Federal Officers were noted around the Lorraine Motel." There is no further elaboration.

HSCA was ignorant of another FBI source of data about King. The Bureau had its own spy inside King's Southern Christian Leadership Conference (SCLC). Political Scientist David J. Garrow revealed in his 1981 book *The FBI and Martin Luther King, Jr.* that: "most material gathered by the FBI on King and the SCLC from mid 1966 to the time of King's death came from one human informant."[69] James A. Harrison joined the SCLC in 1964 and was recruited almost immediately to spy for the Bureau. Lured by a weekly stipend and the chance to play spook, he provided intelligence via weekly meetings with his FBI handlers.[70]

On April 3, 1968, Harrison arrived in Memphis at 10:30 A.M. He immediately checked in with Robert Jensen, head of the FBI field office. Harrison promised he would phone in any worthwhile intelligence.[71] He departed Memphis that same day, at 7:30 P.M. What, if anything, he knew about King's April 4 agenda and whether he reported anything to the Bureau remain unknown. HSCA pointed to the alleged absence of physical and electronic surveillance of King on April 3 and 4 as strong evidence that the FBI did not have "foreknowledge" of events relating to the assassination.[72] The committee failed to note, or did not know, that the FBI had penetrated King's organization.

The Bureau was not the only federal entity that could have manipulated the Memphis police through strong linkages with the department. The CIA had an operational interest in monitoring King's activities, and the agency had received intelligence portraying him as a major potential threat to national security. Moreover, a CIA file (obtained by the author in 1982 under the Freedom of Information Act) reveals that, during the 1960s, the Agency had clandestine relationships with an unknown number of police intelligence units throughout the country. Although Memphis was not specifically mentioned in the 362 pages of heavily deleted documents, the released file (Domestic Police Training File) is by no means a complete reflection of CIA-police linkages. The names of certain cities were deleted from some of the documents. In some cases, police conducted break-ins and surveillance at the behest of the Agency. Friendly departments extricated CIA employees from legal difficulties. In return, police were provided with sophisticated training and gadgetry as well as largess that included free trips to CIA headquarters with drinks, meals, and recreation paid for by the Agency. All of this, secret from the public, the Congress and, in some cases, the administrative higher-ups in the departments involved.[73]

HSCA set out to investigate an intelligence dimension that did not surface during the 1968 investigation. The 23-year-old black man who rushed to King's side after the shooting was not a member of the Invaders, a militant black political group. He was instead an undercover police officer from MPD's intelligence unit. There are two significant conspiracy-related questions regarding Marrell McCullough's presence at the Lorraine. First, what did he know about King's agenda? Could he have passed on—however unwittingly, as a normal part of his surveillance—information that King would be exiting the motel during the early evening? Second, did any federal authorities or networks have access to McCullough's intelligence data?

Concerning a possible federal linkage, HSCA narrowed the question to whether McCullough had some personal connection with the FBI. The committee concluded that he did not, in part because:

In an interview by the FBI shortly after the assassination, McCullough was treated no differently than other eyewitnesses, indicating that the FBI was unaware of his ties to the Memphis Police Department. Thus, the committee found that McCullough was not employed by the FBI or any federal agency. Nor did he have knowledge, so far as the Committee could determine, that his information was being transmitted to the Bureau or the federal government.[74]

Of course, the fact that McCullough's FBI interview appeared normal could mean that the Bureau wanted to protect his cover, or that the interviewing agent was unaware of his spy status while other FBI agents were aware. The crucial question is not whether McCullough was "employed" by a federal agency, nor is it whether he was aware that his data was being passed on to the feds. It is whether he had information that, if it ended up in federal channels, could have been tapped by conspirators in order to plan the assassination.

E. H. Arkin reported extensively to the Bureau on King's activities in Memphis. He was McCullough's control. According to McCullough, the two men met "not every day but we tried to keep it every other day at least."[75] An FBI memo provided to the author by Professor Gerald McKnight, who has studied the Bureau's file on McCullough,[76] reveals that Arkin disseminated to the FBI data gathered by McCullough on April second and third.[77] This included intelligence on what was going on at the Lorraine.[78]

FBI agent William Lawrence testified before HSCA and was asked at what point he learned the identity of MPD's "Max" or "Agent 500" (McCullough's code names). Lawrence's answer was inconclusive.[79]

Lawrence: It would have been sometime during this period. I cannot recall the exact date. It was sometime after the sanitation strike started.

HSCA: Do you recall whether you knew pre or post assassination?

Lawrence: I cannot honestly answer that. It would have been in that time frame, either before or immediately after.

Lawrence was one of the two agents who conducted McCullough's post-assassination interview—the interview in which he was treated like an ordinary witness, thereby indicating to HSCA that the Bureau did not know he was a spy. But a document from the McCullough file shows that the Bureau knew Max's identity as early as March 27. The memo is written by Lawrence. It states that on March 27 Captain Jewell G. Ray of MPD "advised confidentially" that the police had an undercover operative whose code name was Max. The memo describes McCullough's background (Mississippi native, military police experience) and his spying (joining the Invaders).[80] Although McCullough's first name is incorrect (Marion instead of Marrell), this would seem to present no barrier to the Bureau's knowledge of the identity of the "negro rookie" policeman who had "gotten in with strike support leaders" and whose checks were being laundered through an electric company where he was ostensibly employed. (The memo contains other particulars that would help to obviate any confusion created by the inaccurate first name—that McCullough had moved to a new neighborhood, that he had been in Memphis only a short time, and was an Army veteran.)

Did McCullough know that King would emerge from his room at around 6:00 P.M.? Such knowledge, if it reached a federal data network, would be crucial for a well-orchestrated assassination plot hatched by some element of American intelligence. (It is clear from CIA documents obtained by the author that CIA and FBI exchanged intelligence data on King's movements, activities, and associations.) HSCA looked exclusively at the narrower question of whether McCullough was a conspirator rather than whether his information could unwittingly aid a conspiracy. As Committee Chairman Lewis Stokes (Dem. Ohio) put it to McCullough:

You are aware of the speculation that has grown up around Dr. King's having been in some way maneuvered out on the balcony. In light of the fact that it is known that James Earl Ray checked into the rooming house around 3:00 P.M. that afternoon, there was speculation as to how he would know that Dr. King would be out on the balcony and he would thereby be able to shoot him from the bathroom window.[81]

The committee satisfied itself that McCullough could not have lured King onto the balcony: the spy had nothing to do with transporting King to dinner; he was at the Lorraine for the exclusive purpose of meeting with the Invaders.[82]

McCullough's possible knowledge of King's agenda was obscured by the vagueness of questioning and testimony concerning how he ended up at the Lorraine just minutes before the shooting. He told HSCA that he went there to meet with several members of the Invaders, and that he had given a ride to the Reverends James Bevel and James Orange.[83] (James Orange was a member of SCLC's advance team. James Bevel had been assigned by SCLC to work with the Invaders in connection with King's Memphis activities.)[84] McCullough told HSCA that on the afternoon of April 4, Orange needed a ride to go shopping, which McCullough provided "just out of courtesy to him." At 5:30 McCullough drove Orange to the Clayborn Temple to pick up Bevel, then drove both men to the Lorraine (where McCullough happened to be going).[85]

But McCullough admitted that he used transportation as an entré for spying. He had volunteered to become "Minister of Transportation" for the Invaders because, in his words: "I had a car, none of the guys had a car, and I used that to get into the group and to gain their confidence."[86]

An April 13 FBI memo contains reports passed on by Arkin. The data was clearly gathered by McCullough. It was obtained on April 2 when he attended a meeting at the Lorraine, between King's staff and the Invaders. The source of the intelligence is deleted from the memo, but the deletion is three letters—surely the deleted word is MAX, McCullough's code name. The memo provided data on both Bevel and Orange:[87]

With regard to James Bevel, [3 letters deleted] has seen him on two or three occasions and stated Bevel is very militant in his talk with Negro youths.

Also, on April 3, 1968 Arkin reported that [3 letters deleted] had told him that Rev. Orange stated that he would be willing to work with black power groups.

Did McCullough's spying on King's staff give him knowledge of the 6:00 departure? He indicated to HSCA that he had only the vaguest notion of why King emerged from his room shortly before 6:00 P.M.

HSCA: You have never heard it rumored or discussed in terms of people wondering how Dr. King happened to be out on the balcony at that precise time?

McCullough: No, sir. All accounts I have heard he was out talking to the singing group and was making a special request for a song.[88]

It is true that while standing on the balcony, King asked Ben Branch, the leader of the Bread Basket Band, to sing a particular song later that evening. Did McCullough believe that this is *why* King was on the balcony at this precise moment? HSCA's questioning failed to zero in on this key point relating to what federal intelligence could have known.

Kyles had invited "Dr. King and his group" to dinner.[89] This included the SCLC advance staff as well as King's permanent entourage.[90] It seems logical that in McCullough's capacity as a spy posing as Minister of

Transportation he would find out as much as possible about what Bevel, Orange, and King were doing. He stated that he knew that Bevel and Orange were going to the Lorraine to meet King.[91] It seems unlikely that the ministers would ask for a ride yet keep secret the plans for going to dinner. Federal-intelligence foreknowledge of King's six o'clock appearance is a definite possibility.

Nor was McCullough the only possible source for this information. The FBI adamantly insisted to HSCA that it did not bug King's motel room in Memphis, and the committee found no evidence that would refute this claim. McCullough assured HSCA: "I can say that the Memphis Police Department didn't use any electronic surveillance [on King]."[92] If the Bureau had King's phone tapped on April 4, 1968, it would surely work hard to cover this up in the wake of an assassination. It is unlikely that 23-year-old rookie McCullough was privy to everything the MPD intelligence squad did by way of surveillance. (CIA links to police—including police surveillance conducted for CIA, break-ins performed jointly by police and CIA, and CIA agents posing as police (with police help)—were usually kept secret from all but a very few of the most trusted officers in the departments involved.) Around four o'clock on April 4, Ralph Abernathy called Kyles's house from the Lorraine to discuss the dinner plans.[93]

As to who in the MPD-federal intelligence network knew what and did what, the search for information, and the games of disinformation, continue unabated. In 1986 I was given access to a secret MPD report by a source formerly with the Memphis city government. The 140-page document was written within a year after the assassination and originated with the MPD. It purports to be a day-by-day account of MPD's law-enforcement and intelligence activities during the period of the March 28 demonstration and the assassination—a summary of raw intelligence files and memos. So far as I can determine, it has not been seen by anyone beyond an elite group of Memphis officials.

I was given access in order to influence my view of MPD's role. The document is provocative not for what it says but for what it omits. The authors of the report could not have envisioned that a congressional investigation and FBI releases under the Freedom of Information Act would expose its omissions and inaccuracies, examples of which follow.

• The King party's alleged lack of cooperation with the security detail is discussed at length. The removal of the detail is never mentioned, much less explained.

• All police intelligence data gathered on King on April 3 and 4 is attributed to the surveillance team inside the firehouse. Undercover operative Marrell McCullough does not appear anywhere in the report, not even by his code names. He is written out of events as if by Hollywood script writers.

At approximately 5:38 P.M. a car arrived in the courtyard of the Lorraine Motel and Rev. James Orange and Rev. James Bevel of the Southern Christian Leadership Conference were observed disembarking from it along with a Female Negro known as Clara Estes.

McCullough drove the car, disembarked, and stood chatting with the others.

• The treatment of the Reddit affair is most curious.

"At 5 P.M. a confidential report from outside Memphis arrived" advising that a radical group "had plans to assassinate Detective E. E. Reddit . . . and a security plan was laid out for him." There is no inkling that the information was inaccurate.

I was surprised to find that in volume four of HSCA's exhibits, there were what appeared to be published excerpts from this same report.[94] The title was the same: "Civil Disorders, Memphis, Tennessee, February 12–April 16, 1968." There was no date either on the congressional excerpts or the report I had seen in Memphis. I had been assured by my source that neither Congress nor anyone else beyond a small clique of Memphians had seen the report. A closer analysis of HSCA's published excerpts revealed a significant difference.

Congress had been given a sanitized version, apparently devoid of footnotes (my source claimed that they were withheld and there are no footnotes or footnote numbers in HSCA's published excerpts). The source said "the footnotes tell all." This is not true, because the footnoted report was often selective and inaccurate, as previously described. Still, the 40 pages of citations offer a rich description of the memos, files, and sources which purportedly back up the report. Had HSCA gotten the notes, it would have had a much clearer sense of what documents to pursue and what questions to ask of MPD.

Many items contained in the original report were missing from HSCA's version. In both reports, items are listed chronologically, by day and within a particular day. In HSCA's published excerpts covering April 1 through April 5, there were items missing from each day. For example, on April 3 six items dealing with black political activity are missing. On April 4 twelve items are missing. They deal with police activities at the crime scene within minutes after the shooting and with post-assassination violence.

The congressional version manifests what appears to be some editorial license designed to make the "civil disorders" look worse. A March 21 item from the full version reads:

And at a meeting sponsored by the Union and the Ministers Alliance at the Mt. Olive C.M.E. Church there were talks about how teachers could participate in the march without being docked in their pay for being off work.

In HSCA's version the item reads:

And at a meeting sponsored by the Union and the Minister's Alliance at the Mt. Olive C.M.E. Church *there was talk of firebombs and burning* [emphasis added].

Nowhere in the full report is there any reference to "firebombs and burning" on March 21.

HSCA's version has an April 4 item about "16 reported incidents of strike oriented vandalism." No such reference is contained under April 4 in the longer version. An April 2 item in the full version states: "There were only four reported incidents of harassment and vandalism." In HSCA's version the item is precisely the same, except the number of incidents is upped to seven.

MPD intelligence files cited in the 40 pages of footnotes accompanying the report I was given access to, could contain information vital to pursuing this case. This is especially true of MPD's "Martin Luther King Security and Surveillance File." But these files were allegedly destroyed in 1976. The Memphis American Civil Liberties Union (ACLU) launched successful legal action to obtain certain police intelligence files, including the King files. ACLU lawyers arrived at police headquarters 15 minutes too late: the documents had been burned, or so it is widely believed. The Reverend Samuel Kyles told me that he suspected that "they exist somewhere." His suspicion may be correct.

My efforts to locate the files finally led me to a Memphis man who claims to have them in his possession. He would not give me access. After stating firmly that he had them, he smiled wryly and served up the standard disclaimers. "But maybe I'm wrong about that. Maybe I'm mistaken."

Of all the previously examined elements in the mosaic of collapsing law-enforcement and mysterious data networks, only the withdrawal of security can be dismissed as logically unrelated to an assassination conspiracy. The other elements need further resolution before the possibility of conspiratorial manipulation of MPD, or usurpation of data, can be logically eliminated.

9   The Evidence Reexamined

"James Earl Ray fired one shot at Dr. Martin Luther King, Jr., the shot killed Dr. King."

Final Report, House Select Committee on
Assassinations, 1978 (p. 370)

The Lorraine Hotel, whose proprietors were black, was anything but luxurious. The two-story, L-shaped building, located in one of the seedier sections of Memphis, faced onto the motel's parking lot and swimming pool.[1] A balcony ran along the outside of the second story and was accessible from second-floor rooms as well as from stairways ascending from the parking lot.

Across Mulberry Street was a row of ramshackle buildings, including Bessie Brewer's boarding house, from which the shot was allegedly fired. Also located across from the Lorraine was Fire Station no. 2, which on April 4, 1968, was being used by a Memphis police intelligence squad to spy on King.

Brewer's boarding house, at 418–422 ½ Main Street, was a run-down brick building with a wooden interior, set in the midst of a block of storefronts. On the Main Street side, a narrow door opened onto a set of stairs that led to the second floor. At the top of the stairs a long hallway stretched to the opposite side of the building, facing the Lorraine. At the end of the hallway was a tiny, common bathroom with a single window that commanded a view of the Lorraine and of King's room. This window, from which the shot was allegedly fired, was at the extreme left rear of the building, in the north wing.

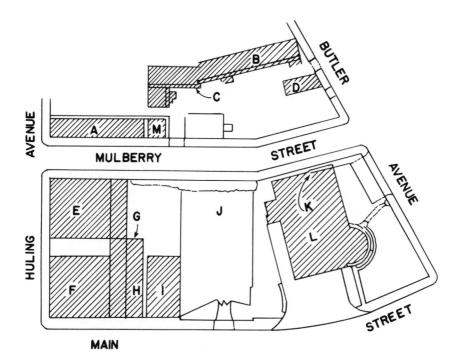

Photo 1. Crime Scene, Assassination of Dr. Martin Luther King, Jr., Memphis, Tennessee. Credit: Jim Freeley, adapted from House Select Committee on Assassinations Final Report. (A) Lorraine Hotel; (B) Lorraine Motel; (C) Room 306; (D) One-story Brick Cafe; (E) U.S. Fixture Company; (F) U.S. Fixture Company; (G) Bathroom Window; (H) Rooming House (North Wing) and Jim's Grill; (I) Rooming House (South Wing) and Canipe's Amusements Co.; (J) Parking Area; (K) Memphis Police Surveillance; (L) Memphis Fire Station No. 2; (M) Motel Office.

That this general location is the crime scene for the assassination of Dr. King is not in doubt. Beyond that, however, the doubts are numerous and serious. Where was the shot fired from? Did Ray fire it? By what modus operandi was the murder perpetrated? Unfortunately, the available evidence (forensic, ballistic, fingerprint, eyewitness, polygraph) is far from conclusive, thus rendering thee case murkier than official investigations have claimed. In this chapter we will examine in detail each of these areas of evidence.

One problem lies in the absence of the kind of evidence that tends to make a case open and shut. Not one witness saw the actual firing of the shot. Ray was not caught with the smoking gun in hand. Instead, he eluded authorities for two months. Photographic evidence that might establish King's precise location at the time of the shooting is non-existent. There are no known sound recordings of the event, as there are of the assassinations of President Kennedy and of his brother Robert. Thus a clear evidentiary baseline for determining time and motion and the origin of the shot does not exist (there is nothing analogous to the Zapruder film of JFK's assassination).

In reaching its conclusions concerning Ray's guilt and his modus op-erandi, HSCA tended to oversell the evidence, glossing over inconsist-encies and gaps in order to achieve an investigative closure. Moreover, the committee did not operate under an adversarial paradigm in which its interpretations were subject to challenge or cross-examination.

THE SNIPER'S LOCATION

Despite extensive efforts, HSCA could not determine the exact location from which the shot was fired.[2] One reason for this is that Dr. King's precise position is indeterminate. While it is clear that he was standing on the balcony outside his motel room and was facing in the general direction of the boarding house, he was also bent slightly forward and was looking downward, as he conversed with colleagues in the parking lot below.[3] The degree to which King was leaning forward or turning his head affects trajectory calculations concerning the origin of the shot.

Even more damning to the accuracy of such calculations is the fact that the path of the fatal bullet was not probed during the autopsy. Dr. Jerry T. Francisco, Shelby County, Tennessee medical examiner, per-formed the autopsy at 10:45 P.M. on the night of the shooting.[4] He removed a flattened bullet from King's back, numbered it, photographed it, and gave it to FBI agents. Francisco concluded that the cause of death was "a single gunshot wound to the chin and neck with a total tran-section of the lower cervical and upper thoracic spinal cord and other structures of the neck"; he also noted that death occurred shortly after the wound was inflicted.[5] The bullet struck the right side of King's face on a tangent.[6] It entered the mouth, fractured the jawbone, exited on the lower right side of the chin, then reentered the base of the chin just above the collarbone, tearing the suit jacket and shirt collar as it went. The bullet continued its penetration (right to left, front to back, and slightly downward), passing through the spinal cord and finally lodging itself near the left shoulder blade.[7] King's right cheek was blown open by the impact, leaving a gaping hole three inches long. Yet, with all this information, the precise path of the bullet remains unknown.

In 1978 Dr. Francisco was interviewed by HSCA. He indicated that it was not because of constraints imposed by Dr. King's aides or his widow that he did not dissect the wound and trace the path of the bullet; but, rather, it was because of his own sensitivities concerning the treatment of the dead. HSCA concluded that the decision not to probe the wound was Dr. Francisco's alone, based upon his desire not to further deform the body, and that there was no outside interference.[8]

In the absence of this vital information, calculations about the origin of the shot are all the more at the mercy of estimates of King's position at the moment of impact. Since the bullet had entered from the right at a slightly downward angle and since King was facing forward, some possibilities could be eliminated: this precluded a shot from the fire station, located across Mulberry Street to King's left, or from the parking lot or the street below King.

Debate has centered on whether the shot was fired from the bathroom window of the boarding house or from the bushes below the window. Three other windows in the north wing of the boarding house faced King's room (the windows in the south wing were boarded over from the inside). The two windows to the right of the bathroom were in a room occupied by two tenants during the shooting. The three windows to the left were in a building occupied by a furniture company. At least one of these windows appears to afford a clear view of King's room.

Regarding the primary controversy of whether the shot originated from the bathroom window or from the bushes below, there is only one reliable witness who claimed to see movement in the bushes. Solomon Jones, King's chauffeur, was in the parking lot of the Lorraine waiting to drive King to dinner. Jones told the FBI that immediately following the shooting, he caught a glimpse of a man who had his back toward the Lorraine. The figure was in a grassy area in the yard behind the boarding house, an area separated from Mulberry Street by a retaining wall and shielded from the Lorraine by shrubs and bushes.[9] Jones was questioned by HSCA. The committee concluded that since he had been pushed to the ground seconds after the shooting, and since by the time he got up police officers stationed in the nearby firehouse had "almost" arrived at the Lorraine, that the man seen by Jones "may have been a law enforcement officer responding to the shot."[10]

Harold Carter, a tenant in the boarding house, reportedly saw a man with a rifle running from the bushes. But Bessie Brewer, Carter's landlady, implicitly questioned his reliability as a witness when she described him to the FBI as a man who "drank considerably."[11]

In contradiction to Jones and Carter, Memphis Police Officer Torrence B. Landers claimed that shortly after the shot was fired, he rushed into the backyard of the boarding house and searched for footprints. It had rained the previous day, and Landers claimed that the ground was soft: If anyone had been in the area, it would have been easy to observe their footprints. Landers found only two footprints, near the cellar door of the rooming house.[12] Plaster casts were made, but the results of this effort, if any, are unknown.[13]

The committee retained an Albuquerque, New Mexico, firm which used "sophisticated scientific equipment" to conduct an engineering survey.[14] As sophisticated as the equipment may have been, the survey was still hindered by not knowing precisely either the path of the wound or King's position. The engineers simulated "the probable posture of Dr. King at the instant of impact," which was described as "head forward looking down into the parking area and with a slight forward bend at the waist."[15] The accuracy of this simulation is further compromised by the possible movement of King's head. Memphis Fire Fighter George W. Loenneke was in the fire station across from the Lorraine. He was looking at King through the peephole made by police surveillers (a hole in the newspaper covering the window). Loenneke claimed that he actually saw King get shot and that King was turning slowly to the left when the bullet struck.[16]

Given the absence of firm baselines, it is not surprising that the engineering survey was inconclusive: The geometric data was consistent with a shot from either the bathroom window or the shrubbery.[17] The engineers also concluded that if in fact the shot originated from the yard below the window, it could only have been fired by someone standing, because a prone or kneeling rifleman could not have fired from a point high enough to produce the downward trajectory of the King bullet.[18]

Still, HSCA was very sure of itself in asserting that the assassin fired from the bathroom: "Although the scientific evidence did not independently establish the location of the assassin, when it was combined with witness testimony, it pointed strongly to the rear of the rooming house."[19] The only witnesses cited by HSCA were Charles Stephens and William Anschutz, whose statements HSCA described as "mutually corroborative."[20] That Stephens was used by HSCA to bolster the conclusion that the shot came from the bathroom while Solomon Jones was dismissed as probably having seen a police officer instead of an assassin tells us a great deal about HSCA's biases. However tenuous and inconclusive Jones's account, his sobriety was not in question—unlike Stephens. (Stephens and Anschutz's statements will be examined in detail later in this chapter.)

THE CASE AGAINST JAMES EARL RAY

Official investigators present a powerful, albeit circumstantial, case that James Earl Ray assassinated Martin Luther King, Jr. A variety of different kinds of evidence implicates Ray. If we summarize the case as would a prosecuting attorney, or HSCA, the litany of evidence reads as follows.[21]

Ray arrived in Memphis the day before the crime and checked into the New Rebel Motel using the alias Eric S. Galt. A Memphis newspaper found among the artifacts allegedly left at the crime scene by the fleeing assassin a front-page article on King which told of his arrival on April 3. April 4 Ray rented a room at the boarding house across from the Lorraine, using the alias John Willard. He rejected a room that had no view of King's motel in favor of one that did. He purchased a pair of binoculars after renting the room. After the shooting, the landlady reported that the furniture in Ray's room had been moved: a dresser had been moved away from the window and a chair drawn up to the window, indicating that the occupant was rearranging the furniture in order to surveil King.[22] Binocular straps were found in the room.

One witness inside the rooming house, William Anschutz, claimed that in the hours just before the shooting, he had tried to use the bathroom on two occasions, only to find it occupied. Another tenant, Charles Stephens, told Anschutz that the bathroom was being occupied by the new boarder (Ray/Willard).[23] After hearing the shot, both Stephens and Anschutz ran into the hallway and saw a man carrying a bundle running away from the bathroom.

Within minutes after the shot, a bundle was dropped in the doorway of Canipe's Amusement Company, next door to the boarding house. Guy Canipe heard the thud of the bundle dropping and glimpsed a man passing his store. The man wore a dark suit and looked clean and neat.[24] Ray was wearing a dark brown suit and appeared neat and clean in comparison with the local population. Julius Graham, a customer at Canipe's, saw a man pass the store and heard the sound of the bundle dropping.[25] Bernell Finley, another customer, heard the shot and then a thud. He saw a man in a dark suit walking hurriedly past Canipe's.[26]

Graham told HSCA that after the thud, a white Mustang pulled away from the curb near Canipe's. Finley saw it too.[27] Canipe saw a car pull away but did not identify the make. Memphis Police Officer Vernon Dollahite told the FBI that when he arrived at Canipe's minutes after the shooting, there was an empty parking space just north of the doorway and there were skid marks in the street, apparently made by an escaping vehicle.[28] Ray was driving a white Mustang on April 4, 1968.

In the bundle found in Canipe's doorway, police discovered a 30.06 rifle, binoculars, ammunition, and a portable radio. The serial number of the rifle matched the one purchased by Ray in Birmingham, Alabama. The radio had an identification number which was partially scratched off, but the FBI was able to decipher it: It was Ray's inmate number at Missouri State Penitentiary.[29] Ray's prints were found on several items contained in the bundle.

Ray's alibi has no corroboration. He admits that he rented a room at the boarding house, purchased the rifle and the binoculars, and fled

Memphis in a white Mustang shortly after the shooting. He claims that these purchases and his presence in Memphis were directed by the shadowy Raoul in connection with what Ray thought was a gunrunning scheme. Ray asserts that he was not in the boarding house at the time of the shooting but was at a gas station several blocks away, trying to fix a tire. He contends that he drove back to the boarding house shortly after the shooting and confronted a police roadblock.[30] As a fugitive who had broken out of prison, he fled Memphis. Ray asserts that he was not aware of King's murder until later, but thought that something had gone awry with Raoul's gunrunning caper.

During the HSCA hearings, Ray's then attorney Mark Lane claimed to have found corroboration for Ray's presence at the gas station at the time of the shooting. But when HSCA questioned the witness, Coy Dean Cowden, he stated that he was actually 400 miles from Memphis on April 4, 1968, and had fabricated his story.[31] There is no evidence that HSCA conducted a systematic investigation of Ray's alleged presence at a gas station.

HSCA pointed out that not only does Ray's story lack corroboration, but it has changed significantly over the years. His first alibi, told to his then attorney Arthur Hanes, Sr., in 1969, was that he was sitting in his parked Mustang outside the boarding house at about 6:00 P.M. when Raoul came running out of the building, jumped into the backseat, covered himself with a sheet and told Ray to drive away. After riding a few blocks, Raoul jumped out, never to be seen again.[32]

After changing lawyers (Hanes to Percy Foreman), Ray's alibi changed to the gas station story. When asked about the inconsistency, Ray responded that the story about Raoul covering himself with a sheet was intended as a joke at the expense of author William Bradford Huie, who was writing a book on the case when Hanes was Ray's attorney; because, said Ray, Huie had an interest in the Ku Klux Klan.[33] Ray claimed that he did not reveal the gas station alibi to Hanes or Huie for fear that they would leak it to the FBI, which would then work to discredit it.[34]

HSCA found it incredible that Ray would purposely withhold his alibi and give a false story to his attorney in a case that could earn him the death penalty. Ray asserted that he had intended to tell his story directly to the jury, surprising his attorney. HSCA concluded that the only explanation for such risky tactics was that Ray had no alibi.[35]

The Polygraph Tests

HSCA employed a panel of polygraph experts to review the results of two lie detector tests Ray had taken voluntarily in 1977—one for *Playboy* magazine, another for columnist Jack Anderson.[36] The panel noted that the tests were seriously flawed. There were "outside noises" and frequent interruptions by Ray's attorney, which created a poor environment for one of the tests. There were inadequacies in some of the questions—the use of dramatic words like "kill"—and in the design of the control questions, as well as in the establishment of baseline response patterns.[37] The tests were administered almost back to back and in the early morning hours, creating a possible "fatigue" factor.

The HSCA panel also noted what it described as "an apparent attempt by Ray to create artificial reactions to control questions." It appeared that "Ray had studied polygraph technique and attempted to produce lie-type reactions to the control questions," in order to hide his real lies.[38] (This is done by the subject depressing his arm in the "cardio cuff" thereby producing an upward surge of blood pressure of the kind typically associated with an untruthful response.)

With all of these deficiencies, it is surprising that the HSCA experts could reach any conclusions about the substance of the data. But they did. The panel opined that Ray was deceptive when answering two questions negatively: "Do you know who shot Dr. Martin Luther King, Jr.?" and "Did you shoot Dr. Martin Luther King, Jr.?"[39]

As compelling as the previously described case against Ray may seem, it is not nearly as conclusive when the specifics of the evidence are closely examined.

Renting the Room

In its final report, HSCA describes Ray's renting of a room at Brewer's boarding house in a way that makes it appear, at least implicitly, to be part of his assassination plan.

Mrs. Brewer recalled renting room 5-B to John Willard. She also noted that the tenant rejected the first room shown to him, one equipped with light housekeeping facilities, saying he only wanted a sleeping room Willard accepted 5-B, Mrs. Brewer recalled, which was in the rear of the building near the bathroom and which offered a view of the Lorraine Motel.[40]

This bare-bones description is factually accurate, but it is much more damning to Ray than the detailed record on which it is supposedly based.

If, as HSCA implies, Ray was already planning to shoot King from the boarding house when he rented the room, he certainly made no attempt to be inconspicuous. Bessie Brewer told the FBI that her initial impression of Ray/Willard was that he did not "fit in" with the other tenants and looked as though he could have obtained lodging in "nicer surroundings."[41] This is an understatement. Into this dingy flophouse, populated by what Mrs. Brewer described as "alcoholics," walked a neatly groomed man wearing, of all things, a dark brown business suit complete with tie. The only more conspicuous attire Ray could have worn to this seedy den of intoxication would have been a clown suit. Virtually everyone who saw "Willard" or the "new tenant" clearly remembered the neatly dressed man in the dark suit. As shall be described later in this chapter, Charles Stephens, on whose testimony HSCA relied, was drinking on the day of the assassination. His common-law wife Grace had a criminal record that included two alcohol-related arrests. FBI reports concerning several other tenants indicated consumption of alcohol on the day of the assassination. Howard Vance "said he was 'intoxicated' for the two days of April 3 and 4." Mr. Frank M. Marley was home all day on April 4 but "he had been drinking heavily all afternoon and did not get out of bed to see what was happening." Alfred W. Eaton, who was in his room on April 4, "had been drinking that afternoon."

Even Ray's demeanor was conspicuous, and not as a nervous novice killer or as a mean-faced murderer. According to Mrs. Brewer, he unnerved her when he first appeared at her door because he had an unusual smile on his face—a "sneer" or "smirk." She remembered this because it seemed to her as if the man was trying to smile for no reason (she did not interpret the smile as an attempt to be flirtatious).[42]

From Mrs. Brewer's account of the rental transaction, Ray was either supremely cool in his premeditated attempt to obtain a room from which to surveil and shoot King—and, despite his attire and his smirk, to do so without arousing suspicion—or his rental of the room had nothing to do with King.

According to Brewer, Ray came to her door and asked "Do you have a room for rent?" She answered affirmatively and asked if he wanted it by the day or the week, to which he replied: "By the week."[43]

At this point, without further conversation, she led Ray directly to room number 8, located in the south wing of the boarding house about 20 feet from her door. If Ray had already cased the boarding house vis-à-vis the Lorraine, he would have known that there were no windows in the south wing that offered a view of the Lorraine: therefore, he might have asked for a room in the north wing. He was already so conspicuous by his attire and his smirk that there would be little additional risk in requesting a room well-situated for his plan of assassination. Ray followed Mrs. Brewer to room number 8 and looked inside without entering. He then said: "Well, I won't need the stove and refrigerator since I won't be doing any cooking. I was thinking more of a sleeping room."[44]

While it is literally true that Ray rejected this first room, which did not afford a view of the Lorraine, it is also true that there was another logical reason for the rejection: room 8 was not a private room, was not partitioned from 6 and 7.[45] Ray was a fugitive from the law who contends that he was there to do some gunrunning, both of which made privacy very desirable if not essential.

Mrs. Brewer told Ray that there was only one vacant "sleeping room" with no stove and refrigerator—5-B in the north wing. The door to 5-B had been padlocked until she opened it up for Ray. He immediately said he would take the room (without checking the view from the window), for he had no choice if he wanted to stay at Brewer's.

Unless Ray had already decided that he would shoot King from the common bathroom, he might have at least taken a look at the view before paying for the room. The window of 5-B faced directly onto the south wing of the boarding house, separated from it by a narrow alley way. In order to see King's room it was necessary to lean out the window, at least slightly, thereby becoming conspicuous.[46]

In a picture of the inside of 5-B taken after the assassination, a chair is next to the window and situated as if someone was sitting in it and watching the Lorraine. Chair or not, the surveillant would still have to thrust his head out of the window and could not sit back comfortably and observe.

It was also true, as HSCA points out, that the room Ray ultimately selected was much nearer to the bathroom than the room he rejected. Had Ray already decided to shoot from the bathroom, before trying to rent a room? Mrs. Brewer recalled that after saying he would take 5-B, Ray asked her where the bathroom facilities were. She pointed to the door down the hallway.[47] If Ray already knew that the bathroom was to be his sniper's nest, as HSCA implies, then he had no real need to ask such a question. If he asked the question because he was a wily criminal attempting to hide his foreknowledge of the bathroom, his self-interest would have been much better served had he dressed and acted in a less conspicuous manner.

If Ray did indeed plan to assassinate King from the boarding house, his planning seems quite sketchy. No matter how inexperienced at murder or unimaginative at crime Ray may have been, he knew he needed an accessible window with sight lines to the Lorraine. The window in his room forced the sniper to expose himself, which made a steady rifle shot exceedingly difficult and greatly increased the risk of detection (as either a surveillant or a sniper).

The bathroom window could only be used if the assassin positioned himself inside an old-fashioned bathtub with steeply sloping sides, and then only if he could be in the bathroom at the right time, when King was visible. This common bathroom served 13 persons besides Ray. Given the fact that nearly half of them were heavy drinkers, the facilities may have been used quite frequently. While Ray could not know the exact number of tenants or their habits, the sheer number of rooms and doors might have given him pause if he planned to shoot from the bathroom.

HSCA viewed Ray's renting of a room as a clear indication of both guilt and premeditation. A close examination of that transaction raises as many questions as it answers about Ray's intent and his plan—if any.

The Witnesses

With five exceptions, the crime scene witnesses provided only general, often vague, information. The three whose statements relate to the dropping of the bundle containing the rifle will be discussed later. The two most crucial witnesses are boarding house tenants Stephens and Anschutz, whose statements will be discussed shortly. No witness claimed to have seen Ray, or anyone else, shoot King.

Several witnesses in the parking lot of the Lorraine saw or heard something relevant. As described earlier, Solomon Jones thought he saw someone moving in the bushes below the bathroom window. Several persons who were standing outside the Lorraine believed that the shot came from the general direction of the row of buildings across Mulberry Street. Undercover Police Officer Marrell McCullough told the FBI that the shot came from "the series of old buildings located just west of the motel."[48] James H. Laue, who occupied the room next to King's and was in his room when the shot was fired, thought the sound was that of a firecracker exploding in the motel courtyard below his room.[49]

Memphis Police Officer Barney G. Wright was inside the fire station located across from the Lorraine and south of the boarding house. He did not hear the shot but remembered that the plate glass window in the lounge of the fire station "rattled."[50]

Inside the boarding house, D. L. Reeves was in his room in the south wing when he heard what sounded like a gunshot. (The bathroom was in the north wing. The two wings of the boarding house were connected by an enclosed walkway located on the Main Street side of the structure.) He went into the hall where he encountered Mr. and Mrs. Brewer, but no one else.[51]

Bessie Brewer and her husband Frank were eating dinner in their apartment and watching the television show "Rawhide" when she heard what sounded like a gun shot; her husband thought it was a firecracker.[52] The couple went into the hall and headed toward the back door, which faced the Lorraine. Mr. Brewer ran to the door and exited onto a wooden porch. A law-enforcement officer ordered him to "get back in the house and lock the door." Neither of the Brewers saw any fleeing suspects.

Charles Stephens and William Anschutz were in their respective rooms in the north wing when the shot was fired. Both their rooms adjoined Ray's. Stephens and his wife Grace were in room 6-B, which adjoined not only Ray's room but the bathroom.

Mrs. Stephens told the FBI that she was in bed ill all day, but that she heard a noise that sounded like a firecracker and seemed to come from the yard behind the building. She also claimed to have heard soft footsteps coming out of the bathroom and proceeding rapidly down the hallway.[53] Later, Grace Stephens would assert that she saw the fleeing fugitive and that it was not Ray.[54] The record indicates that Mrs. Stephens's sobriety is in question, as is her husband's. This, combined with her conflicting descriptions of what she saw and her having been committed to a mental hospital shortly after the assassination, led HSCA to conclude that her observation of someone other than Ray leaving the boarding house was "not worthy of belief."[55] The author agrees, and extends this to all of her observations and not simply those that are exculpatory of Ray.

William Anschutz, an employee of the Firestone Rubber Company, was in room 4-B, next to Ray's (on the opposite side from the Stephenses). He was watching TV when he heard a shot. He could not tell precisely where it came from, but he believed that it originated from either Ray's room or the bathroom.[56] According to Anschutz, he opened his door and immediately saw a man running down the hall, hiding his face by holding his arm over it. The man was carrying something long that appeared to be wrapped in a blanket. As the man ran past, Anschutz claims to have said, "I thought I heard a shot." The man replied, "Yeah, it was a shot."

Anschutz thought the man had entered the hall from Ray's room but was not certain. He saw the man for only a few seconds and the face was hidden. Anschutz described the fugitive as six feet tall, slim, and in his early thirties. The witness's only recall about the man's clothing was that he did not seem to be wearing a "coat." Ray wore a dark suit which had a suit jacket, but no overcoat.

Anschutz told the FBI that he was not drinking on the day of the assassination, and that he had given up drinking for health reasons. This would certainly make him one of the potentially more reliable witnesses at Brewer's.

The witness whose statements are the most implicative of Ray is Charles Stephens. In 1968 the 46-year-old Stephens told the FBI that he was sitting in his kitchen repairing a radio when he heard a loud noise which he was sure was a gun shot.[57] Unlike other earwitnesses, Stephens claimed to be certain about the origin of the shot: it came from the bathroom next door, only a few feet away from where he was sitting. He asserted that upon hearing the shot, he immediately ran to his door (10 to 12 feet from where he was sitting). When he opened the door, he saw a man running down the hall away from the bathroom. The man carried a package three to four feet long and six to eight inches thick, wrapped in what appeared to be a newspaper. Stephens claimed he was in the hall before Anschutz and saw Anschutz come out of his apartment and say something to the fleeing man.

Stephens told the FBI that the fugitive "closely resembled" the man who had earlier rented room 5-B (Willard/Ray). He described the suspect as a white male, 5 feet 10 inches to 5 feet 11 inches tall, 165 pounds, slender, with dark complexion, sandy or slightly dark hair, wearing a dark suit. Stephens added that he only glimpsed the man from behind, and did not get a look at his face.[58]

Stephens further stated that he expected to hear a "scuffle" emanating from the bathroom if someone had fired a shot from there, but he heard no such "scuffling" sound.[59] He could not determine whether the man came directly from the bathroom or went from the bathroom to room 5-B and then ran down the hallway, because Stephens did not see the man enter the hallway.[60]

For Ray, one of the most damning parts of Stephens's statement is what he claims to have heard before the shooting. He said that on several occasions during the afternoon, he heard the door to Ray's room open and heard footsteps go down the hall and into the bathroom. The person remained in the bathroom for "a considerable period of time."[61] Yet, during these visits, Stephens heard the commode flush only once. On the last visit to the bathroom, Stephens estimated that the individual stayed there for 20 to 30 minutes.

During the course of the afternoon, William Anschutz tried on two occasions to get into the bathroom, to empty some dish water into the sink. He found it occupied both times. He could not pinpoint the times but said they were only a few minutes apart.[62] After the second attempt he knocked on Stephens's door and inquired, somewhat angrily, as to who was using the bathroom. According to Anschutz, Stephens told him it was the tenant in 5-B (Ray).[63]

HSCA's final report relied heavily on Stephens (and, to a lesser extent, Anschutz) in seeking to explain what happened at the crime scene: "Because the medical and engineering evidence was not conclusive as to the precise origin of the shot, the committee used the testimony of witnesses at the crime scene to determine the most likely origin."[64]

The report then discusses the statements of Stephens and Anschutz, because the other earwitnesses had only vague notions, except for the less-than-credible Grace Stephens who thought the shot came from the yard below. The reader will recall that Anschutz was not sure whether the shot came from 5-B or the bathroom; only Stephens was positive that it was the bathroom.

Neither Stephens nor Anschutz were sure whether the fleeing stranger came into the hall from the bathroom or from 5-B, for neither of them saw the man actually enter the hall. Anschutz could not identify the fleeing suspect. Anschutz's only link between the tenant in 5-B and the visits to the bathroom was on the basis of what Stephens told him. It is only Charles Stephens who asserts that the shot definitely came from the bathroom, that the new tenant was spending a lot of time in the bathroom, and that the fleeing figure "closely resembled" the new tenant.

HSCA attempted to gloss over its implicit reliance on Stephens by stating: "Stephens' sobriety on the afternoon of April 4 was called into question by a number of sources, and the committee did not rely on his testimony for an eyewitness identification of the assassin."[65] In fact, however, HSCA did rely on Stephens to link Ray to the bathroom and to establish that the shot came from the bathroom, even though Stephens's liabilities as a witness appear so formidable that one wonders why the committee would rely on him for any information.

HSCA interviewed both Stephens and Anschutz. Neither could recall the details of the bathroom visits (time, sequence, duration). While this lack of recall is easily explained by the passage of time and does not, ipso facto, reflect negatively on the credibility of the witnesses, it does mean that they were unable to provide any information that would bolster or reaffirm the notion that Ray was staked out in the bathroom.[66]

Although the committee did not rely on Stephens for a positive identification of Ray as the fleeing suspect, the evolution of Stephens's statements on this crucial point is relevant to his overall credibility as a witness.

In 1968 Stephens told the FBI, in two separate interviews conducted within a week of the assassination, that he saw the fleeing suspect only from the rear and that this man "closely resembled" the man who earlier had checked into 5-B. Two months later, Stephens provided an affidavit used by U.S. authorities in extraditing Ray from England. The closest Stephens would come to a positive identification of the fugitive was to say: "I think it was the same man I saw earlier with Mrs. Brewer looking at 5-B."[67]

Then, in 1974, Stephens initiated a court proceeding to press his claim for a total of $185,000 in reward money that had been offered by three different sources for information leading to the arrest and conviction of King's killer.[68] Stephens's attorney claimed that his client's description was "the prime factor" in putting Ray behind bars. Stephens claimed that he had positively identified Ray as the fleeing suspect, from a photo provided by police after Ray's arrest.[69] This, despite the fact that he originally stated that he never saw the suspect's face, and despite his extradition affidavit which stated, rather weakly, "I think" it was Ray.

Even more interesting than Stephens's escalation of certainty regarding his identification of Ray is his description of events. In 1974, just two years before HSCA interviewed him, he testified in court during his unsuccessful pursuit of the reward money. His account was significantly different from his 1968 FBI statements.

Stephens stated in 1974: "I tried to get in the bathroom several times before but I couldn't."[70]

In 1968 Stephens told the FBI that he heard someone go into the bathroom from room 5-B but that it was William Anschutz who tried to get into the bathroom. Stephens never mentioned trying to get into the bathroom himself.

1974: "This time [immediately after the shot] I went to the bathroom, opened the door, glanced in and then down the hall. This guy was just turning the corner down the hall."

In 1968 Stephens never mentioned checking out the bathroom before sighting the fleeing figure. Instead, he stated that as soon as he opened the door to his apartment he saw the man running down the hall.[71]

In Stephens's first FBI interview (April 7, 1968), he asserted that he actually saw the fugitive leave the bathroom This conflicts with Stephens's assertion, in that same interview, that he only saw the fugitive from the rear: The man would have been running toward Stephens if Stephens had seen him depart the bathroom. In his second FBI interview three days later, he stated that he "had no way of knowing" whether the man entered the hall from the bathroom or from room 5-B. In his extradition affidavit three months later, Stephens stated that he opened the door to his apartment, entered the hall and "looked toward the bathroom and I saw that the door was open and it was empty." In 1974 Stephens said that he went to the bathroom and opened the door and looked inside before seeing the fugitive run down the hall.

HSCA went to great lengths to chronicle Ray's inconsistencies as well as those of Mrs. Grace Stephens, and then used these as a primary reason for dismissing their stories. There was no mention of Charles Stephens's inconsistencies. It is not as if these matters were trivial, since the nature and sequence of the events recalled by Stephens—the sound of footsteps, the silent commode—are central to the implicative nature of his testimony against Ray. Moreover, the man whose earwitness testimony was relied upon by HSCA told the FBI in 1968 that his "hearing is not the best."[72]

Wherever Stephens's encounter with the suspect began, the man was moving rapidly away from him down a dimly lit hallway about 50 feet long.[73] But the most striking impediment to Stephens's accuracy as a witness is not deficient hearing or lighting, but his alleged drinking. HSCA raised the question of Stephens's sobriety only in connection with his ability to positively identify Ray, as if that were the only facet of Stephens's story that could be invalidated by his alcoholic consumption.

HSCA's final report, which makes brief reference to the fact that Stephen's sobriety was "questioned" by a number of sources, downplays the severity of the problem.[74] A committee staff report on Stephens, which was not quoted in the final report but was published in volume 13 of the committee's hearings and exhibits, describes Stephens as "well known on South Main Street for his excessive drinking habits."[75] The staff report states that on the day of the assassination, Stephens had been in Jim's Grill (located below the north wing of Brewer's boarding house) "drinking—like always."[76]

Having relied on Stephens's testimony to prop up its case against Ray, HSCA then tried to prop up Stephens's credibility—to imply that since Stephens could prop himself up on April 4, his drinking did not impinge upon the accuracy of his statements.[77] The HSCA staff report pointed out that Memphis Police Lieutenant James Papia told the committee that he had questioned Stephens only minutes after the assassination and that although Stephens had obviously been drinking, he was "neither incoherent nor staggering." Lieutenant Glen King also interviewed Stephens and found him "coherent." Lloyd Jowers, the proprietor of Jim's Grill, told HSCA that on April 4 Stephens "was in control of himself and knew what he was saying or doing"; and, furthermore, that although Stephens drank beer "all the time by the quart," Jowers had never seen him pass out.

Evidently HSCA established for Stephens a sobriety test whose standards would surely put a chill into anyone concerned with drunk driving; that, so long as Stephens was not staggering or incoherent, his drinking did not preclude his accurately perceiving and reporting on the crucial events of the afternoon.

Not only is there a marked difference between being able to avoid staggering or babbling and accurately reporting on a series of interrelated events, but two sources allege to have had encounters with Stephens which raise the question of whether he could have witnessed *anything* accurately.[78] Taxi driver James McGraw told HSCA that he had observed Stephens lying on the bed in 6-B in a "drunken stupor." Captain Tony D. Smith of the Memphis police homicide squad observed that Stephens and his wife were "intoxicated." He did not question them.

Stephens's shifting accounts, his pursuit of financial reward, and his alleged drinking made him the kind of prosecution witness whose testimony would be severely discredited, if not torn to shreds, by any competent defense lawyer. But in the nonadversary context of HSCA's investigation, Stephens's notions about what happened at the crime scene became a pillar of the committee's reconstruction.

FINGERPRINTS

In its final report HSCA states: "No prints, either identifiable or unidentifiable, other than Ray's, were found on the rifle."[79] The report's summary description of the fingerprint evidence is misleading. It neglects some intriguing absences of Ray's prints and overstates their presence.

The committee retained fingerprint expert Victor J. Scalice of Forensic Control Systems of New York. He made a positive identification of Ray's prints on the following items contained in the bundle dropped at the crime scene—the rifle, the binoculars, the newspaper, and a Schlitz beer can.[80] He found that the original photograph of the print taken from the telescopic sight was too poor in quality to afford an identification.[81] Because of Scalice's other commitments, he was unable to do all of the work requested by HSCA; so the committee hired two experts from the Washington, D.C. Metropolitan Police Department—Ray H. Holbrook and Darrell D. Linville, both of whom had done fingerprint analysis in the 1972 Watergate burglary case.[82]

This duo of experts , whom HSCA referred to as "the panel," concluded that Ray's prints could be identified on the following items from the bundle: the telescopic sight, the bottle of after shave lotion.[83] The "panel" did not agree with Scalice's positive identification of a Ray print on the rifle nor with Scalice's findings that Ray's prints were on the newspaper, the beer can, and the binoculars.

HSCA's final report is, at best, simplistic; at worst, misleading. It concludes badly that Ray's "prints were on the rifle." This completely ignores the conflicting judgments of the experts.

Positive Identification of Ray's Prints on Items Contained in the Bundle

Scalice	Holbrook and Linville (the Panel)
rifle	telescopic sight
binoculars	bottle of after-shave lotion
newspaper	
beer can	

HSCA ignored the fact that two of its three experts could not render positive identifications on four of the six items, including the rifle. Instead, it presented Scalice's findings as definitive, as if *any* positive identification of a Ray fingerprint was valid, even if the finding was supported by only one of three experts.

After stating, without qualification or elaboration, that Ray's prints were on the rifle, HSCA further stated that "No prints, either identifiable or unidentifiable, other than Ray's were on the rifle."[84] As part of its investigation into possible conspiracies, the committee asked the panel to compare the prints on the rifle to those of several individuals other than Ray[85]—Ray's brothers John and Jerry, Randy Rosenson (named by Ray as a possible associate of Raoul), Jesse B. Stoner (president of the segregationist National States Rights Party and an associate of Jerry Ray), and Gus Proch (an alleged gunrunner who had purchased weapons in Birmingham, Alabama).[86] No prints from any of these five men matched the prints on the rifle.

There were two fingerprints and one palm print found on the rifle and photographed by the FBI in 1968. Scalice concluded that all three prints were Ray's. This is the basis for HSCA's statement that no prints other than Ray's, either identifiable or unidentifiable, were found on the rifle.

Subsequent to Scalice's analysis, Holbrook and Linville could not positively identify any of the three rifle prints as belonging to Ray; neither could they identify them as belonging to any of the other five men.

Our examination of HSCA's use of fingerprint evidence reveals that the committee failed to treat the data objectively and instead selectively used it to bolster the presumption of Ray's guilt. The panel's failure to corroborate Scalice's identification of Ray's prints was ignored; the panel's inability to match the rifle prints with any of the five individuals tested was embraced as further evidence that no prints other than Ray's were found on the rifle. In fact, the panel's findings clearly refute HSCA's assertions: The findings suggest that the prints could belong to someone other than the six men tested.

It is interesting to note the absence of Ray's fingerprints in places where they might have shown up, according to HSCA's version of the crime. A spent cartridge was found in the rifle, and it is assumed by HSCA that this cartridge held the bullet that killed King. The cartridge was hand-loaded into the rifle (according to HSCA's ballistics experts), and its surface would retain fingerprints rather well, as surfaces go.[87] There were no prints at all, identifiable or unidentifiable, on the cartridge case. Did Ray carefully avoid putting his prints on the cartridge case while loading it into the rifle, yet fail to wipe his prints from the scope or other artifacts? Nor were Ray's prints on any of the nine bullets contained in a box found in the bundle, even though the bullets were of two different types and four had been placed in the box by someone other than the manufacturer.

According to Mrs. Brewer, the dresser in Ray's room had been moved away from the window, allegedly by Ray, as part of his attempts to monitor King. Ray's prints were nowhere on the dresser: The only print belonged to a Memphis police officer.[88]

Memphis police lifted a total of ten prints from the boarding house (Ray's room and the bathroom) and sent them to the FBI for analysis. Only two were clear enough to permit comparison: the policeman's print on the dresser and a print from the fireplace in Ray's room. The latter was not Ray's print and was not identified.[89] The cardboard box in which the rifle was found yielded but one print—that of Donald Wood, the clerk at the gun shop where Ray originally purchased the rifle.[90] The bathroom windowsill was removed and sent to the FBI laboratory. The only print found was that of an FBI agent.[91]

The fingerprint evidence is not nearly as extensive or conclusive as HSCA's final report makes it appear.

Ballistics

Ballistics data is often the linchpin of the prosecution's case, tying the defendant's gun conclusively to the murder. HSCA's final report states: "While the firearms panel could not say conclusively that the rifle found in Canipe's, the one with Ray's fingerprints on the stock and scope, fired the fatal shot, it did conclude that it was possible for the shot to have been fired from that rifle."[92] "Possibility" is far from certainty. The ballistics data does not prove that the bullet that killed King was fired by the rifle purchased by Ray. When closely examined, the data raises a number of puzzling questions about Ray's alleged modus operandi.

The bullet taken from King's body was in three fragments. Two were judged to be so badly distorted that no identification was possible. The third fragment, the base portion of the bullet, manifested the class characteristics (six grooves, six lands, right twist) of a .30–06 caliber bullet of Remington Peters manufacture—the same *type* of bullet used by the rifle found at the crime scene.[93] This fragment allegedly could not be positively identified as having been fired by the rifle found at the crime scene, as opposed to any other Remington Gamemaster. (This was said to be because the rifle made different markings on every bullet, thus precluding the specific comparisons needed to determine whether a particular bullet was or was not fired from it.)[94] Therefore, the fatal bullet could have been fired from another rifle.

The firearms panel concluded that the spent cartridge case found in the rifle did bear the distinct markings of the firing pin of that rifle; therefore, it had been fired by that rifle (the one purchased by Ray).[95] There exists no scientific test by which a bullet can be linked to a particular spent cartridge, thus there is no way to prove that the empty cartridge found in the weapon actually launched the fatal bullet. The only certainty is that the cartridge found in the rifle launched a bullet, at some indeterminate time.

In the bundle dropped at the crime scene was a box of ammunition, a Peters cartridge box that originally contained 20 rounds.[96] The nine bullets found in the box were of two different types. Five were .30–06 Springfield caliber commercial-type ammunition, the same type of ammunition as the fatal bullet, and the same type as the empty cartridge found in the rifle.[97] The other four rounds were military-type ammunition manufactured by Remington Arms, a different type than the fatal bullet or the spent cartridge.[98] The panel further determined that the military-type bullets found in the commercial-type box bore markings which indicated that, previously, "they may have been loaded into disintegrating-type machine gun link belts or an eight-round clip for the MI Gerand rifle."[99]

The unanswered questions are: Where was this ammunition obtained? By whom? And why were two different types found in one box? One possibility, of course, is that Ray purchased two different kinds of ammunition and used much of it in target practice, then put the remnants into one box. There is no direct evidence of any purchase or practice. No prints were found on the box or the shells.

If Ray was the assassin, he must have been either extremely confident of his abilities as a marksman or extremely forgetful or inept, for he loaded only one bullet into the rifle. None of the nine rounds found in the ammunition box had ever been loaded into the chamber or the magazine of Ray's rifle or any other rifle.[100] As originally purchased, the rifle had a five-shot capacity—an ammunition clip held four shots and one additional bullet could be hand loaded into the chamber. No clip was ever found: not in the rifle, the bundle, nor anywhere else. Absent the clip, Ray's only possibility for a second shot was to hand load the weapon (a time-consuming and therefore risky method).

Harold Weisberg has noted that the standard instructions provided with Ray's rifle clearly show how to load and use the clip.[101] If Ray was so inept as to lose the clip or so incompetent that he could not master its use, one cannot help but wonder how hc mustered the technical savvy and confidence to pull off the assassination. Conversely, it is difficult to imagine that a would-be assassin who, so far as we know, had never before shot at another human being and was not a skilled marksman would have the confidence to assume that he needed only one shot.

Having failed to prove, through its ballistics experts, that Ray's rifle fired the shot that killed King, HSCA was in no mood to conduct further scientific tests that might create additional doubts rather than quiet them. The committee decided not to conduct a neutron activation test.

In this test, samples of bullets to be compared are bombarded with neutrons. Their radioactive characteristics are then compared in terms of the trace elements that make up each bullet or fragment.[102] By comparing the number and proportion of various trace elements (copper, silver, sodium, antimony, chlorine, etc.), it is possible to determine the probability of common origin; whether fragments came from the same bullet or bullets came from the same batch of manufacture. The greater the variation in composition, the less likely bullets or fragments had a common origin.

In 1968 the FBI conducted a neutron activation test on the five commercial-type bullets found in the bundle, the spent cartridge found in the rifle, and the fragments of the fatal bullet. The Bureau hoped to find that all of these items had come from the same batch of ammunition. The five commercial bullets found in the box were made by the same manufacturer, as their imprint indicated. But the FBI found that their elemental composition varied to such an extent that they could not be used as a "standard" against which to compare the fatal bullet.[103] Nearly a decade later, despite improvements in the technology of the test, HSCA declined to conduct its own analysis:

After considering the results of the FBI's neutron activation test, the Committee decided not to conduct further examinations of this type. Because the elemental composition of the five Peters cartridge box commercial-type cartridges differed, they could not be used as standards of comparison with the bullet recovered from Dr. King's body.[104]

The specific results of the 1968 FBI test remained classified, so we do not know the range and proportion of variance. Still, it would appear that new tests might have yielded important data, even in the absence of a match among the five bullets sufficient to produce a "standard."

Depending upon the amount and kind of variance, one possibility is that the five commercial-type bullets came from several different batches, their presence in the same box notwithstanding. We already know that the four military-type bullets found in this box were of different origin.

The five bullets may not have been similar, but basic comparisons could still be made: fragments of the fatal bullet could be compared to each of the five bullets, the empty cartridge found in the rifle could be compared to the cartridge cases of the five bullets. The presence, in the empty cartridge or in the fatal bullet, of a trace element not found in any of the five bullets or cartridges—or the presence of the same elements but in vastly smaller or larger quantities—would tend to indicate that the fatal bullet or the empty cartridge did not come from the same batch(es) of ammunition as the five bullets found in the box.[105]

A close examination of the fingerprint, ballistics, and eyewitness evidence reveals that it is neither as rich nor as conclusive as HSCA's final report portrays it. The gaps and inconsistencies raise serious questions concerning the validity of the HSCA's version of the crime. Moreover, the committee's handling of the evidence manifested a pattern of selectivity which was clearly biased toward establishing Ray's guilt.

10

Time and Motion:
The Double Image of
James Earl Ray

This is a most unusual case. It was so from the beginning. As it goes on, it gets more and more unusual.

Judge W. Preston Battle
Shelby County, Tenn., Dec. 18, 1968

There is no indication that any official investigators, from 1968 to the present, bothered to attempt a systematic, logical reconstruction of Ray's alleged time and motion. This is probably because they never had any serious doubts about how the crime was perpetrated, even though they should have. This chapter will present such an analysis.

All official investigations have concluded that Ray fired from the bathroom window. We will now examine this possibility, on the basis of the available evidence. HSCA implied that Ray surveilled King from room 5-B, by moving the dresser away from the window, pulling up a chair, then leaning slightly out the window to observe King (using the newly purchased binoculars). HSCA also believed that the testimony of Stephens and Anschutz implicated Ray, in part because it indicated that he spent a conspicuous amount of time in the bathroom.

If Ray was surveilling from his room, then, at the moment King appeared, Ray had to gather up the bundle containing the radio, beer cans, and cartridges, add the binoculars, and go up the hall to the bathroom, hoping that one of the 13 tenants was not occupying it. If Ray did not take the bundle with him into the bathroom, then presumably he had to go back to his room after the shooting in order to retrieve it—a sequence which would add to the time needed for a clean escape and

would create the risk of being permanently separated from his possessions, should the presence of people in the hall or the desperateness of
his escape render it impossible for him to detour to retrieve the bundle.
Moreover, unless he brought the rifle box to the bathroom (while leaving
the rest of his possessions in the room) he would risk being seen carrying
a rifle.

If, as Stephens and Anschutz's testimony implies, Ray was waiting
in the bathroom watching for King, then this too creates problems for
the assassin. Presumably, if Ray intended both to monitor and shoot
from the bathroom, he had to carry the weapon and the binoculars with
him on each visit (unless Ray's "plan" was so ill-conceived that he would
end up rushing back to his room to get the rifle). It is risky, and cum-
bersome, to make several trips back and forth to the bathroom carrying
binoculars and a rifle—even if the weapon was in a rifle box (with a
brand name on it). If Ray carried his entire trove of equipment and
possessions on each trip to the bathroom, this too would look odd and
might arouse suspicion even among the denizens of Brewer's boarding
house.

What if Ray was ensconced in the bathroom with his rifle and a fellow
tenant who found the bathroom occupied decided to camp in the hall
and wait, reasonably expecting that whoever was inside might be there
for only two or three minutes rather than twenty? Ray might have come
face to face with someone as he went back to his room carrying his
equipment, or as he fled after shooting King.

Both Stephens and Anschutz claim to have had a conversation about
the bathroom being occupied.[1] Anschutz, presumably holding his basin
of dishwater, went to Stephens's door, which is only a few feet across
the hall from the bathroom. Anschutz asked—somewhat angrily, if we
are to believe Stephens—who was it that was using the bathroom? Stephens allegedly replied that it was the new tenant. If this is true, then
surely Ray could overhear the conversation. It would serve as a clear
warning about the liabilities of using the bathroom, if Ray was not
already aware of them. Ray might have expected Anschutz or some
other tenant to knock on the bathroom door and inquire about obtaining
access. Simply the prospect of such an incident should have been unsettling to a novice assassin.

Given all this, one wonders why Ray might not have preferred to take
his chances surveilling and shooting from his room. While it is true that
he would have had to lean out the window in a somewhat awkward
manner in order to shoot, thus exposing himself to view, there is some
indication that the bathroom too may have required an awkward posture
for shooting. In his room, his marksmanship could remain undisturbed
(by a knock at the door or by the angry voice of someone attempting to
access the bathroom).

The bathroom was hardly the perfect sniper's nest. The tiny room was approximately seven feet wide and there was a distance of only two feet between the window and the left wall, as one faced the Lorraine. The only way an assassin could fire at King was to step into the bathtub and angle the rifle toward the right (resting it on the sill). The tub was an old-fashioned one with steeply sloping sides.[2] After the shooting, scuff marks were found in the bathtub; but there was no way to determine whether they were made by police, a tenant, or an assassin.

It is important to examine Ray's alleged time and motion in relation to King's, although HSCA did not do so. Regarding Ray's alleged surveillance of King, HSCA concluded:

Ray admitted purchasing binoculars on the afternoon of April 4, 1968. Although inexpensive, they would have enabled Ray to keep a close watch on movement at the Lorraine Motel from the rear of the rooming house. Ray could have observed the Lorraine either from room 5-B, by leaning slightly out the window, or from the bathroom at the end of the hall.[3]

Ray checked into the boarding house between three and three-thirty in the afternoon, then purchased the binoculars at the York Arms Co. at approximately four o'clock.[4] While HSCA viewed this purchase as part of Ray's assassination plan, the distances and logistics involved raise serious questions as to why Ray would believe that binoculars were so essential that he would interrupt or defer his surveillance of King in order to go out and procure them.

HSCA implied that the binoculars were necessary in order to keep "close watch on movement at the Lorraine." The distance from the bathroom window to King's room was approximately 207 feet;[5] from Ray's room, about 25 feet more. At those distances, one can clearly "monitor" movement with the naked eye: when someone opened a door or stepped onto the balcony, this could be easily seen. The case can be made that binoculars would be helpful in identifying King, that the assassin might not be very familiar with King's face or might perceive all blacks as looking alike. But Ray could easily peer through his telescopic sight to make sure of his target.

According to HSCA's scenario, Ray got his binoculars at four o'clock and was then ready to return to the rooming house and monitor King. The committee seemed to believe Charles Stephens's claim that the tenant in 5-B (Ray) was spending a conspicuous amount of time in the bathroom. HSCA has completely overlooked the fact that King stepped out onto the balcony of the Lorraine on a separate occasion *prior* to the shooting.[6]

Sometime during the afternoon, King left his room, walked along the balcony to the stairs and went down to his brother A. D.'s first-floor room. After several hours of telephone calls and meetings, King and Abernathy returned to King's room, somewhere between 5:30 and 5:50 P.M. King was shot at 6:01 P.M.

King's first appearance was much briefer than when he stood chatting prior to the shooting, and he was moving most of the time. Nevertheless, as he walked from the stairs to his door (a distance of about eight to ten feet), he was visible from the bathroom window long enough for someone to have fired.

King's chauffeur, Solomon Jones, saw King depart the first-floor room and return to his own room. As King was about to enter his room, he turned to Jones, who was waiting in the parking lot below, and instructed him to start the car so that they could drive to dinner.[7]

In HSCA's scenario, Ray was presumably ensconced in the bathroom and ready to fire. Why didn't he shoot? He had no way of knowing that, minutes later, King would reappear for a longer time; although other assassins or conspirators could have had foreknowledge of King's impending departure for a six o'clock dinner.

The duration of King's first exposure was probably only 10 to 15 seconds, but that was sufficient time to take a shot, if Ray was already waiting. Evidently, Ray was not tempted by the first appearance of his target but calmly waited for a better, less hurried shot, despite the potential hazards of trying to hold down the bathroom for extended periods of time.

If the assassin was someone other than Ray and knew that King would emerge at six o'clock and walk across the balcony, descend to the parking lot, and enter a car, this assassin might well have opted for the second, less-rushed opportunity (or may not have been set up in time for the earlier opportunity).

Returning to the scenario whereby Ray was holed up in the bathroom, perhaps more puzzling than why Ray did not shoot during King's first appearance is why he waited so long to shoot during King's second appearance. A close examination of the record reveals that King was standing on the balcony for a period that, to a waiting sniper, was impressively long; and King was basically a stationary target as he stood at the railing looking down into the parking lot below. He was shot during the last moment that he was stationary, just before he was about to turn and walk along the balcony to the stairs.[8]

The duration of King's presence on the balcony cannot be precisely determined from witness recall, but a rough estimate is possible. If we examine the statements of all of the witnesses who observed King while he was on the balcony, his actions were as follows.[9]

King left his room and stepped onto the balcony. He then called to SCLC attorney Chauncy Eskridge, who was in the parking lot, and asked that Jesse Jackson be invited to dinner. Samuel Kyles, who was hosting the dinner, recalled telling King not to invite too many people because there might not be enough food.

King spotted the Reverends Orange and Bevel wrestling playfully in the parking lot. "Don't let them hurt you," King called out.

Solomon Jones urged King to bring a topcoat because it was chilly. King looked down and replied: "Solomon, you really know how to take care of me."

King called down to Ben Branch, leader of the Bread Basket Band. "Ben, make sure you play 'Precious Lord, Take My Hand' at the meeting tonight. Sing it real pretty."

"OK, Doc, I will," Branch replied.

According to Kyles, King asked Ralph Abernathy to get a topcoat for him.

King saw Jesse Jackson. "Jesse, I want you to go to dinner with us this evening." King then cautioned Jackson not to bring along the entire Bread Basket Band. Kyles chided King: "Doc, Jesse had arranged that even before you had."

Then Kyles said to King: "Come on, it's time to go." Kyles started to walk along the balcony toward the stairs. After a few steps, he called down to Chauncy Eskridge: "Chauncy, are you going with me? I'm going to get the car."

Kyles had progressed several doors from King's room when he heard the shot.

Obviously, the mood among King's entourage was a relaxed one. At minimum, the previously described conversations would take two to three minutes, allowing for brief pauses of transition as King spoke to one person, spotted another, then spoke to them. Kyles states that it was approximately 5:30 when he first went to King's room. They chatted while King finished dressing, then went onto the balcony—at 5:55, Kyles estimated. King was shot at 6:01.[10] Chauncy Eskridge believed that King stepped into view as early as 5:45 and was on the balcony a full 10 to 15 minutes prior to the shooting.[11]

Considering that a shot could be squeezed off in seconds, the sniper appears to have waited an eternity. Perhaps James Earl Ray had to work up the nerve to kill a man for the first time. If nerves were a problem, he certainly overcame them—firing a perfect shot. Perhaps a sniper other than Ray was getting into position for a six o'clock shot and did not have much lead time. Perhaps such a sniper was taking the time to do what expert marksmen do: lining up the shot, adjusting the sight, "doping the wind" (observing the wind direction and estimating its possible effect on the shot. According to National Weather Service data obtained by the author, there was a 12 kilometer crosswind at 6:00 P.M.).

There is no evidence that Ray possessed any sophisticated expertise regarding firearms. Nor did he seem to possess any innate technical competence. The clerk who sold him the binoculars remembered that Ray made a point of asking if the "instructions" were in the box. The clerk replied that there wasn't much a person needed to know to operate binoculars, other than holding them up to your eyes and adjusting them.[12]

According to HSCA's reconstruction, Ray fired the shot, ran down the hall to the stairs, exited onto Main Street, dropped the bundle containing the rifle, then got into his white Mustang and sped away. Shelby County Deputy Sheriff Judson Ghormley was the first law-enforcement officer to reach the scene of Ray's alleged escape. Ghormley arrived on Main Street just moments after the white Mustang sped away, although he did not see the escaping fugitive or hear the car depart.[13]

Ghormley was stationed in the firehouse. Upon hearing the shot, he ran outside toward the Lorraine, then circled the fire station back to Main Street, heading south until he discovered the bundle outside Canipe's record store. Ghormley estimated that the elapsed time between the shot and the discovery of the bundle was "no more than two to three minutes."[14] Bernell Finley, a customer inside Canipe's, heard the bundle drop "within a matter of a minute or so" after the shot.[15]

Ghormley told the FBI that the next officer to arrive at the escape scene was "Officer Douglas," who drove up in a cruiser and parked outside Canipe's. Memphis Police Officer Barney G. Wright, who was riding with Douglas, estimated that he arrived in front of Canipe's within two to three minutes after the shooting.[16]

Patrolman Vernon Dollahite also ran out of the fire station at the sound of the shot. He went to the Lorraine, then proceeded onto Main Street from Huling Street, north of the boarding house. He rushed past the boarding house to Canipe's, from the opposite direction in which Ghormley had come.[17] Dollahite's 1968 FBI statement provided no estimate of elapsed time, but he did not see the white Mustang nor did he hear the screech of tires. Dollahite arrived after Ghormley (who also did not see or hear the escaping vehicle).

Talmidge Martin, an employee of the furniture company located on Main Street two doors north of the boarding house, saw a man wearing a brown shirt run past his door just after the shooting. Martin speculated that the man might have been a sheriff, because personnel of the Shelby County sheriff's office wore brown uniforms. It seems certain that Martin saw Vernon Dollahite, who was with the sheriff's office and wore a brown uniform. Martin told the FBI he was uncertain as to the elapsed time between the shot and the sighting of the officer, but he felt that it was "within thirty seconds to as late as two minutes."[18]

It seems clear that, as HSCA's final report described, the departure of the Mustang "preceded the arrival on South Main of two officers from tact [tactual unit] 10 by only a matter of seconds."[19] The officers seem to have arrived between one to three minutes after the shooting, and neither saw or heard the escape. The witnesses inside Canipe's heard the screeching of tires. Ghormley and Dollahite did not. The white Mustang was cleanly away from the crime scene before either officer arrived.

If we estimate the specifics of time and motion necessary for Ray's escape (according to HSCA's scenario) they are as follows:

- a brief pause after the shot to see that the target was down (1 to 2 seconds)
- step out of the high-sided bathtub
- put the rifle inside the cardboard box
- gather up the bundle [if he had to detour to his room to get it, then securing the bundle would take longer]
- burst into the hallway and run approximately 85 feet to the stairs
- descend one flight of stairs and exit onto the sidewalk
- travel approximately 45 feet to the Mustang, pausing to drop the bundle. According to two of the witnesses inside Canipe's, this was done at a fast walk, not a run. After dropping the bundle, Ray would then have to circle around to the driver's side of the Mustang.
- put the key in the ignition, start the car, and peel away.

It is indeed physically possible to accomplish these tasks in under two minutes. But if Ray did do it this way, he could not afford any confusion or hesitation that would interrupt the flow of his escape, for he missed a confrontation with Ghormley or Dollahite by a matter of seconds.

It is not simply that all of these movements had to have been performed within a one to three minute time frame, but that they had to be completed soon enough so that the escaping vehicle was out of earshot and out of sight of the converging officers. Once Ghormley sprinted past the slight curve that ended at the firehouse driveway, his view extended to a distance of approximately 200 feet to Canipe's door and another 200 feet from Canipe's to the intersection of Main and Huling (the first possible turn off for a vehicle proceeding north on Main Street).

THE BUNDLE DROP

There is no doubt that within minutes after the shooting, a bundle containing items linked to Ray was dropped in the doorway of Canipe's Amusement Company, next door to the boarding house. The bundle contained: an April 4 Memphis newspaper, a box of cartridges, a rifle (contained in a cardboard box), a bottle of after-shave lotion, a pair of binoculars, and a portable radio bearing a scratched identification number that turned out to be Ray's Missouri State Penitentiary inmate number.[20] The questions are: Who dropped it, and why? The FBI and HSCA concluded that Ray dropped it as he fled in panic. Some assassination researchers believe that Ray would not be so stupid as to leave such incriminating evidence at the crime scene, and that a conspirator collected Ray's belongings and purposely dropped them as part of a frame-up.

There were three relevant witnesses. All were inside Canipe's. At about 6:00 P.M., Bernell Finley was browsing through popular records when he heard a shot. "A minute or so later" he heard a second noise emanating from the front door.[21] He glimpsed a man "walking rapidly" by. Then he heard the screech of tires and saw a white car speed past, heading north on Main. Finley saw only the rear portion of the car—the roof line and the trunk—but he told the FBI he was certain it was a Mustang.

He saw the passing figure for only an instant and viewed only the left side of the man's face, but Finley was sure that the man was white and wore a dark suit.

Julias Graham was with Finley.[22] He did not hear the shot, but he did hear the sound of heavy footsteps, of "a running man." He looked toward the front door and saw a man drop a bundle outside. Then he heard screeching tires and saw a white Mustang speed away.

In 1968 Graham told the FBI that he saw only the man's left side and only for a moment. He described the suspect as a white male, 25 to 35 years old, 165 pounds, wearing dark clothes (either a dark suit or dark dress-type jacket and slacks). In 1977 Graham told HSCA that he could not recall the suspect's description, but he did recall that a white Mustang went past Canipe's just after the bundle was dropped.[23]

The third witness was Guy Canipe, the store owner. He heard a "thud" outside the front door and saw a man "walking" south.[24] He went to the door and saw a small white car drive by ("possibly a compact"). There was only one man in the car. Canipe caught only a brief glimpse of the man and saw little of his face, except possibly a bit of the left side.

Canipe's first description was given to Shelby County Deputy Sheriff Judson Ghormley, who reported the data to the FBI:[25] a white male, tall, a little on the heavy side, dark hair, wearing a dark suit (possibly black) complete with shirt and tie. Six days later, Canipe was interviewed directly by FBI agents. He described the suspect as a white male, 25 to 30 years old (possibly older), five feet ten inches to six feet tall, dark hair, neat and clean, wearing a dark-colored suit. Canipe also stated it was his impression the man was "chunky." In 1977 Canipe told HSCA that the man was a white male, five feet ten inches to six feet tall, neat and clean, wearing a dark suit. He reiterated that the fugitive had a "chunky build"[26]—an impression not shared by the other witnesses—and added that the man was "dark skinned," although Caucasian.[27]

Given the apparent discrepancy between Canipe's description and Ray, I attempted to interview Canipe in Memphis in 1986, to put the question to him directly as to whether he thought it was Ray. Canipe asserted, with some irritation, that the case had been "thoroughly investigated by local authorities." He begged the question by stating: "I wouldn't know Ray any more than I know you." He refused to talk further.*

Finley and Graham seem to be describing someone who looks like Ray; Canipe's "chunky," dark-skinned man seems unlike Ray. Ray wore a dark suit when he checked into the boarding house.

Most implicative for Ray is the fact that all three witnesses associate the bundle drop with the screeching departure of a white car. Finley and Graham specifically identified the vehicle as a white Mustang. Ray admits driving away from the crime scene in his white Mustang, but alleges a different set of circumstances.

One of the puzzling questions is why Ray, as opposed to someone trying to frame him, would dump such a trove of incriminating evidence. It had been theorized that he dropped the bundle to insure that he would go down in history as a famous assassin, but even HSCA rejected this theory.[28] Instead, the committee concluded,

an official police car protruded onto the sidewalk on the east side of south Main Street and would have been clearly visible to Ray as he fled south from the rooming house. The committee believed that Ray threw the bundle of evidence down in a moment of panic, probably triggered by his seeing police activity or a police vehicle.[29]

The panic scenario was apparently first put forth in 1968 by Memphis Police Officer William E. Gross, who was inside the fire station when the shooting occurred. He told the FBI that the first thing that a fleeing suspect would have seen as he exited the boarding house and ran south on Main was a police car parked in the driveway of the fire station, thus prompting the bundle drop.[30]

Three police cars were parked in the firehouse driveway, approximately 200 feet from the boarding house.[31] Although the cars were unmanned at the time, it is certainly possible that their mere presence would unnerve a fleeing assassin. (Police Officer Barney Wright stated that two vehicles were parked side by side with the third police car parked behind the other two. This may have made it difficult, from Ray's position, to see that the cruiser farthest away from him was unmanned.)[32]

---

*Another key crime scene witness refused the author's request for an interview citing fear of harassment by Memphis police.

HSCA raised the possibility that Ray may have seen a police officer as well as a vacant police car, since several officers were stationed inside the firehouse and ran outside immediately after the shooting. However, the data seem to preclude this possibility. An examination of the FBI interviews with TACT–10 officers indicates that all of them exited the firehouse and ran east toward the Lorraine, rather than west onto Main Street. The firehouse was set approximately 40 feet back from Main Street, so that neither the exiting of the officers nor their subsequent rushing around would be visible from the section of Main Street where Canipe's or the boarding house were located. While Officers Ghormley and Dollahite did run onto Main Street after going to the Lorraine, they both arrived after the bundle was dropped and neither saw or heard the white Mustang.

This was further confirmed by the author's interview with Fire Fighter George W. Leonneke.[33] He was observing King from inside the firehouse at the time of the shooting. When King fell, he ran throughout the building telling police King had been shot and exhorting them to get to the Lorraine. According to Leonneke: "Every one of the police—I told them all—and they all run out the back door or the side door to the Lorraine." Shortly after the police rushed away from Main Street and toward the Lorraine, Leonneke looked out the window and observed Main Street: he saw no one—no police, no fire fighters, no pedestrians, no cars. Because the firehouse was set back, he could not see the section of Main Street where Ray would have been, but Leonneke's observations confirm that Ray would not have seen any police officers.

The panic explanation has the same seductive quality as the insanity explanation: it serves as an ipso facto cause for all kinds of otherwise illogical or inconsistent behavior; that is, since Ray was panicked, there is no necessity to logically analyze the dropping of the bundle. But a close look at the evidence raises serious questions about the validity of the panic theory.

Allegedly, Ray's Mustang was parked beyond Canipe's on the same side of the street. The car faced north as Ray approached from the south. His fastest escape route was to go directly into the street and head, at an angle, toward the driver's side of the car. Walking along the sidewalk and dropping the bundle—perhaps even pausing momentarily to select a drop site or to execute the drop—created a delay, however brief, in terms of getting to the car. One wonders if the most likely response to panic might not be to sprint directly to the car rather than walking rapidly, dropping the bundle, then circling into the street to get to the driver's side. Formidable panic would seem to dictate a run instead of the walk. If Ray believed that the cruiser 200 feet away was a direct threat, then the goal should have been to distance himself from it as fast as possible, no matter how suspicious he might appear.

The doorway to Canipe's was located in an angular recess, a few feet back from the edge of the sidewalk. According to Julias Graham, who saw the drop, the man "stepped to the left and dropped the bundle in the recess"[34]—a definite detour of time and motion.

What HSCA serves up is not a panic theory so much as a theory of selective panic. Ray does not break stride and run, and he does not simply dump the bundle any old place. Instead, he briefly detours away from his escape vehicle and carries the bundle to what appears to be a rather purposeful drop, as opposed to dropping it instantly on the sidewalk in front of the boarding house.

If Ray had the presence of mind not to drop the bundle instantly and not to break into a run that might arouse suspicion, then the question is: Why he didn't have the cool to hang on to the bundle? Did he really believe that his escape would be aided by jettisoning it? Did he think that if he did not have the incriminating evidence with him, he might be let go if he were stopped? As an escapee from Missouri State Penitentiary, he was hardly in a position to be set free after any competent law-enforcement check following his being picked up, even absent the murder weapon in his car. Why not take the bundle with him and ditch it in some bucolic setting, thereby delaying the discovery of the incriminating evidence? Panic, says HSCA.

One psychological consequence of panic can be to cling irrationally to belongings thought to be important, as with persons who delay their escape from a burning building in order to retrieve some precious possession. Ray surely had a proprietary interest in the bundle. According to HSCA's logic, he had carefully assembled all of his belongings in it and had either risked drawing attention to himself by transporting it to the bathroom or had delayed his escape to go back to his room to get it.

While fleeing down the hallway, Ray supposedly had the foresight to cover his face with his arm; and he had the chutzpah to respond to Anschutz's observation about the noise sounding like a shot: "Yeah, it was a shot."[35] This seems fairly composed on Ray's part. Yet, at the sight of a police car 200 feet away, he allegedly lost his cool and abandoned his all-important bundle, leaving his prints, prison serial number, and the murder weapon in a place where it was sure to be instantly discovered by police.

In terms of the risk of immediate apprehension, dropping the bundle may have been more dangerous than keeping it. The police car may have been empty but Canipe's store was not: There were three people inside. There was a large, glass storefront window and the door was open (the bundle extended into the doorway, so the door must have been opened when the drop occurred). Julias Graham actually saw the bundle being dropped.

Ray allegedly paused to come toward men who, so far as he knew, might be potential pursuers. Someone could have run out of the store after him, connecting his presence with the sound of the shot; someone from the store might have rushed out and caught the number of Ray's license plate.

Ray had not taken the precaution of wiping his prints from all of the items in the bundle nor had he handled them only with gloves. Even Ray's simplistic criminal mind could understand that it was one thing to drop a "clean" bundle (devoid of prints) but that to leave his prints was one of the surest ways to precipitate capture.

TWO WHITE MUSTANGS

Ray contends that his white Mustang was not parked outside Canipe's but was at a nearby gas station. He then drove back to the crime scene, saw that there was trouble and fled.

No evidence has been generated that corroborates his alibi. There is no indication that HSCA, the FBI, MPD, or Ray's lawyers ever conducted a systematic investigation of gas stations within a reasonable radius of the boarding house. On the other hand, the frame-up version of the bundle drop requires the presence of two white Mustangs.

Although neither of the official inquiries mentioned it, the press had described the presence of two white Mustangs on Main Street during the hours preceding the assassination. The Associated Press reported that "two of them, both 1966 models, were parked within 100 feet of the rooming house entrance. . . . "[36] The *Memphis Commercial Appeal* carried a drawing of the crime scene which pictured two white Mustangs parked on Main Street.[37] White Mustangs were very common in the Memphis area in 1968. Frank Holloman, Memphis public safety director, defended the failure to put out an immediate APB by stating that: "You had a large number of white Mustangs" in the area.[38] In the aftermath of the shooting, Memphis police estimated that they stopped 50 to 60 such cars while searching for the fugitive.[39] The *Minneapolis Tribune* quoted a Tennessee Ford dealer who estimated that "600 of them were sold and 400 are still on the street."[40]

FBI interviews and witness statements to the press seem firmly to establish that there were two white Mustangs present at the crime scene: one parked almost directly in front of Jim's Grill (next door to the boarding house); the other, several car lengths south, near the doorway to Canipe's. Lloyd Jowers, the owner of Jim's Grill, arrived at work at approximately 3:55 P.M. He parked his Cadillac directly behind a white Mustang that was "parked on the street directly in front" of the grill.[41] Jowers noticed that the car had an out-of-state plate (Mississippi, he thought; Ray's was Alabama).

David Wood was sitting in Jim's Grill having a beer at about five o'clock. He recalled seeing a white Mustang parked in front of the grill. He noted that it had no front license plate and no inspection sticker on the windshield, indicating that the vehicle was from out of state.[42] Gilbert Cupples arrived at Jim's shortly after five. He parked across the street. As he crossed to enter the grill, he saw a white Mustang parked directly in front of Jowers's Cadillac.[43]

At 5:15 to 5:30, two customers departed the grill together after finishing their dinner. Ray Hendrix, an employee of the Army Corps of Engineers, forgot his jacket and went back inside to retrieve it. His companion, William Reed, a salesman for a photography firm, waited outside and passed the time by checking out the car parked "almost in front of Jim's Grill." It was a white Mustang. Reed's interest stemmed from the fact that he was looking for a car to buy.[44]

Late in the afternoon of April 4, parking places were scarce in this area of Main Street. Had this Mustang departed, it is very likely that the spot would quickly have been filled. For example, Harold Parker arrived at Jim's Grill at about 4:20. He had to park further down Main Street because the spaces near Jim's were all taken (he did not recall the types of cars).[45]

The second white Mustang was seen by employees of the Seabrook Wallpaper Company, located at 421 Main Street, across from Canipe's. (Jim's Grill was 418; the boarding house, 420–422 ½; Canipe's, 424.) At about 4:30 the Seabrook employees had finished work and several were waiting for rides home. Elizabeth Copeland, who worked in customer services, saw a white car pull up and park "across the street," between 4:30 and 4:45. This location was several doors and several car lengths south of Jim's Grill. Mrs. Copeland summoned fellow employee Peggy Hurley, who was waiting for her husband to pick her up. But when Mrs. Hurley looked at the car across the street, she said it was not her husband's Falcon: it was a Mustang.[46] Elizabeth Copeland looked at the car again and noticed a white male with dark hair sitting behind the wheel. She believed that the man was wearing a dark coat.

Francis B. Thompson, the company's bookkeeper, had finished work and was waiting for her daughter to pick her up. She too saw a white car drive up and park "across the street . . . in front of Canipe's Amusement Co.," at 4:30 or 4:45.[47] She overheard the exchange between Elizabeth Copeland and Peggy Hurley and corroborated that Hurley had described the vehicle as a Mustang.

At approximately 4:45, Francis Thompson's ride arrived. As Mrs. Thompson got into her daughter's car, she noticed there was a white male sitting in the Mustang. She could provide no further description.[48]

The man was still behind the wheel when Peggy Hurley's husband finally arrived, sometime after five. Mr. Hurley later told the *Memphis*

Commercial Appeal that he parked behind a white Mustang about 20 feet south of Canipe's and that there was a "young" man sitting in the car (Ray was nearly 40 years old)[49] Hurley also remembered that the car had a red and white plate, which he believed was from Arkansas (both Arkansas and Alabama had red and white plates in 1968).

At approximately 5:20, Elizabeth Copeland's husband pulled up. He double-parked next to the car which, earlier, Peggy Hurley had said was a Mustang. When Mrs. Copeland crossed the street and got into her husband's car, she noticed there was no longer anyone sitting in the other car.[50]

The Mustang outside of Jim's Grill was never seen with anyone in it. It was seen by two customers (Cupples and Wood) at around 5:00 P.M. This overlaps with the sightings of the occupied Mustang in front of Canipe's, which arrived at approximately 4:45 and was still occupied after 5:00 when Peggy Hurley's husband parked behind it.

If we relate the Mustang sightings to Ray's known and alleged movements during this period, we have Ray checking in at Brewer's at about 3:30. Ralph Carpenter, the clerk at the York Arms Company who sold Ray the binoculars, places the purchase at "about 4:00."[51]

Lloyd Jowers was more certain of the time at which he saw a white Mustang in front of his grill—3:55. Since Carpenter's estimate is somewhat more vague, and since York Arms was located only a mile and a half from the boarding house and the grill, it is very possible that the Mustang parked in front of Jim's Grill was Ray's.

It seems far less likely that the second Mustang, parked near Canipe's, could belong to Ray. If he had arrived and parked at 4:45, this would leave a large gap in his movements following the purchase of the binoculars (at around four o'clock). Supposedly, Ray bought the binoculars in order to monitor King. What would he do for 45 minutes, presumably away from the boarding house? Why would he sit in the car from four forty-five until after five o'clock when he could be in his room or the bathroom setting up the kill?

Ray claims he departed the boarding house and drove to a gas station. It appears that one of the two Mustangs did leave the area before six o'clock. The reader will recall that Ray Hendrix and William Reed left Jim's Grill sometime between five-fifteen and five-thirty. While Hendrix went back for his jacket, Reed checked out the Mustang parked in front of the grill. When Hendrix returned, both men walked north along Main Street (in the opposite direction from the boarding house and Canipe's).[52]

They approached the corner of Main and Vance and were about to step off the curb and cross the street when Reed looked to see if there were any cars approaching.[53] He saw a white Mustang about to turn off of Main onto Vance. Reed pulled Hendrix back onto the sidewalk.

Both men identified the car as a white Mustang. It turned and passed directly in front of them. According to Hendrix, it was not moving fast and did not squeal as it rounded the corner. The vehicle proceeded east on Vance and disappeared from view.[54]

As for the driver, Reed was vague: a white male with a white shirt, not young, not old. Reed did not notice whether the man wore a tie or a hat. Hendrix saw only that there was one white male in the car.

Was this James Earl Ray, driving away from the crime scene as he claims he did? If so, it is difficult to imagine him being in sync with HSCA's assassination scenario. It would mean that, as the assassin, Ray interrupted his efforts to set up the kill in order to take a ride for no apparent reason.

If the first Mustang did belong to Ray, it was parked in a much better position than the second one in terms of a fast getaway from the boarding house. With his car parked in front of Jim's Grill, Ray could exit the boarding house and reach it very quickly, without having to walk up the street past Canipe's

The second Mustang—the one seen by the Hurleys, Thompson, and Copeland—would seem to be the one that screeched away directly after the bundle was dropped. According to Charles Hurley, this Mustang was located 20 feet south of Canipe's (toward the firehouse). It will be recalled that Canipe, Graham, and Finley saw a man pass Canipe's store as the bundle was dropped then continue up the sidewalk (south) and out of view. Within moments they also heard the screech of tires and saw a white car speed by the store, heading north.

TWO DARK SUITS

After the assassination, police picked up a man who had been in the area of Brewer's boarding house and who was wearing a dark suit. The man was subsequently released: Police and FBI concluded that he had no involvement in the crime. A close examination of the strange case of then 41-year-old Ted Andrews (a pseudonym provided by the author) raises a host of unanswered questions about the handling of his case by authorities.

At 8:00 A.M. the morning after the assassination, Lloyd Jowers, the owner of Jim's Grill, alerted police to the presence of a mysterious stranger who was eating breakfast and "acting strange": he seemed "very calm" while everyone else seemed agitated over the shooting.[55] Jowers had noticed this same man at about four o'clock the previous day, when Jowers parked his Cadillac behind the white Mustang and entered the grill. The stranger ordered a meal and was conspicuous because most of Jowers's customers were locals who frequented the grill regularly.

Jowers described the man as a white male, five feet eight to five feet nine inches, heavy (about 160 pounds), with a ruddy complexion and sandy hair, and wearing a dark suit.[56] The man finished his meal on the afternoon of the assassination and departed the grill. Jowers did not notice where he went but was sure that he did not get into the parked Mustang.

On the morning of April 5, Andrews was stopped by police as he left Jim's Grill. He was taken to headquarters for questioning. Andrews was carrying a briefcase and a cardboard box containing a new portable radio. His story was as bizarre as it was incongruous.

According to Helen Wynne, who ran a rooming house at 390 ½ Main Street, Andrews checked in at two o'clock on the afternoon of the assassination, one and a half hours before Ray/Willard checked in at Brewers (at 420 Main Street).[57] Mrs. Wynne knew Andrews: his father had been a permanent tenant and the son had rented a room on four or five occasions. This time, he had no luggage except a small briefcase. She described him as a man who usually kept to himself and did not talk with the other tenants; a man who never smoked, cursed, or drank— "very much a gentleman." But Mrs. Wynne knew nothing of his family life or employment and he gave no indication of why he was in Memphis or where he was going.

Mrs. Wynne clearly recalled that sometime during the afternoon of April 4, probably around three-thirty, Andrews told her he was very tired and was going to take a nap. He instructed her to awaken him at five-fifty, because he had some phone calls to make. She woke him as requested, and he went out. Mrs. Wynne had no idea where he went or precisely when he returned, although he did spend the night in his room and was talking with other tenants about the assassination.

She did not have a pay phone in her house but did have a private phone which she would have allowed Andrews to use if he had asked. But he did not ask, Mrs. Wynne observed, even though he had specifically mentioned that "the reason he wanted to get up was in order to make some telephone calls."[58]

When interviewed by the FBI, Andrews provided a most singular narrative of his life and times and of his visit to Memphis.[59] He claimed to have left his home in Tennessee and hitchhiked all night to get to Memphis, catching a ride in a truck hauling pigs and arriving at seven-thirty on the morning of April 4. He had only a couple of dollars in his pocket, so he sold a pint of blood for $15 at Baptist Memorial Hospital, a transaction for which he proffered a receipt. Ostensibly weak from loss of blood yet flush with the profit, Andrews took a taxi directly to Mrs. Wynne's. He claimed to have arrived between 9:30 and 10:00 A.M. Mrs. Wynne placed his time of arrival at 2:00 P.M.

Andrews described how he had a meal at Jim's Grill at around 2:00 P.M. Lloyd Jowers, the owner of Jim's Grill, fixes his sighting of Andrews eating at 4:00.

Andrews stated that he made a number of early morning calls from the hospital to "various persons and firms," attempting to find someone who wanted a car driven to California. One person he called suggested that he call back at 6:00 P.M. to clarify whether there was a car available.

Asserting that he had not wanted to bother Mrs. Wynne for the use of her phone, Andrews said that, just prior to six o'clock he walked to the Ambassador Hotel (one block north of Mrs. Wynne's) and placed some phone calls.

Andrews claimed to have left the Ambassador at around six and walked back to his room. There was considerable excitement in the area, and he saw an ambulance pass by. He did not see any fleeing cars or persons nor any Mustangs.[60]

Andrews told his FBI interviewers that he would gladly furnish any information or cooperate in any manner, in order that he could immediately be eliminated as having anything to do with the shooting of Dr. King.[61] He then offered to display the contents of his briefcase—described by the FBI as "various papers, toilet articles, two dirty shirts, undergarments and socks, and a new radio inside cellophane paper."[62]

Andrews's comments about his "luggage" hardly helped to bolster the credibility of his story. The FBI reported that he claimed he always "traveled light" because he expected to be hitchhiking and could not afford to carry much clothing. Yet, it would seem that someone interested in driving two-thirds of the way across the US might have packed an additional bag or put several more shirts in the briefcase. Andrews claimed that he had traded for the new radio "a day or so before" in Little Rock, Arkansas, and that he carried it with him so he could pawn it to buy food en route to California.

Little Rock is several hundred miles west of his home in Tennessee. Andrews's thumb must have had quite a workout, since his story places him in Little Rock "a day or so" before April 4 and in Tennessee on the night of April 3, when he left and hitchhiked all night in the rain to arrive in Memphis at 7:30 A.M. on April 4. He never explained the apparent geographic illogic of his travels. Little Rock is several hundred miles closer to his alleged California destination; yet, instead of heading west from there, he backtracked to Tennessee then traveled northeast to Memphis.

Equally curious is Andrews's claim, made later in his FBI interview, that on March 27 he purchased a 1958 Ford station wagon for $49 in Little Rock—he produced a receipt—and that the car was now at his father-in-law's house in Tennessee.[63] This is an odd purchase for a man so strapped for the cash needed to sustain him while driving someone else's car to California that he would pawn a radio and sell blood.

The FBI's handling of Andrews is instructive concerning the Bureau's approach to the case. It is not that there is any evidence that Andrews was in any way involved, but that the fragmentary fugitive description and the odd nature of his story could easily have rendered him more of a prime suspect, at least temporarily.

Andrews was cleared because, according to the FBI, "it appeared that he did not fit the available description of the unknown assailant and that information furnished by him as to his identity and activities in Memphis had been sufficiently verified to eliminate him as a suspect."[64] Moreover, "his presence in a rooming house other than the one from which the shots were made" had been established.[65]

What the Bureau meant here is that it was looking for Willard (Ray), the man who checked in at Brewer's boarding house. The FBI report on Andrews described him as five feet seven inches tall, 150 pounds, light brown hair, blue eyes, 41 years old, wearing a white shirt, a tie, and a gray hounds-tooth check suit (no hat). The suspect who checked into Brewer's was taller and thinner and wore a brown suit.

In their 1968 interviews with the FBI, the three witnesses from Canipe's store provided rather vague, somewhat conflicting descriptions of the man who dropped the bundle—descriptions that do not seem to fit Ray much better than Andrews (and in some ways seem to fit neither of them). Julius Graham gave the following description: age—25–30; height—five feet seven to five feet eight inches; hair—black or dark brown; clothing: either a dark suit or a dress-type jacket and slacks, no hat, did not notice a shirt or tie; neat and clean in appearance. Bernell Finley gave this description: age—unsure, not an old man; weight— around 160 pounds; height—first estimate, five feet six to five feet eight inches, then changed to five feet ten inches; hair—could not recall; clothing—wearing a dark suit. Guy Canipe, Jr. offered this account: age—25 to 30, possibly older; weight—175 to 200 pounds, "chunky" build; height—five feet ten inches to six feet (uncertain estimate); clothing— dark colored suit, neat and clean-cut.

Both Ray and Andrews wore dark suits, had blue eyes and brown hair (Ray's was darker), and were described as neat and clean. Andrews is described by the FBI as five feet seven inches tall, 150 pounds—three inches shorter and 20 pounds lighter than Ray. Andrews was a year older. It is not clear whether this is Andrews's self-description or is based on the observations of the interviewing agents. Lloyd Jowers, who had observed Andrews on two occasions at Jim's Grill, described him as five feet eight to five feet nine inches tall, 160 pounds, "heavy," age 27 to 30.

In dismissing Andrews, the FBI seemed to place great weight on the fact that his "presence" in a rooming house other than Brewer's was verified. But this relates primarily to the renting of a room, since he was not present there the entire time. If the Bureau really believed that his "activities in Memphis" had been verified, it must have simply taken Andrews's word as gospel and neglected the apparent conflicts. He claimed to have checked in on April 4 four hours before his landlady said he did; he claimed to have eaten at Jim's Grill two hours before Jowers recalled seeing him there.

One FBI memo states that the only further action planned was to obtain Andrews's fingerprints, by using his Navy serial number, so that they could be "compared with those available in this case as one more step in eliminating him as a suspect."[66] If the Bureau followed through on this, the results remain unknown. It is odd that the FBI would not fingerprint Andrews while he was in custody and compare these prints (unless there was doubt as to his real identity).

The Bureau itself fuels one's curiosity about its handling of Andrews by its conspicuous deletions in two documents pertaining to him. One excision is two and one-half lines long: "As will be noted from the FD–302 of Andrews, his presence near the scene around the time of the shooting [two and one-half lines deleted] indicated the desirability of his being questioned as a general suspect."[67] The bottom of this same page refers to an "FD–302 stencil (To Be Destroyed)."[68]

Of the three other deletions in the 15 pages of documents on Andrews, two relate to his military service.

Served in U.S. Navy under Navy Serial No. [deleted] on two different occasions, first from about January 1945 to June 1946 and again entered the military service September 1, 1959, during Korean War. Stated volunteered both times [approximately 12 to 15 words deleted].[69]

On the next page of this same document, Andrews's selective service number is deleted, while the number of his Tennessee driver's license is provided. Two pages later, an entire category of data is deleted—heading as well as the data—comprising one-third of a page.

What is so sensitive about Andrews's military service? The deletions were surely not for reasons of privacy: These same documents provide the names and addresses of his relatives, his driver's license number, his home address and telephone number, and his employment record.

The author's interviews with both Andrews and his wife produced more, rather than less, uncertainty about his story. Mrs. Ellen Andrews, his wife of nine years (in 1968), recounted how she had been contacted by police following her husband's detention in Memphis.[70] She had to identify him and corroborate that they were married.

"They thought he was the killer," she told the author. "They told me he looked like him [the killer]." Mrs. Andrews further recalled that when she first saw a picture of James Earl Ray flashed on her television screen, she remarked that her husband did indeed look "somewhat" like Ray, although shorter. "There is a resemblance," she told the author, while offering the caveat that the two men did not look exactly alike.

Mrs. Andrews claimed that she had no idea her husband was in Memphis until after the police contacted her. Nor, she said, did she know anything about his plan to go to California. But she asserted that this was not unusual, that he had a habit of going away on business, to sell various products, and not telling her where he was headed or when he would return.

Mrs. Andrews said that after he was released by authorities, he was sent home by bus. According to Mrs. Andrews, he stayed for a few days and then departed suddenly, without explanation. She claimed that she heard nothing from him for five years.

She also remembered what she perceived as an odd incident which she did not directly relate to the day before the assassination but which parallels Andrews FBI statement concerning how he got to Memphis.

"One time, he left and bought a car, and left it in mother's driveway. He left his clothes and wedding ring [in the car], then rode with hogs."

Had Mrs. Andrews known of her husband's announced intention to get to California, she might have found his purchase and abandonment of the car, and his discarding of the clothes, even more puzzling.

Mrs. Andrews described Ted's Navy service as "strange." "A lot of things happened," she asserted; but she claimed to know only "bits and pieces" of it—recounting that he once jumped ship.

When the author contacted Andrews, he was understandably reluctant to discuss an incident in which he had been detained as a murder suspect, however briefly. He told the author that in 1968 he was a salesman and had gone to Memphis "on business" for "a day or two," that he had been "detained after breakfast." He stated that he had been having no luck as a salesman and had decided to hitchhike to California, to his company's headquarters.

In his 1968 FBI interview, Andrews said that he had his landlady awaken him and then went to a nearby hotel in order to make some phone calls in connection with driving someone else's car to California. Now, 17 years later, Andrews gave the author a quite different account: he was "in a hotel restaurant eating dinner at the time [of the assassination]," and he then exited onto the street and saw the ambulance pass by.

Andrews repeated this version no fewer than three times. His assertion concerning his presence in the hotel restaurant was delivered without qualification or hesitation; his tone was not one of clouded, distant recollection but of certainty.

There was no mention of telephone calls or of finding a car to drive west (central elements in Andrews's 1968 story). One might expect that his memory concerning *What were you doing when Martin Luther King was shot?* would remain sharp, considering that he was compelled to account for his activities because he was a suspect.

Andrews's landlady stated that she woke him, per his instruction, at 5:50 P.M. Then, according to Andrews, he walked one block to the Ambassador Hotel. King was shot at 6:01; the ambulance arrived at the Lorraine at 6:06 and departed very shortly thereafter.[71] Andrews's putative dinner must have been one of the fastest on record, requiring him to walk to the hotel, order, eat, and stroll out onto the sidewalk—all in less than 20 minutes.

I asked him: "Were you anything special in the Navy?" He paused before answering: "Just that I was my mama's little boy."

"Why would the FBI delete information about your Navy service?" I asked.

"No idea."

The FBI's secrecy about Andrews's military background, coupled with the conflicting nature of his story, should have caused HSCA to take an interest in him, if only to discover more about how the Bureau cleared him as a suspect in 1968.

THE PARADOXICAL RAY

An in-depth analysis of the available evidence has rendered James Earl Ray a more, rather than less, puzzling figure. The crime scene evidence is similar to the evidence from the fugitive phase of the case (Toronto, London, Portugal), presenting a double image: Ray the wily, ice-cool hit man; Ray the fumbling, incompetent amateur. The "Ray" at the crime scene is indeed a paradoxical mixture of genius and stupidity.

Ray's alleged shooting of King was a spectacular success. According to HSCA's scenario, he selected a sniper's nest, waited patiently for the right moment (when his target would be stationary and exposed for a considerable period of time); dispatched King with a single, nearly perfect shot to the head; escaped the boarding house, escaped Memphis. No U.S. assassin (convicted or alleged) escaped farther from the crime scene, and none remained at large for as long a time.

Political Scientist James W. Clarke, in his book *American Assassins*, refers to Ray as "a coldly rational and shrewd, if not highly competent hit man" who engineered an "ingenious escape."[72] This is the same James Earl Ray whose criminal career prior to the assassination is described by Clarke as "a record of bungled and ludicrously inept robberies and burglaries."[73] This is the same Ray whom a former, fellow-inmate labeled as a "hayseed" and a "born loser."[74]

Ray had to transcend more than his previous criminal ineptitude in order to successfully assassinate King. His technical proficiency and firearms skills are problematic. There is no evidence that Ray had ever shot at another human being much less killed one, or that he was violence prone. Yet he allegedly became a cold-blooded killer for hire.

It is revealing to note how HSCA dealt with the latter paradox. With regard to Lee Harvey Oswald, it asserted:

The Committee also considered the question of whether Oswald's words or actions indicated that he possessed a "capacity for violence." The presence of such a trait would not, in and of itself, prove much. *Nevertheless, the absence of any such words or actions by Oswald that indicated a capacity for violence would be inconsistent with the conclusion that Oswald assassinated the president and would be of some significance* (emphasis added). In this regard, the Committee noted that Oswald had on more than one occasion exhibited such behavior.[75]

And what of Ray? Clarke described Ray's previous criminal career as one in which "no one was ever hurt or seriously threatened with bodily harm."[76] Nor is there any evidence that Ray was violence prone outside of his criminal career. Absent any indication that he possessed a "capacity for violence," HSCA simply decided to drop this trait as a necessary prerequisite for guilt; and the committee moved on to talk about money, ego-gratification, and "lack of sympathy for Blacks" as factors which motivated Ray.[77]

HSCA's assassination scenario presents us with a Ray so cool yet so panic prone, so capable yet so inept, that he seems almost schizoid:

—The man with the cool of the Jackal, who set up and executed a one-shot kill, panicked at the sight of an empty police car 200 feet away and dumped evidence that would assure his identification, if not his eventual capture.

—The man whose criminal planning included undergoing plastic surgery in order to hide his identity as the assassin not only arrived at the crime scene wearing the most conspicuous attire possible but insisted on wearing it all throughout the commission of the crime.

—The man, who was so frugal that he carried with him to the crime scene an old portable radio bearing his thinly disguised prison serial number, went out two hours before the murder and purchased a forty-dollar pair of binoculars, when he was easily able to observe the Lorraine with the naked eye and to identify King with the telescopic sight.

—The man who carefully assembled nearly every artifact in his possession (including a beer can) and placed them in a bundle, left behind two binocular straps which were found in his room.[78]

In a June 20, 1968, memo summarizing the case, J. Edgar Hoover described Ray as a wily criminal.[79]

The Attorney General asked how we thought Ray got the three names he used. I said this again shows his astuteness as all three are living people residing in Canada who never knew him and never heard of him. I said on the other hand, Ray spent last year, when he was wandering around the country, a great portion of the time in Canada and I thought he was planning this thing and seeking a double identity like Sneyd, Galt, and Bridgeman and checking out those names so if there were any check made on his application for a birth certificate, they could ascertain such a person existed. I said this shows his shrewdness. I said I think we are dealing with a man who is not an ordinary criminal in the usual sense, but a man capable of doing any kind of a sly act. The Attorney General said he was exceptionally clever.

The best evidence suggests that Ray was an unexceptional criminal who had exceptionally clever help.

11   Motive: The Peking-Line King

A [CIA informant] feels that somewhere in the negro movement, at the top, there must be a negro leader who is "clean" who could step into the vacuum and chaos if Martin Luther King were either exposed or assassinated.

CIA memo, May 11, 1965

Why, Martin's Vietnam views alone were enough to get him murdered. Others have been shot for less.

Rev. Jesse Jackson, 1976[1]

In a typical murder case the discovery of a clear motive on the part of a suspect can be a major step in solving the case. A la Perry Mason, when it is learned that the victim's spouse recently took out a million-dollar insurance policy on the deceased, the investigation becomes better focused. But the assassination of a prominent political figure is very different. Motive always abounds, and to such an extent that it is more useful in weeding out suspects than in pointing to the guilty party.

For example, a case can easily be made that each of the following groups or interests had a motive to assassinate President John F. Kennedy (although some are far more compelling than others): the Mafia, anti-Castro Cubans, the KGB, Texas oil barons, right-wing fanatics, Fidel Castro. Here, as with the King case, the primary utility of motive is to exclude from investigation the groups or interests who did not possess one: the Democratic Party, the Sons of Ireland, the Girl Scouts of America.

When HSCA opened its investigation, there was a new addition to the list of organizations that had motive—Hoover's FBI. There was no good evidence in 1968 that the FBI had motive, but subsequent revelations concerning the Bureau's vendetta against King (Hoover's venomous, pathological hatred of King; the Bureau's attempts to destroy "the Black Messiah" personally and politically) clearly placed the FBI on the suspect list.

The committee never looked beyond the FBI to other agencies or networks within the U.S. intelligence community. It should have: There was motive within elements of the CIA and, quite probably, military intelligence as well. The full list of entities possessing a motive is not known; what is known is that it definitely extends beyond the FBI.

While other agencies may have lacked the personalist enmity of the Hoover vendetta—the perverse combination of racism, abuse of power, and an intense personal hatred of King—there was another motive which, while less personal and more *businesslike*, was equally compelling. It was spawned not by the psychological hang-ups and dictatorial style of a particular agency head but by vivid and dire warnings from intelligence data about King and his political plans.

As the CIA's own documents demonstrate, Martin Luther King, Jr. was perceived to be one of the most dangerous domestic threats to U.S. national security. The logical bottom line of the Agency's reports, given its working assumptions about the interface of domestic and international politics, was that Hanoi had in King a direct pipeline through which to subvert the United States' Vietnam War effort.

The FBI believed that King had significant Communist ties.[2] A typical top secret Bureau memorandum dated March 29, 1968 (only five days before the assassination), is entitled "Communist Infiltration of Southern Christian Leadership Conference" (the organization headed by King). But CIA had its own data on King's putative Communist ties.[3]

From 1965 throughout the remainder of King's life, a highly respected CIA source who had close ties to the civil rights movement, Jay Richard Kennedy, reported to the Agency concerning alleged communist infiltration of that movement.[4] One 1965 CIA report on Kennedy's inputs warns that :

The Communist left is making an all out drive to get into the Negro movement. . . . Communists or Negro elements who will be directed by the Communists may be in a position to, if not take over the Negro movement, completely disrupt it and cause extremely critical problems for the Government of the United States.[5]

A similar report written that same year warns of Communist "efforts at corrupting and seizing the Negro Civil Rights Movement." The report also conveys Jay Richard Kennedy's belief that this was not a matter that should be handled by the FBI alone, as a domestic problem, but should be considered by the CIA to be an "international situation."

Regarding King himself, Kennedy warned in 1965 that the civil rights leader was vulnerable to blackmail and corruption by the Communists because of three principle areas of alleged liability: highly derogatory personal information about King's private life, a theft of Southern Christian Leadership Conference funds, associations with Communist or pro-Communist types.[6] Kennedy claimed that the real danger lay with "Peking-line communists" who were increasingly influential in the civil rights movement.[7]

On at least two occasions in 1965, Kennedy called his CIA contact to further discuss the "Peking-line" menace, especially as it related to opposition to the Vietnam War from within the movement. One CIA report conveys Kennedy's warning that,

so called leaders like Martin Luther King, Jr. and [deleted] have very clearly started blending the Negro Civil Rights Movement into a merger with their attacks on the government policy in Vietnam and, even to a lesser degree, attacks on Government policy in the Dominican Republic.[8]

Professor David J. Garrow wrote of Kennedy's inputs:

The fact that the CIA treated Kennedy's observation and analyses with the utmost seriousness is far more important than the issue of whether many of Kennedy's impressions bore any close resemblance to what actually was happening within the civil rights movement. The CIA officer was just as fascinated with "Peking-line Communists" as was Kennedy, and how many officials in the higher echelons of the Agency were as captivated with Kennedy's views as was his immediate friend [the CIA officer to whom he reported] remains unknown.[9]

Despite the restrictions of its 1947 charter regarding domestic spying, the CIA had an active operational interest in King. Perhaps the Agency decided to take Kennedy's advise and view King as an "international" problem rather than a domestic one, because of the alleged influence of foreign Communists. That King was a subject of serious concern is indicated not only by CIA documents relating directly to him but also by other documents which reveal the Agency's perceptions and activities during the 1960s.

The CIA viewed the civil rights movement with a trepidation that is best described as paranoic. The Agency believed that it was, or inevitably would be, Communist inspired if not Communist directed. It viewed "black power groups" as somehow posing a direct threat to its mission. One 1967 memo describes such groups as posing "a new threat" to CIA operations abroad and to its "image in the United States," because of what the Agency perceived as increasing hostility toward it on the part of some blacks.[10]

In response to this nebulous threat, the Agency targeted black political groups with a zeal that, until the revelations of the 1970s, most observers assumed was reserved for foreign Communist parties that challenged "friendly" dictatorships. In the late 1960s the CIA infiltrated black groups participating in the Resurrection City encampment in Washington, D.C.; photographed the participants at a Malcolm X day rally in the Capitol, and had an informer planted inside the Washington, D.C. school system to report on increasing militancy among black youths.[11]

In January 1984, in response to an FOIA request, I obtained 134 pages of CIA documents pertaining to the rubrics "Dr. Martin Luther King, Jr." and "Southern Christian Leadership Conference."* Although the released documents were relatively few in number and were heavily deleted, they reveal much about the CIA's interest in King. One document is a November 28, 1975, internal memorandum which claims: "We have no indication of any Agency surveillance or letter intercept which involved King."[12] Other documents belie this claim.

One Agency memo—subject: "King, Martin Luther," dated November 5, 1967—has a deleted list of "various individuals" whose advice King "has sought and relied upon." This document is extensively deleted, and the protection of "intelligence activities, sources and methods" is one of the main justifications for deletion. In its cover letter accompanying the released documents, the CIA failed to include any explanation of the meaning of the letters (A through G) used to justify various deletions. In response to my request for this crucial data, a CIA information officer first responded that, as a matter of policy, the Agency did not provide such information to FOIA requestors. After I questioned the legality of such a policy, the second response was that this data was impossible to retrieve, given the way in which the Agency's FOIA data system functioned. Finally, the key to the coded deletions was miraculously discovered and provided.

Another 24-page memo, dated March 7, 1968, (a month before King's assassination), is almost totally deleted: 20 pages are devoid of substance except for an occasional heading. The document summarizes data on King under the headings: "addresses," "foreign travel," "Contacts," "Organizations to Which [deleted] Belonged Or Mentioned as Participant in Activities."

CIA has sought to create the impression that it had only a cursory interest in King and the SCLC, and that this interest was largely satisfied

---

*I wish to acknowledge the assistance of Attorney Dan Bernstein of Boston who helped me frame and pursue my request.

by whatever data Hoover shared with the agency.[13] But the released documents suggested an independent, operative interest on the part of CIA. One memo concludes by stating: "This summary is based on FBI reports and Agency reports all of which are filed in [deleted]."

Documents released to the author indicate that in at least two instances, CIA passed data to the FBI rather than vice versa. An October 5, 1967, report on King's Chicago activities states: "The Bureau may pass the above report to appropriate field offices for background use only." Of course, the amount of intelligence passed on to the Bureau was probably as much a function of the CIA's attempt to present a low domestic-spying profile to the turf-conscious Hoover as it was a function of the quantity of intelligence that the Agency had collected on King.

Another CIA file obtained by the author in 1982, the Domestic Police Training File, reveals that during the 1960s and 1970s, the Agency had a clandestine relationship with many local police departments. In return for largesse, training, and gratis equipment, police would sometimes conduct surveillance and break-ins on behalf of the CIA. In four of the cities named on King's notes and receipts—New York, Chicago, Miami, and Washington, D.C.—CIA had a working relationship with police.[14]

One of the most intriguing documents is a July 10, 1966, dispatch. It is extensively deleted, including the identities of the sources and recipients. It contains a potpourri of notes and receipts apparently obtained from King himself. It is not clear whether the data was passed on by the FBI, was contributed by the intelligence squads of certain metropolitan police departments, was obtained directly by CIA, or all three.

The 12-page dispatch contains photocopies of several scrawled notes, apparently made by King or members of his staff. One is written on hotel stationery. There are also: photocopies of several Diners Club card receipts in King's name, lists of phone calls placed from his Miami hotel room during a two-day period, sales receipts for ties and handkerchiefs, and an assortment of business cards. There is also a page from an appointment calendar, and it contains a message for King.

This material was a rich find. By the author's count, there were 24 names, most often accompanied by address and/or phone number, of persons who were in contact with King. These individuals included a Chicago minister, a South Korean newspaper editor, an Atlanta attorney, an advisor to the Governor of New York, and a Miami private detective.

The dates on the slips and notes range between December 23, 1965, and May 20, 1966. It cannot be determined from the released document what means were used to gather this data. One possibility would be clandestine "garbology" (sifting through the trash after King had checked out of a hotel room); another would be a break-and-enter, seizing the material before it was discarded. The receipts were definitely obtained from King himself rather than from vendors: The Diners Club receipts are customer copies. Unless King had a habit of consigning his collected business cards, phone numbers, and customer receipts to the trash, a break-and-enter seems a likely possibility.

Professor David J. Garrow's analysis of this data differs from mine. Garrow cites FBI rather than CIA documents and assumes that the data was gathered by Dade County Police and passed to the FBI, neglecting the possibility of direct or indirect CIA involvement in gathering and/ or transmitting the information.[15] The fact that the data went to the Bureau does not preclude its simultaneous or prior possession by CIA. Garrow states that the Agency "made no effort to explain how it acquired" this data and further states that Dade County Police "somehow managed to acquire" it, but he does not include the possibility of CIA involvement.[16]

Some of the receipts are photographed on backing paper which seems to come from a federal intelligence agency. The paper is apparently a form for analyzing documents. It is marked "Secret (when filled in)." Although the exact origin of the backing paper cannot be deciphered, its presence suggests that at least some of the receipts were in the physical possession of a federal intelligence agency.

CIA characterizations of its King file imply that the material is routine, foreign-oriented, and centers on world reaction to King's death. The released documents refute these claims.

The U.S. intelligence community's original concern about King was the potential danger created by his alleged Communist ties. Subsequently, his antiwar stance, coupled with his plan for massive domestic demonstrations against poverty, must have been viewed as both the final proof of Peking-line influence and the ultimate domestic threat to national security. America's most formidable political activist was being used by the Communists (through blackmail, ideological leverage or both) to subvert the United States' Vietnam War effort by creating turmoil.

King's emerging opposition to the war escalated very sharply one year to the day before his assassination. On April 4, 1967, he unleashed a blistering condemnation, delivered at the Riverside Church in New York City. King charged that the United States was "the greatest purveyor of violence in the world today." He referred to U.S.-fortified hamlets as "concentration camps."[17] *Life* magazine characterized the speech as sounding like "a script for Radio Hanoi."[18]

In mid to late April of 1967, newspapers speculated on the possibility that King might launch a third-party presidential candidacy with himself and Dr. Benjamin Spock campaigning on an antiwar platform. The FBI kept the Johnson White House informed about this prospect, through information gathered from a wiretap on the phone of King aide Stanley Levison, who was considered by the Bureau to constitute a Communist influence on King.[19] The possibility of a King/Spock ticket was surely of concern to other intelligence agencies besides the FBI. In mid May of 1967, the FBI began to gear up "countermeasures" to deal with a possible King candidacy. FBI headquarters asked several field offices to submit plans for clandestine harassment.

An April 19 report from Hoover's office to President Johnson's personal secretary, Mildred Stegall, described King as "an instrument in the hands of subversive forces seeking to undermine our nation."[20] This view was undoubtedly shared by many other intelligence officers.

A CIA memo dated October 5, 1967, reports on the "domestic racial situation" and on the New Politics Convention.[21] It states that at this convention, the Communists were very eager to obtain support for the proposed King/Spock antiwar ticket but failed to do so. (This three-page memo is extensively deleted and contains no fewer than 14 deletions justified on the grounds of protecting "intelligence activities, sources, or methods.")

King ultimately decided against pursuing a presidential candidacy, but his opposition to the war continued unabated until it was silenced by a bullet in Memphis. Only four days before his death he delivered an impassioned speech at National Cathedral in Washington, expressing his views on the economic and moral bankruptcy of America's war policies:[22]

Our involvement in the war in Vietnam has torn up progress in Geneva ... strengthened the military industrial complex. It has strengthened the forces of reactionaries in our nation. It has put us against the self-determination of the vast majority of people. Put us in a position of protection of a corrupt regime that is stacked against this world. It played havoc with our domestic destiny. This day we are spending $500,000 to kill every Vietcong soldier and every time we kill one, we spend about $500,000. While we spend only $53 a year for every person trying to rise in poverty-stricken or so-called poverty programs which is not even a good skirmish against poverty. Not only that, it has put us in a position of appearing to the world that here we are ten thousand miles away from home, fighting for the so-called freedom of the Vietnamese people, when we do not even put our own house in order. We force young black men, young white men, to fight and kill in brutal soldiering, yet when they come back home, they can't hardly live on the block together.

Moreover, King's plans for the spring of 1968 were guaranteed to have a chilling effect upon even the icy mentalities of the intelligence community's cold warriors. FBI memos describe King's plans for massive demonstrations. His spring offensive may well have been perceived by elements of U.S. intelligence as nothing less than a major, Communist-directed attempt to destabilize the United States.

An FBI memo of January 2, 1968, offers a dire warning:

Martin Luther King, Jr., President of the Southern Christian Leadership Conference (SCLC) has publicly stated that he will create massive civil disobedience in the Nation's Capitol and in 10 to 15 major cities throughout the United States in the Spring of 1968 if certain commitments are not forthcoming from Congress in the civil rights field. An aide of King has stated "Jail will be the safest place in Washington, D.C. this Spring."[23]

Another Bureau memo asserts:

King has warned that these massive demonstrations may result in riots. Because of this we should be in a position to obtain intelligence so that appropriate countermeasures can be taken to protect the internal security of the United States.[24]

A top secret Bureau memo dated two days before King's assassination states:

Despite this violence in Memphis Levison [King aide Stanley Levison, alleged by the Bureau to be a communist influence] and King are continuing their plans for massive civil disobedience to start in the later part of April 1968, in Washington, D.C.[25]

The specter of massive civil disobedience and riots spurred by Peking-line Communists in order to undermine America's war policies could easily have prompted some group of clandestine cold warriors to employ the most extreme of "countermeasures."

Ironically, events after King's death provided striking confirmation of the intelligence community's worst fears regarding his potential for creating political chaos, for destabilizing America's cities. Following the assassination, there were several days of turmoil—arson, rioting, looting, shooting by snipers and police. Riots occurred in over 100 cities throughout the United States; 37 people were killed. For the first time in our history, the White House situation room (the windowless cavern under the West Wing where the president and his closest advisors had gathered to deal with crises in Vietnam, the Middle East, and eastern Europe) was activated to monitor a *domestic* crisis.[26]

When the riots were quelled and the smoke had cleared, not only was the immediate threat gone, but so was its source. King's fearsome ability to put people into the streets would never again be a problem for "internal security" or "national security" (or for the political security of Vietnam War policies).

12   Threads from the Web of Conspiracy

> Like the Mafia, the Agency [CIA] forms a true brotherhood—one for all and all for one—except that, in the clutch, alas, everyone is expendable. But up to that final point, the members of the Company will do anything for each other—lie, cheat, steal, kidnap, suborn perjury, bribe, corrupt, subvert, kill, and kill again.
>
> Harrison Salisbury[1]

Given the present state of the evidence, any attempt to outline certain dimensions of the plot must necessarily be speculative. But speculation has its place in exploring the meaning of known data and pointing the way for further investigation. At least the following analysis is labeled as speculation. In 1968 the FBI labeled myth as truth (that Ray was a lone assassin). In 1978 HSCA offered up "circumstantial evidence" of probable conspiracy, when, in reality, the scenario was little more than speculation.

The similarity between James Earl Ray and his four Toronto aliases, especially Galt, were surely the result of conspiratorial planning rather than coincidence. This was beyond the capacities of a small-time loser like Ray. As for HSCA's alleged St. Louis conspiracy, putting up $50,000 to recruit a hit man is a fairly primitive way to go about the business of assassinating a major political figure. The precision manifested in the selection of Galt as a cover bespeaks of a sophistication and an access to data that seems beyond the grasp of the alleged St. Louis plotters.

On April 23, 1967 (approximately one year before the assassination), Ray escaped from prison. Whether his escape was engineered as part of his recruitment as an assassin or a patsy is problematic. Whether Ray knew it or not, he was—or was soon to be—enmeshed in a web that would ultimately be spun into an assassination conspiracy. He began to use the Galt alias only three months after he broke out. HSCA denied that Ray's escape was connected to an assassination plot, but the committee did believe that the adoption of the Galt alias was related to the assassination, although HSCA failed to understand how. James Earl Ray, whose stunted criminal imagination and shaky power of memory led him to use as aliases the names of associates or family names, suddenly had an alias that departed from this pattern and that was strikingly compatible.

Four months before the assassination, Ray had plastic surgery in Los Angeles. The operation, performed by Dr. Russell C. Hadley, eliminated Ray's very distinctive pointy nose. HSCA viewed this as related to the crime, as part of a "concerted effort to avoid identification as the assassin."[2] What the committee missed is that—again, whether Ray knew it or not—the surgery had the effect of rendering his appearance more compatible with that of the real Galt and with those of the other Toronto aliases. The surgery may well have been related to the plot but at a more sophisticated level than HSCA imagined.

If Ray himself was dreaming up ways to avoid detection as an assassin, there were surely less painful, less expensive alternatives than surgery— alternatives more typical of Ray's fairly conventional, petty-criminal mentality. He could have affected a beard or moustache or dyed his hair or reverted to the brush cut he wore in 1966. Any of these options would have rendered him less compatible with Galt and the other aliases as well as rendering him different from the pre-assassination James Earl Ray. In contrast, the surgery had the effect of making his appearance more compatible with Galt's

The Galt name was more than just another alias: It was his false identity during the nine months preceding the assassination. It was the name for which Ray had the most documentation. It was his cover. Whether Ray was the assassin or the fall guy, the plan would seem to have been to implicate the real Eric S. Galt just long enough to allow Ray to escape to Angola, where he could be comfortably disposed of.

Once the main cover was selected, other aliases were chosen on the basis of general physical compatibility with Ray and with the real Galt. Their geographic proximity to Galt was designed to further implicate him, to create the impression that he was using as aliases the names of men who lived so close to him that he could easily have spotted their physical resemblance and usurped their names.

The three secondary aliases could have been picked via physical surveillance of the general area around Galt's home. Or they could have come from disparate file sources rather than from a common source:

Willard, through the passport office; Sneyd through Toronto police files; Bridgeman, through files on municipal employees (he worked for the Toronto Board of Education). Or they could have been selected from a more generic data bank: driver's license applications, for example.

Peter Dale Scott, a former Canadian diplomat with expertise concerning the intelligence agencies, suggested to the author that selecting three or four names having basically similar physical characteristics can be done fairly easily by anyone with access to government files. Scott points out that the aliases could have been obtained by the CIA from the RCMP as a favor or in trade. He notes that friendly Western intelligence agencies sometimes swap data or dossiers to be used as covers in each other's operations, and may do so without knowing the nature of those operations.[3]

Simple usurpation of a man's name in connection with a crime is not necessarily enough to seriously implicate him. For example, Ramon George Sneyd was not only one of Toronto's finest (and thus had a leg up on establishing the credibility of his character references) but it was clear that his name was not used before or during the commission of the crime, only afterwards (as a false identity for the fleeing assassin). Eric S. Galt was in a different situation. "Galt" was Ray's primary alias, and it was used before the crime and in direct connection with its perpetration.

In addition to Galt's physical resemblance to Ray, there was skilled marksmanship and visits to Memphis and Birmingham, Alabama (where the rifle found at the crime scene was purchased). Galt was more than simply a cover: He was a man who could be implicated in the crime, at least temporarily while Ray made his escape. The real Galt was fortunate not to have been arrested as the prime suspect.

Consider his situation. For two weeks after the assassination, what the press described as "the greatest manhunt in history" pursued not James Earl Ray but Eric S. Galt.[4] As a Memphis newspaper described the day after the shooting:

Police . . . almost immediately broadcast a description of the sniper: a white male, 30 to 32 years old, five feet ten inches tall, 165 pounds, dark to sandy hair, medium build, ruddy complexion as if he worked outside, wearing a black suit and white shirt.[5]

Except for the fact that Galt was in his early fifties (but was often taken to be ten years younger), the description fit Galt as well as it did Ray. Galt's outdoorsmanship (scuba diving and shooting) surpassed Ray's, and his complexion was ruddier. It made sense to authorities that a man plotting an assassination would use aliases for activities directly connected to the crime. They deduced that the suspect's real name was Galt, using the alias Lowmeyer to buy the rifle and Willard to rent a room near King.[6] Authorities soon discovered a clear trail of activities and credentials fleshing out "Eric S. Galt." An abandoned white Mustang thought to be the get-away vehicle had been purchased under that name.

Ray fled to the city where the real Galt lived. There, Ray used as aliases the names of two men (Bridgeman and Sneyd) who lived only a short distance from Galt, as did John Willard. Ray took a room under the name of Paul Bridgeman in the 100 block of Ossington Street—only 220 yards away from the room where Eric Galt's scuba club held its meetings,[7] and across the street from the auto body shop frequented by Willard.

There was only one Eric S. Galt in all of Canada in 1968.[8] The trail of evidence led to him. Authorities might easily have hypothesized that Galt shot King and then fled back to Toronto, using as aliases the names of solid citizens who lived near him. Law officers have been known to fix upon someone as the prime suspect with considerably less to go on than they had in Galt's case, especially when there is enormous pressure to solve the case. What apparently saved the real Galt from being targeted as the prime suspect was the slothfulness of law enforcement. From the night of the April fourth assassination until sometime on or near April 18, authorities found neither Ray nor the real Galt.

It was not until April 19 that the FBI finally identified the fingerprints found on the items dropped at the crime scene. Then the Bureau knew for the first time that the real suspect was convicted robber James Earl Ray.

On April 17, only 48 hours before Ray was identified, the Justice Department issued a press release designed to focus increased attention on the hunt for "Galt." The department filed a complaint with the U.S. Commissioner in Birmingham, Alabama, charging "Eric S. Galt" with conspiring to interfere with King's constitutional rights. This was done to secure an arrest warrant and to generate additional publicity for the flagging manhunt.[9]

CIA documents obtained by the author under the Freedom of Information Act show that on April 18, the day before Ray was finally identified, the Agency cabled its field offices enlisting them in the search for: "the suspected assassin of Martin Luther King, Jr. name Eric Starvo Galt, alias Harvey Lowmeyer, alias John Willard . . . considered armed and extremely dangerous." Headquarters told the field offices: "Galt's current whereabouts unknown. While have no reasons believe Galt headed for your area, desire cover all possibilities. Request addressees make every effort determine if Galt is or has been in your area."[10]

On April 18, only hours before the Bureau would finally identify Ray as the real suspect, there was an important break in the case. The Kansas City field office sent an "urgent" cable to FBI Director Hoover and to the Memphis field office, at 4:04 P.M.:

Review of March, nineteen sixty-eight Toronto, Ontario, Canada telephone directory reveals a listing for one Eric Galt, four nine Leahann Drive, Telephone No. Seven five nine six nine three two. Kansas City is unaware of any Bureau instructions to check Canadian directories, therefore this is being furnished for Bureaus information.[11]

At the time this cable was received, the real Galt had not been questioned by any authorities, either American or Canadian.[12] Therefore, his alibi had not in any way been established. Apparently Galt was saved from being targeted and grilled as the suspect only by the fact that within hours of this cable, the FBI's ponderous fingerprint search finally identified Ray. But there is indication that upon receiving the above cable, the Bureau began to investigate Galt, before Ray was identified.

A handwritten notation appears on the headquarters' copy of cable. It is faint and scrawled in the style of a doctor writing a prescription. The author could not decipher the substance, other than that it contained the name "Eric Galt." Eric Galt was more successful. When I mailed him a copy, he instantly recognized two family names other than his own.[13]

As best it can be deciphered, the notation reads: "[deleted] [deleted] advises he believes [unintelligible] is Shaddoff [unintelligible] Garry Eric Galt and will [unintelligible] out. [unintelligible] 610 P [for P.M.] 4/18/68"

Garry Eric Galt is Galt's son. Shaddoff was the maiden name of Garry Eric's wife, from whom he had separated some years previously. Like his father, Garry Eric had worked at Union Carbide in Toronto, but only for a brief period in the mid 1960s and not in any department relating to the proximity fuse.

The exact significance of the notation is not clear. Neither is the origin of the information, since the source is deleted. Perhaps some source or data system erroneously brought forth information on Galt's son instead of Galt. The senior Galt was, in fact, listed in the 1968 Toronto telephone directory as Eric Galt rather than Eric S. Galt, as the FBI's Kansas City office correctly reported. A Bureau query for information on Eric Galt (no middle initial) could have increased the chances of erroneously getting data on his son. Or, perhaps the notation reflects the first phases of a background check on Eric S. Galt. What is clear is that by 6:10 P.M. on April 18, Eric Galt was more to the FBI than simply a Canadian telephone listing. Within hours, however, the Bureau was to discover

a piece of information that would render superfluous any data on Galt—
that the suspect was James Earl Ray.

It was shortly after all this had transpired that the real Eric Galt first
became aware of his connection to the case. His best recollection is that
this was two to three weeks after the crime. One of his friends read the
fugitive description for "Eric Starvo Galt" in a Toronto newspaper.
"Boy" remarked Galt's friend, "that's pretty damn close, isn't it?"[14] By
the time Galt was aware of the linkage, Ray's prints had been identified.
Ray was about 15 miles from Galt's house, renting a room in downtown
Toronto.

"Pretty damn close" is right. Although James Earl Ray had been identified as the suspect, authorities grilled Galt about his whereabouts during the crime. Fortunately for him, he had what would appear to be a
perfect alibi: He was working at Carbide the day of the assassination
and for several days before and after. Even with all this, Canadian
authorities were, for a time, dubious about the claims of Carbide workers
who vouched for Galt. It was suggested that his coworkers might be
lying to cover for him.[15]

Suspicions about Galt would have escalated dramatically had he lacked
an ironclad alibi—if he had been absent from work or, worse, if he had
been motoring through the southern United States to go scuba diving
or rock hunting. He regularly went south in the warm weather (spring
or summer).[16] Even in Toronto things could have been worse for Galt.
He frequently carried rifles and pistols back and forth between his home
and the shooting range at the gun club, at the same time that authorities
were hunting the "armed and dangerous" "Eric Starvo Galt" or "Eric
S. Galt."

Imagine what Galt might have faced if the FBI had discovered him
earlier on, or if the Bureau's glacial fingerprint-identification process had
taken longer to discover Ray. Galt would surely have been a prime
suspect, at least for a while. An interrogation might have led the Mounties to think they really had their man.

Galt's father was a prominent private detective in South Africa who
emigrated to Canada before Galt was born.[17] Having family roots in one
of the world's most racist societies would not be advantageous to anyone
being questioned about the murder of a black political leader. To authorities, this family background might easily have been perceived as
constituting motive. As with the other details of Galt's life, his family
ties to South Africa were documented in his Carbide security file.

Under the Freedom of Information Act, the author obtained a letter,
ostensibly written by Ray, that seems very provocative in terms of his
linkage to the assassination plot. On the FBI's 1968 list of fingerprint
evidence appears item Q334: "letter from Galt to South African Counsel."

It is dated December 12, 1967, and signed "Eric S. Galt." (Two news-papers mistakenly reported in 1968 that the letter was signed "Eric Starvo Galt" instead of Eric S. Galt.) It bears the return address of Ray's Los Angeles apartment, and it states:

My reason for writing is that I am considering immigrating to Rhodesia, however there are a couple legal questions involved. One: The U.S. government will not issue a passport for travel to Rhodesia. Two: would there be any way to enter Rhodesia legally (from the Rhodesian government point of view). I would ap-preciate any information you could give me on the above subject or any other information on Rhodesia.

The American South African Counsel, which promoted the apartheid policies of the Ian Smith regime, never responded to "Galt." Nor was there any follow-up letter from "Galt" either to the counsel or to the Rhodesian government.

There are several important points regarding this letter, the first of which is that it is dated four months prior to King's assassination. Ac-cording to all of the available evidence, James Earl Ray was not possessed by a virulent racism; nor did he manifest any horror at interacting with blacks in bars, etc. He had never expressed any desire to leave the country permanently. Ray was a petty criminal born in the United States, and had never traveled farther than Mexico or Canada. After the assas-sination, however, his ultimate destination was Angola. It is difficult to believe that Ray's sudden interest in joining the world's most racist society was unrelated to the impending assassination of America's preeminent black leader.

Moreover, it was during this same period, while Ray was in Los Angeles, that he had plastic surgery to dull his pointed nose. Also while Ray was in Los Angeles, someone in Birmingham, Alabama, obtained a duplicate driver's license in the name of Eric S. Galt.

It seems likely that Ray's letter about Rhodesia reflects premeditation. But whose? Was it Ray's, or did someone encourage him to write the letter? If Ray wrote it without any outside urging, it would appear to indicate that he knew that he would soon have to flee the country under conditions that would make a repressive, racist society an ideal location.

If he wrote the letter at the behest of someone else, he could have done so without knowing about the assassination. Although Ray could not have known it, the letter could have added to official suspicions of the real Galt, if it had surfaced before Ray was identified. Galt was a Canadian rather than an American citizen, but he had traveled fre-quently and extensively throughout the United States. The South African Counsel discovered the letter in its files and turned it over to the FBI in May, before Ray was captured but after his fingerprints had been iden-tified.

Could the letter have been written by someone besides Ray? We know that someone other than Ray was generating "Galt" paper (the Alabama driver's license). In 1968 the FBI concluded that all of the "Galt" letters in its possession were signed by Ray. HSCA decided not to reexamine the signatures because, said the committee, "since Ray admitted using the Galt, Raynes, and Sneyd aliases there was little controversy about the origin of the writings."[18] Given the incident of the driver's license, however, the assumption that Ray's use of the Galt alias meant that he produced all of the "Galt" artifacts seems unwarranted. Expert analysis of the handwriting should have been conducted, especially given the inconclusiveness of the fingerprint evidence. HSCA's fingerprint panel found that the letter had four latent prints of sufficient quality to test. Three belonged to the same "unidentified" person.[19] None belonged to Ray, even though the letter was typed and presumably subject to considerable manual manipulation.

I wrote to Ray and asked him about the letter. He responded: "I don't actually recall writing the letter you enclosed but I probably did."[20] I also asked why he wrote it. Ray stated that he had seen an ad in a magazine soliciting immigrants to Rhodesia, but he ignored the real question of what motivated him to respond.

Ray's final destination was Angola. He flew to London, then to Lisbon, where he stayed from May 12 through 17. There, he lived in a series of cheap hotels and kept to himself.[21] When he left Portugal and returned to London, he was finally arrested on June 8, as he was about to board a plane for Brussels. Lisbon, where Ray had been, and Brussels, where he was headed, were then the centers of mercenary activity in Europe if not the world. Portugal was fighting its colonial war in Angola by using mercenary troops. Belgium had lost its precious colony in the Congo, but Brussels remained Europe's main recruitment center for mercenaries.[22]

In 1968 authorities and the press speculated that Ray thought he would be warmly received by white mercenaries fighting in black Africa, because he was the accused assassin of a famous black leader. Although mercenary sources in Brussels told reporters that this was not so—because Ray would constitute too much of a stigma and his visibility would be unwelcome[23]—he could not be expected to know this.

Having failed to make appropriate mercenary contacts in Lisbon, Ray returned to London and sought help. He phoned Ian Colvin, an editorial writer for the *London Daily Telegraph* who had recently written a book mentioning Major Alistair Wicks, a mercenary leader in the Congo.[24]

Colvin recalled that Ray spoke rapidly and in a high-pitched, singsong fashion. "I'm a Canadian in London for a while," said Ray. "I'm trying to reach my brother who is with these people in Angola." Ray asked for Major Wicks's telephone number, which Colvin refused to divulge.

Colvin did offer to pass along Ray's request for information. Ray identified himself as Ramon Sneyd and gave the name of the hotel where he was staying.

Two days later Ray phoned again.[25] Colvin asked if Ray had heard from Major Wicks. Ray said that he had not, but he also said that he had changed hotels without leaving a forwarding address or phone number. According to Colvin, Ray sounded "highly distraught." That was the last Colvin heard from the fugitive.

In Ontario, Canada, the RCMP had been doggedly sifting through hundreds of thousands of passports. They finally spotted Ray's picture on a false passport issued under the name Ramon George Sneyd. RCMP quickly identified the real Sneyd, then put the word out to watch for anyone traveling under that name.

In London Ray booked a flight to Brussels. By routine, a duplicate copy of the plane's passenger list went to Heathrow Airport inspectors. An officer checking the list spotted the name "Sneyd."[26] Police were alerted and a stakeout was set up. At 11:30 A.M. on June 8, Ray arrived at the airport to catch his flight to the mercenary mecca of Europe. He was quickly arrested. He offered no resistance, except to quietly insist that he was Sneyd.[27]

The unseen hand that guided James Earl Ray along his eleven-month odyssey to historical infamy had failed him. From the time he escaped prison a year before the assassination, the unseen hand had been there: It had given him his aliases, directed him, assisted him.

One instance in which Ray's handlers most likely provided guidance was in Toronto, sometime between April 19 and 21. It was on April 19 that the FBI first identified Ray's fingerprints. On April 20 Ray had a phone call. He was not in his room on Ossington Street when the call came, and no message was left. Quick word of the FBI's discovery and/ or counsel concerning how to deal with it may have reached Ray by some other means of contact, for he swiftly erected another barrier between himself and the law.

On April 18 he had rented a room on Dundas Street, and on April 21 Ray moved to that address. He changed aliases, from Bridgeman to Sneyd. Cameron Smith, who in 1968 was a reporter for the *Toronto Globe and Mail*, described to the author his gut feeling about Ray's stay in Toronto:

He was a hop, skip and a jump ahead of everyone. I consider it unlikely that a person who was in Toronto for his first time could move with the speed and agility that Ray did without help.

The trial was there. Ray's identity and appearance were known. It was one thing for reporters not to be able to catch up with him. But the Metropolitan police force is large and highly skilled as is the RCMP, and considering the intensity with which the search was on, I find it inconceivable that a person totally unfamiliar with the city, whose face was being published in the newspapers, could avoid apprehension all by his lonesome.[28]

But in London there were no more smart moves, only dumb ones. After a miraculous flight from Memphis, a cunningly successful month-long hole up in Toronto, and an escape from Toronto to London, Ray fell just short of getting to Brussels and fleeing to Angola. The nearly flawless, highly professional fugitive performances turned in by Ray in Memphis and Toronto degenerated into amateur bungling as soon as he crossed the Atlantic.

At the Lisbon Airport he proffered a Canadian passport in the name of Ramon George Sney*a* (instead of Sney*d*). Ray had filled out an identification form in the name of Sneyd. This obvious discrepancy did not escape the attention of Portuguese authorities, who queried Ray about it. He told them that his real name was Sneyd; his passport was wrong.[29] Authorities bought the story.

Upon arriving in London, Ray went to the Canadian Embassy where he requested a new, corrected passport. He was given one. This occurred while the RCMP back in Ottawa were feverishly searching to find Ray's picture on a phony passport. His action red-flagged his passport and might have gotten him caught instantly. Even though it didn't, it was not a smart move.

Ray's behavior in London and Portugal contrasted rather strikingly with his smooth, competent fugitive activities in Toronto. In Toronto, right after the FBI had discovered his identity, he quickly changed his name and address. In Toronto he purchased a round-trip plane ticket to London, to appear more like a tourist than a fugitive. In London, however, he practically turned himself in to Canadian authorities while seeking to repair a glitch in his passport that had already been successfully explained away to Portuguese authorities.

In Toronto Ray was quiet and withdrawn to the point of being mole-like. In Lisbon he got into an argument with the proprietor of the rooming house where he was staying. He allegedly tried to bring a woman into his room. When the landlord refused to allow it, Ray got into a heated argument.[30] Such conspicuous behavior is counterproductive for any fugitive, to say the least.

Further evidence that Ray had lost his lifeline and was desperate is provided by his possible participation in a London bank robbery, four days before his capture. The thief stole 95 pounds by passing a note to the teller: "Place all 5–10 pound notes in this bag." The handwriting on the note cannot be identified because it was thick, block printing. Both the FBI (in 1968) and HSCA's experts identified a thumb print on the note as belonging to Ray.[31] He denies the crime.

Lone-assassin mythologists would probably tell us that in Europe Ray's desire for the ego gratification as a famous assassin finally came to the fore (that is, he wanted to get caught). Within the mosaic of conspiratorial intrigue that surrounded Ray, there is a much better explanation for the contrast in his behavior: He had somehow lost contact with his handlers and was on his own for the first time during his fugitive odyssey.

Ian Colvin, whom Ray contacted in London, described him as sounding "highly distraught." After Ray's arrest, authorities found a syringe in his London hotel room and speculated that he may have been taking drugs.[32] Whether Ray lost his cool because he lost contact with his handlers or lost contact because he lost his cool, the unseen hand was gone. In Toronto Ray was visited by the fat man and the slight man and drank with another man on several occasions. In Portugal Ray's only reported contact was the woman whom he tried to bring into his room. He hung out in a sleazy Lisbon bar where he drank beer and chatted with the girls who worked there, but he was always seen alone.[33] (One witness at a London hotel did report that when Ray checked in he was accompanied by another man who seemed to be a "friend," but there were no corroborating witnesses.)

What would have happened if Ray had succeeded in getting to Angola? Whatever he thought he might find there—a safe hiding place, a hero's welcome, a payoff, all of the above—there is the likelihood that he would have been murdered.

If the alleged assassin were murdered in Toronto or London, the aura of conspiracy already surrounding the case would become almost palpable to many reporters and law officers, as well as to an increasingly broad segment of the public. This would be true even if Ray could be eliminated without a hitch. But if authorities had traced Ray to mercenary legions in Africa, where he was found murdered or, more likely, was never found at all, the conspiratorial fallout would be much less intense. That a violence-prone lone assassin, driven by racism and ego gratification, sought out the company of other violent men in one of the world's most politically tumultuous areas, and that he perished doing so, would be viewed by many as not only believable but fitting.

The question arises as to how a sophisticated assassination conspiracy clever enough to match Ray and Galt, kill King, and guide Ray through Toronto could be inept enough to allow him to be captured alive in London. It is only in James Bond novels that operations always go smoothly. In the real world, even the most carefully planned assassination plots crafted by experts have failed or have been plagued with operational problems.

Consider, for example, the CIA's string of unsuccessful attempts to assassinate Fidel Castro in the early 1960s.[34] One plot involved spiking Castro's favorite cigars with a deadly botulism toxin; another involved a ballpoint pen that would explode a poison dart into el presidente when he went to sign his name. Despite the best efforts of the CIA's Technical Services Division, the Executive Action Unit (formed to eliminate troublesome foreign leaders) and the Agency's friends in organized crime, none of these Bondian plots succeeded.

Nor are failures confined to plots employing sophisticated methods. In late 1960 the CIA dispatched its premier hit man, code name QJ/WINN, to the Congo to eliminate Patrice Lamumba. The plan was for QJ/WINN to "pierce both Congolese and U.N. guards" who protected Lamumba, enter Lamumba's residence, and spirit him away. QJ/WINN would penetrate the security forces by "making the acquaintance of a U.N. guard."[35] The plan called for Lamumba to be turned over to his political rivals for final disposition. The murder would appear indigenous. Just as the plan was about to be operationalized, Lamumba suddenly moved to Stanleyville where he would be much more difficult to kidnap, and another plan had to be devised.

The operatives who plan and execute assassinations for intelligence agencies do not always possess the cunning and the icy demeanor of Frederick Forsyth's fictional hit man, the Jackal. QJ/WINN, while serving as the CIA's first-string hit man, got involved in narcotics smuggling and faced charges in an undisclosed country.[36] One CIA cable poses the possibility of "quashing" the charges or otherwise "salvaging" QJ/WINN. One of QJ/WINN's colleagues in the CIA's Executive Action Program was code named WI/Rogue. Rogue was very difficult to control, as a CIA cable describes. "Concerned by WI/Rogue freewheeling and lack security. Station has enough headaches without worrying about agent who not able handle finances and who not willing follow instructions."[37]

Then there was William K. Harvey, the 250-pound, gravel-voiced CIA officer who formed the Agency's Executive Action Unit in the early 1960s. One might expect that the man who headed such an operation would be cool, detached, and businesslike; not so. Harvey allegedly behaved like a character from a John Wayne western. A true clandestine cowboy, the gun-toting Harvey was legendary for his four-martini lunches and his bluster, and what some regarded as his loose-cannon activities.[38]

The fact that Ray did not get to Angola, or that his competence as a fugitive seemed to evaporate on the other side of the Atlantic, or that he lived to stand trial, cannot be used to dismiss the involvement of American intelligence or its networks or offshoots. In reality, intelligence-based assassination plots are not always as flawless as their fictional counterparts.

Also, it must be remembered that the conspiracy to assassinate Martin Luther King, Jr., was successful, despite its flaws. King *was* terminated. The conspirators behind Ray have never been caught.

13 An Interview with James Earl Ray

I'm not lookin' for no favorable interview. You write what ya want.
. . . You *will*.

James Earl Ray to the author, Dec. 1, 1984

Tennessee State Penitentiary is a large, white Gothic structure nestled near the Cumberland River. It rose out of the morning fog like a medieval castle, except that it was encircled by barbed wire instead of a moat. There was not a single sign to guide the visitor to its location (until the visitor was already there), nor did the facility appear on any maps issued by the state or city. It was as if the city that calls itself "the country music capitol of America" would rather forget both "Tenn. Pen." and its most infamous occupant.

I had been warned by sources in Nashville that having obtained written permission to visit might not be synonymous with getting in to visit. To my chagrin, the prison bureaucracy seemed to have had a memory lapse about my visit.

Fortunately, Hollywood benignly intervened. Because a film crew was shooting a scene with actress Sissy Spacek for the movie *Marie*, Warden Michael Dutton was already at the checkpoint where I was stalled; and he was effusively accommodating, since good public relations was already the order of the day.

Security was intense. After leaving behind all personal effects (save one ID and some writing materials), I was searched with a handheld metal detector and subjected to a meticulous body frisk (at times I had to look down at my clothes to make sure it wasn't a strip search). There were nine checkpoints, nine locked gates between Ray and freedom. He was being kept in what prison authorities termed, not without irony, "segregation," isolated from the rest of the prison population and locked in his quarters 24 hours a day.

To get to Ray, the visitor was escorted across the prison yard by a guard (while inmates stared curiously), to a low brick building resembling a bunker. The bunker was ringed by its own set of bars; its door unlocked only from the inside. I entered and was greeted by five uniformed guards, one of whom escorted me to a room containing a table and four chairs. After several minutes, the door opened and Ray was ushered in. The door then closed and was locked from the outside.

Ray appeared quite different from the last photos I had seen (circa 1977). His hair was grayer, but still thick. He seemed thinner and shorter than I expected, almost slight in build. He was strikingly pale (a by-product of segregation, no doubt). His eyes were clear and blue. The scar over his left eye was still visible, as was Eric Galt's.

We shook hands. He was clad in an orange jumpsuit—not his choice of attire but the prison's. Should Ray somehow break out of segregation, he could easily be spotted.

It is important that the reader understand Ray's demeanor, as a context for better understanding his answers. He was initially a bit nervous but came well prepared, bringing a folder full of FBI documents, newspaper clippings, and court motions which he had filed on his own behalf. He was businesslike, low key. He spoke in even tones, smiling occasionally. Unlike the very few other inmates I have interviewed, he used no expletives, no prison jargon. During the course of our two and a half hour interview, he never ranted or became irate, even when discussing his "segregated" status or his alleged mistreatment by the HSCA.

I could not help but wonder if this was the new Ray. A lot had happened to him since he was convicted in 1968. He had tried to escape from prison three times and was successful once, remaining at large for two and a half days in 1977. He had married Anna Sandhu, an artist who was assigned by a newspaper to draw sketches at Ray's 1977 trial for escaping prison. He had studied law extensively in the prison library and had launched a flurry of Freedom of Information Act suits and legal motions. In 1981 he had been stabbed 22 times by four inmates while he sat reading in the prison library.

Had Ray evolved into a different person? His letter agreeing to the interview manifested a clarity of syntax that seemed very unlike his past style of written and oral expression. His HSCA interviews frequently revealed him as a syntactical ignoramus who seemed unable to string four words together in logical fashion. His responses sometimes read like botched translations from German; his ability to focus on a question and provide a relevant answer often seemed nonexistent. The Ray I confronted in Nashville seemed much more poised and articulate.

The answer to whether there was a new Ray soon became apparent: there were two James Earl Rays, depending upon the topic under discussion. I was to see a good deal of both of them.

First there was Ray the jail-house lawyer, the practiced interviewee. He was cordial, relaxed, fairly articulate, and clearly focused. This Ray would maintain direct eye contact with the interviewer. He had excellent recall: the names of FBI agents, Memphis police, newspaper reporters, the contents of HSCA volumes, the substance of his previous interviews and testimonies. This Ray appeared when the turf was safe, when we talked of his status in prison, his quest for a new trial, his alleged persecution by HSCA.

When the interviewer steered the conversation to more sensitive areas—the Galt alias, the fat man, the conspirators—the second Ray emerged. This Ray was more like the one manifested in HSCA transcripts. His syntax seemed to degenerate, and his power of memory all but disappeared. His responses were rambling and sometimes only marginally related to the question. He shifted in his chair and appeared nervous; at times, anxious. His lower lip twitched occasionally. He lost eye contact.

Ray attempted to prolong our stay on safe turf. He discoursed at length about his various legal motions; he returned to safe topics whenever there was a pause in the conversation. Finally, however, all of the questions that I had come to ask were asked, although not answered.

ON THE "FAT MAN"

To the author's knowledge, Ray has never been asked about the fat man incident. Certainly HSCA did not ask him. It is a sensitive topic, once one dismisses the Good Samaritan explanation. If, in fact, Ray received an envelope full of money before departing Toronto, this is hardly exculpatory of Ray. Not without considerable explanation on his part, anyway. Also, as we shall see later, Ray refused to talk substantively about anything relating to the conspiracy or the conspirators, except "Raoul."

I began this line of questioning by testing Ray's recognition of Bolton's name. It would be highly unlikely that Ray would know the real name of any courier, or that Ray would admit knowing it even if he did, but I thought it important to test Ray's reaction.

"I tracked down this guy William Bolton," I began. "Does that name ring a bell?"

"No," he replied, showing no reaction.

"He was the guy who came forward to police about finding the letter—Dundas Street, Mrs. Loo's."

There was no verbal response. He shook his head negatively. His often excellent recall about the details of the case seemed to be failing him. The second Ray was emerging. I began to wonder if he would deny that the incident ever occurred.

"The *fat man* articles in the newspaper."

He nodded recognition. "Yes," he said. There was tension in his response.

I told him that the reason I was asking about this was because Bolton had given me a phony story, claiming that the letter dealt with Ray's getting to Portugal and that finding the letter led to Ray's arrest. Ray replied that at that point in time, while he was staying at Dundas Street, he did not know he was going to Portugal.

"What was in the letter?" I asked. "Who was it to?"

"It was a letter of mine, had my name on it. I don't recall much about it. . . . It probably had something to do with getting a passport." This was a most interesting response, to which we will return in a moment.

Ray affirmed that, contrary to what authorities said in 1968, the letter did not have to do with his getting a job. Then I asked the key question.

"Weren't you scared to get the letter, to meet the guy?"

The style of Ray's response differed markedly from his previous answers during this line of questioning, which were delivered almost lackadaisically. This response was swift and forceful, as if there was an urgent point to be made.

"Oh, yes. I was [scared]. I didn't [meet Bolton]. I just told the landlady, she was Chinese, to get it for me. The guy might be a cop or something, yes."

Ray seemed to recognize the implications of admitting that he came downstairs, and this recognition accounted for the zeal with which he answered. But his response lacked credibility.

First, there is Mrs. Loo's detailed account, given to police and the press, in which Ray descended the stairs, met briefly with the stranger, and received the envelope. William Bolton admitted that he had met Ray and given him the envelope.

It is significant that while having opposite stories about whether they met, both Ray and Bolton claim emphatically that Ray was scared. Ray made this point with uncharacteristic urgency. Bolton advanced this claim with a flourish of melodrama, miming Ray's frightened actions upon receiving the letter. If Ray was not scared, the best explanation is that he was expecting a delivery.

The two principals also disagree sharply concerning the contents of the putative letter. As described by police, Bolton's 1968 story was allegedly that the letter dealt with Ray's seeking a job. Bolton's 1984 story was that the letter had sinister conspiratorial overtones relating to Ray's escape to Portugal. Ray thinks it had to do "with getting a passport." One possible explanation for these conflicts is that there was no letter.

Ray's assertion that the letter had to do "with getting a passport" is interesting. Indeed, all indications are that the envelope had a great deal to do with Ray's obtaining his ticket and passport, but not because of any letter.

The reader will recall that all the paperwork for Ray's passport—the passport application, the application for a Sneyd birth certificate—went out on April 6. The passport arrived at the Kennedy Travel Agency in Toronto on April 26. Yet it languished there, along with Ray's airplane ticket, until May 2, just after the fat man's visit. Ray's response about what the envelope had to do with could well be correct: without the money it most likely contained, he could not have picked up his ticket to London, and to pick up the passport and not the ticket might have aroused suspicion and would have done him little good in terms of a getaway.

ON THE GALT ALIAS

To broach this subject I delivered a mini lecture that began with certain assumptions about the Galt alias, assumptions designed to put Ray more at ease. I told him that I believed his claim that he did not know there was a real Eric S. Galt until after the assassination. I also asserted that he could not have ripped off the real Galt's name by any of the methods hypothesized by the press in 1968 (such as from a motel register in the U.S.). Since he did not get the Galt alias off of Galt, I suggested that there were two possibilities: the similarities between himself and Galt were entirely coincidental; someone who knew of the real Galt provided the alias.

I further explained that I had new data extending far beyond the matching scars mentioned by the press in 1968. Ray gave me a puzzled look.

"The matching scars," I reiterated. "You both have them."

There was a pause during which he did not respond. Then he uttered a low, almost grudging "Oh, yeah," as if he was agreeing in order to humor me.[1]

I continued on and told him about Galt's visits to Birmingham and Memphis, about his marksmanship. I reminded Ray about the general physical similarities between himself and Galt, and about the "Starvo" name.[2] Finally, disregarding a good deal of collegial advice, I told him about Galt's security file.

As I laid out the data, he was neither nervous nor passive. Instead, there was a brightness in his eyes and a trace of a smile. I hoped that the sheer weight of the data, and the fact that it was surely new to him, might produce a breakthrough, and that finally he might be willing to abjure his usual evasions and falsehoods about the origin of the Galt alias.

I finished by reminding him that he first used the alias at the same time he alleges to have first met Raoul.

"So," I concluded, "you can see how it's too much to believe in coincidence. Isn't it possible that Raoul or someone else like him gave the Galt alias to you, as a way of setting you up . . . like the rifle? It [the Galt alias] is connected to a sophisticated conspiracy but not by you; they did it."

It was match point for the author, and it turned out to be a moment of supreme frustration. Ray's keen interest was displaced by the reappearance of the second Ray—the vague, evasive Ray like the one in the HSCA transcripts relating to the Galt alias.

His first response was: "I got all these aliases. There were so many, I don't remember. There were two guys in Canada. Sneyd and something . . . two names. Ah, Sneyd and some other."

This was a familiar tactic which I recognized from Ray's HSCA interviews. When asked about the Galt alias he would start talking about another alias. It is incredible that the man who could remember the names of reporters who wrote one article on the case could not recall the Bridgeman name—a name under which he rented an apartment and applied for a birth certificate, a name that received extensive press coverage in 1968, and is referred to dozens of times in HSCA volumes.

I refused to be sidetracked to Bridgeman and Sneyd and pressed on about Galt.

"I wanted simple names," Ray said of the Galt alias.

"But you see my problem," I told him. "It's all coincidence about Galt?"

Ray laughed nervously. He did not flatly assert that it was coincidence.

"I don't know where I got 'em," he continued. "Huie [author William Bradford Huie] says I got Galt off a road sign. Someone said a phone book."

Ray was now passing off his own HSCA testimony as something "someone said." Under repeated questioning by HSCA, it was Ray himself who had suggested that he may have gotten the name from a Birmingham or Chicago phone book.[3] Perhaps the very subject of Galt was so unnerving as to muddle Ray's otherwise impressive recall; perhaps the answer about the phone book was so patently absurd he no longer wanted to embrace it.

"And Willard?" I asked. "There was a real John Willard. He lived a mile and a half from Galt; he fit the description pretty well. He worked on Ossington Street [where Ray rented a room]. That's all coincidence?"

I reminded him, in a challenging tone, that he had used both the Galt and Willard aliases before going to Toronto.

"The Willard name," said Ray. "We got . . . a forged document a long time ago."

Ray contended that he and some unnamed criminal associate robbed "a wino" somewhere and got a "Willard ID off of him."

Ray's response to HSCA concerning the Willard name was as follows:[4]

HSCA: "You don't recall where you got the name John Willard?"

Ray: "Someone else might, no. I don't recall."

In a subsequent HSCA interview Ray said of the Willard name:

Uh, now I have some recollection of that name somewhere. But I don't know where I got it. But it must have been some kind of criminal associate because most of my names were, not most of, but some of them comes [sic] from some type of indirect criminal associate. In other words, maybe somebody, someone else used that name for an alias and I heard about it or something and [Ray did not finish his sentence].

I tried to get at the Galt matter from a different angle. I mentioned that the real Galt could have been in a difficult position—being a marksman, a Memphis visitor, and having a South African father—if the FBI had found him earlier.

In retort to my suggestion Ray responded: "It was two weeks before they found it was my prints. They [the FBI] must have talked to Galt and cleared him early."

I informed Ray that this was not so. He did not respond.

There were only two cracks in the stone wall that Ray erected around the subject of the Galt alias. In a letter to the author dated two days after the interview, there was a single, rather odd reference to the Galt alias. Ray said of HSCA Chief Counsel G. Robert Blakey: "He may very well have suspected that I was someway involved in the 'Galt' matter you mentioned. But since he could not prove it through me decided to say nothing."

This could be an offhand comment about Blakey (although Blakey certainly made it clear to the author that he sees nothing sinister, or even very significant, in the Toronto dimension). Or, this could be Ray's cryptic way of suggesting that there is indeed more to the Galt matter than official investigators know or than he is willing to divulge.

Concerning one Galt-related topic, Ray departed significantly from his standard evasions. I asked him about the duplicate driver's license.

"You never ordered a duplicate driver's license, did you?" I asked. "Did you ever lose yours?"

Ray's response was consistent with what he had told HSCA, unlike his responses about the Galt and Willard aliases.[5] Ray told the author:

I'm almost positive I never got a second driver's license. I got robbed and mugged [in Los Angeles] but lost no driver's license or yellow slip, like a registration. Didn't lose anything [in the mugging], only a watch and a coat.

I asked him who would have ordered and picked up the license. I also reminded him that this incident indicated that someone other than he had an interest in the Galt name.

"I don't know who ordered the driver's license," he answered. "Somebody picked it up off the table in Birmingham [at the rooming house where Ray had stayed]. All the mail came on one table and everyone picked it up."

Ray paused for several seconds. I braced myself for another stone to be added to the wall, expecting that he would try to dispense with the license incident as a coincidence of mistaken mail (which would still not explain the ordering of the duplicate).

At the end of the pause, Ray said quietly: "Maybe Raoul." He paused again, as if he wanted there to be no mistake about what he was saying. "He [Raoul] may have picked it up." This is a suggestion which, to the author's knowledge, Ray has never made before. His tone and demeanor created an ambience of meaningful disclosure.

Thus Ray is willing to admit that the shadowy force in his life ["Raoul"] would obtain an ID in the name of Galt, yet he refuses to admit that the same force had anything to do with the origin of the alias. This inconsistency is not so subtle as to be beyond Ray's grasp. It is likely that he understood it full well and this is why his response about "Raoul" was delivered with a rather dramatic flair.

ON CONSPIRACY AND CONSPIRATORS

By the logic of Ray's version of his role in this case, it was undeniably a conspiracy. He claims to have been set up as a fall guy by the men who murdered King. During the interview, I gave Ray several clear, sympathetic opportunities—if not direct invitations—to ruminate on the conspirators whom he insists framed him. Many observers view Ray as a man who constantly fabricates stories as smoke screens designed to hide his own guilt. By this theory, he should have been eager to impress this interviewer—a professor who writes books, after all—that he was the innocent victim of a frame-up perpetrated by skilled, dangerous conspirators, or that he is a figure worthy of sympathy because the conspirators might kill him.

I made several references to "the sophisticated conspirators who set you up." He would not bite. I asked him directly if he was at risk: "If you get a new trial and open things up again, aren't you afraid you might be lighting a fuse to the conspirators again, rekindling it? And is your life in danger from them? Do you fear for your life?"

Ray responded: "Most of my contacts were in Canada or Mexico, not U.S."

This is a strange answer. Does Ray think the Canadians or Mexicans killed King?

He continued: "No, the only thing left if you think like that is to stay in this place [he nods toward the concrete walls] for the rest of your life."

Ray then recounted how he was stabbed 22 times by four inmates while he sat reading in the prison library. His point is a valid one: prison is a dangerous place to be, apart from any assassination conspirators. Does Ray's rather cavalier comment about conspiracy-related danger reflect his true feelings?

One of Ray's former lawyers, Bernard Fensterwald, Jr., thinks not. He has been quoted in the press and has expressed to the author his belief that Ray is afraid for his life and scared to talk.[6] Harold Weisberg, who has spent many hours with Ray, told the author that he and Ray had correspondence on the topic of conspiratorial danger and that Ray fully understood Weisberg's cryptic reference to *Soul on Ice*, Eldridge Cleaver's book which contains what Weisberg described as "a long section on how to kill in prison in maximum security."[7]

There were two exceptions to Ray's general unwillingness to comment on the conspiracy or the conspirators. I asked him a question which I believe he had never been asked: What are his thoughts concerning the alleged St. Louis-based conspiracy described by HSCA?

Ray smiled. "I think that one of those guys . . . his name . . . well anyway, he asked those guys over [to his house] and he was wearing some Civil War hat, I think it was." He chuckled.

I waited for him to elaborate but he didn't.

"Are you saying that such men could not pull this off?" I asked.

He shrugged, then nodded affirmatively. His smile was gone.

The second exception was more important because it related to Ray's possible jeopardy at the hands of the conspirators, although it concerned past jeopardy rather than present. During my efforts to get him to open up about the Galt alias, I mentioned that one of my hypotheses was that if Ray had succeeded in getting to Angola, the conspirators would have tried to neatly dispose of him there.

Ray's reaction was silent but singularly intense in comparison with the rest of the interview. He looked down and nodded his agreement, firmly and without hesitation—not once but twice. His expression was serious, almost somber.

Logically, if Ray can agree that the conspirators planned to eliminate him in 1968, he cannot be sure that he has nothing to fear now, unless he is sure they are all dead. This seems highly unlikely given that Ray probably does not know their identity.

14   Toward Historical Truth

It seems fitting that in a country where people aspire to two of
everything—cars, kids, and homes—we should have two histories
as well. And we do: a public chronicle or "Disney Version," so widely
available as to be unavoidable . . . and a second one that remains
secret, buried, and unnamed.

                                                                —Jim Hougan[1]

That James Earl Ray has important, undisclosed knowledge is a certainty.
He knows something about the origin of the Galt alias, if only that he
got it from a blind drop, a cutout. Ray surely knows more about the
"fat man" incident, about his bar room companion in Toronto, about
whether "Raoul" is an individual or a composite of shadowy contacts,
and about which elements of the "Raoul" chronicles are real and which
are fiction.

There is a strong motivation for him not to tell what he knows. This
was very apparent during our interview, as he evaded or lied about the
most conspiracy-sensitive matters. Despite his denials, he must know
that, whatever his role was, he was manipulated by a network sufficiently extensive and powerful in 1968 so that it may still be capable of
eliminating him if his actions somehow threaten to expose it. If, for
example, he were to reveal how he got the Galt alias, he might put
himself at risk by providing a lead, however tenuous, to the conspirators.

Moreover, a good deal of whatever Ray knows may be counterproductive to his pursuit of a new trial and to his claims of innocence. The

truth about the Galt alias might make him appear all the more like a clandestine participant in the assassination rather than a mere patsy. Ray is keenly aware of the difference between what benefits him and what will solve the case. When I asked him why he had fired one of his attorneys, he smiled and said that the lawyer "was interested in solving the case. That's different than being my lawyer."

In addition, Ray is a lifelong criminal who does not hold America's political establishment or law-enforcement bureaucracy in particularly high esteem. As Harold Weisberg put it: "Ray won't help the FBI do its work."[2] These factors combine to create in Ray a strong impetus against disclosure.

It has been assumed by most official investigators that Ray is guilty and that it is this fact that prevents him from providing a more complete picture of the assassination. But this assumption is related to another, more implicit one; Ray either acted alone or was the hired gun for a fairly simple conspiracy. By contrast, the kind of conspiracy illuminated here was sophisticated enough to have manipulated Ray through a year-long series of mazes populated by cut-out figures, to the extent that he may have been so well compartmentalized that his knowledge is minimal. This is so whether or not he pulled the trigger. While Ray's secrets are probably not rich enough for him to use them as bargaining chips in seeking a new trial, his knowledge is, in some key areas, superior to that of the FBI, HSCA, and the history books.

Like many prisoners serving extended sentences, Ray has studied law and continues to launch a flurry of Freedom of Information Act suits and legal motions in pursuit of his ultimate goal of exculpating himself. It may be a hopeless, even disingenuous, goal; but it's the only one he has. As he points out, the only alternative is to resign himself to perpetual incarceration, to the boredom of "segregation" and of wearing an orange jumpsuit for the rest of his life.

It is clear to this researcher, from interviewing Ray and corresponding with him, that he plans to pursue his exculpation without providing any information he may possess as to the nature of the conspiracy or the identity of the conspirators. Ideally for Ray, he will uncover some "new" information withheld from him by the authorities, information that will create reasonable doubt about his guilt or point up some procedural flaw in the handling of his case. And he will do so without ever seriously addressing the question of conspiracy. For Ray, trying to zero in on the conspirators is, at best, unhelpful in his pursuit of exculpation—perhaps even counterproductive—and, at worst, dangerous.

After all, HSCA taught Ray a lesson: identifying the probable conspirators, albeit mistakenly in HSCA's case, does not necessarily alter official perceptions of his guilt. Having no incentive to help identify the conspirators or repair the historical record, James Earl Ray will provide no help, unless perhaps he is pressured to do so by the weight of new evidence generated through a competent reinvestigation.

Even without Ray's cooperation, the King assassination can be effectively pursued by investigators possessing sufficient resources, such as subpoena power and an adequate field staff. While HSCA demonstrated that these necessary resources are not sufficient for success, there are important new leads, and neglected old leads, that can and should be investigated.

There are two goals regarding Dr. King's assassination: historical truth and justice. Presently, we have achieved neither. It is possible that it is not yet too late for criminal justice to be achieved: It is possible that leads exist, or could be developed, which would trace back to the conspirators. Whether or not this can be done, the second goal, historical truth, is achievable.

So far, America has been offered two versions of truth: Ray was a lone assassin; a St. Louis conspiracy plotted to assassinate King without the involvement of any government agency. But these are myths, not truths. Myth is a poor substitute for historical understanding, for it cannot provide guidance for the future.

America has two visions. One is of a courageous, charismatic leader struck down in his political prime, and perhaps at the very moment when his country needed him most. The other is of a pale, aging recidivist, a low-life criminal who will probably spend his remaining years serving time as the convicted assassin. If our history is to have meaning for our future, we need to know who is responsible for creating these visions and how, in reality, they are connected to one another. It was not the distorted psyche of James Earl Ray that was fully responsible for King's death and for the political rearrangements and deprivations caused by his death, nor was it the racist megalomania of some shadowy St. Louis cabal. If, as is posited here, responsibility lies with men of clandestine sophistication who viewed King as the penultimate red menace, then we need to know this. The recurrence of past evils can only be prevented if their existence is known and understood.

In 1977 *Time* magazine said:

It would be ideal, of course, if James Earl Ray, finally convinced of the futility of concealing all of the details of his involvement in King's murder and of breaking out of prisons, would lay all the facts on the line in a persuasive way. But after all the twists and turns in his story so far, who would believe him? Moreover, no investigation of any sort is likely to still the doubts of the Mark Lane's and others who live in the mental world of conspiracy.[3]

Our lack of knowledge about the King assassination does not, as *Time* implies, represent the loose ends of our history but, rather, the core of our history. It may well be true that some devotees of American political assassinations "live in a mental world of conspiracy," just as there are those in the national media who live in a mental world of nonconspiracy, or anticonspiracy. What we desperately need to know, however, is what has gone on in the real political world—the world that, regardless of our various political mentalities, we all inhabit.

This assassination constitutes one of the most glaring inefficacies of this country's political and law-enforcement systems. The failures are multiple and are not due to some monolithic, octopuslike conspiracy which controls all. First, the violence and conflicts of the turbulent 1960s were escalated when murder aborted the process of nonviolent political change, and the fact that this was a conspiracy means that the impact on our political order is all the more deep-rooted and sinister. Then there was the failure of law enforcement and of the political establishment, under pressure—pressure to close the case before more cities burned, to control a political system that at times seemed out of control. Thus, there could not be a conspiracy, and so it was promulgated, even before the assassin was known or captured.

As we distanced ourselves from the political strife of the 1960s, other pressures set in, exacerbated by official incompetence—pressures to maintain our image of political stability, to preserve the legitimacy of our law-enforcement system and the credibility of the agencies and political leaders involved. Then, there was HSCA, mired in its own presumptions and incompetence and, in the final analysis, repeating rather than avoiding the mistakes of the Warren Commission—secrecy, superficiality, distortion of evidence.

All of these failures have impacted negatively upon the strength of our democracy. Yet our greatest weakness is our inability or unwillingness to recognize their existence. Political leaders, scholars, law-enforcement agencies, and print and electronic media are quick to understand all of these failures when they are manifested in foreign assassination cases as in the Philippines, Sweden, or South Korea. But in the United States, such understanding too often becomes more of an ideological struggle than an analytical assessment of evidence and events.

If U.S. history were so simplistic and distorted as to dismiss Martin Luther King, Jr., as "a black preacher and interest group advocate," millions of Americans would be outraged. It is intolerable that after 20 years the truth about his tragic assassination remains shrouded in official mythology and official secrecy.

Appendix A: Photographic Evidence, Ray and The Aliases

The physical similarities among the Toronto aliases and between Ray and these aliases was noted by the media in 1968 and by official investigators in 1968 and in 1978 (HSCA). The richness of the similarity extends beyond height, weight, hair color, and general appearance regarding age. As the accompanying photos show, there are other, minor similarities; and, equally as impressive, an absence of striking dissimilarities. These were glossed over in previous investigations and media reports. In comparing Ray and three of the four aliases—a 1968 photo of Willard was never published and is not now available for publication—note the following:

1. *Hairstyle*. In addition to a basic similarity of color, there is a general similarity of thickness (no crew cuts, no balding). Hairlines are also compatible. All have relatively high foreheads over the temples but not as much so in the middle of the forehead. There are no moustaches, beards, or goatees.
2. *Noses*. While there are some observable differences—Galt's appears a bit more flat than Ray's; Sneyd has larger nostrils—there is a basic symmetry. There are no pug noses or conspicuously flat ones; none have outstanding bony protrusions resulting from breaks.
3. *Ears*. Again, there is a rough similarity—fairly large, elongated ears.

Although John Willard bore the least resemblance to Ray, being three inches shorter and 20 pounds lighter, it is clear from observing Willard in 1984 that, in 1968, his nose, ears, and hairline would not have been an exception to the previously described pattern.

It is not that the similarities are such that anyone who knew one of these men would confuse them with any of the others. These are not "look-alikes." But in terms of the general physical description typically provided by witnesses at a crime scene, Ray and his aliases share a striking compatibility.

Photos 2–5 (left to right). Top: Paul Bridgeman; Eric S. Galt.
Bottom: Ramon George Sneyd; and James Earl Ray, circa 1967–68.
Credit: UPI Telephoto.

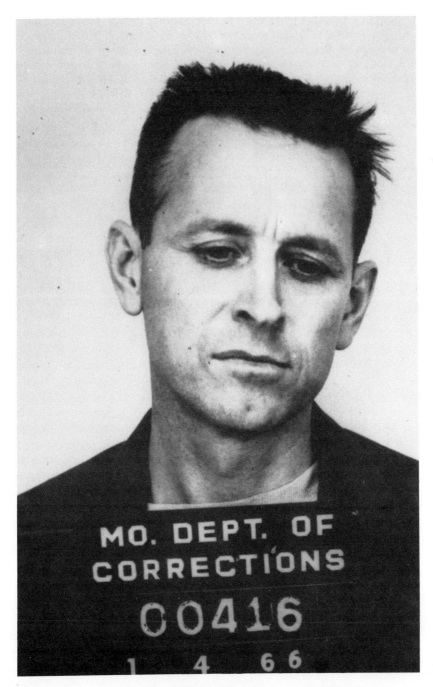

Photo 6. James Earl Ray, Prison Mug Shot, 1966. Credit: UPI Telephoto.

Moreover, the media and official investigators have failed to notice another intriguing fact: Whether by accident or conspiratorial design, James Earl Ray's appearance evolved to become more like those of his aliases. Four months before the assassination, Ray had plastic surgery which honed down his distinctively pointed nose. The pointed nose was not only the kind of feature that witnesses might remember, but it was also something that— from a side view, at least— made Ray less compatible with his aliases, whether Ray knew it or not.

Ray's hairstyle also ended up being much like those of his aliases. Ray's 1966 brush cut was unlike the hairstyles worn by his aliases in 1968. By 1968 Ray had a hairstyle very much like those of the Toronto men.

Appendix B: Chronology of James Earl Ray

March 10, 1928	Born in Alton, Ill.
1944	Obtains a job at a tannery in Hartford, Ill.
January 1946	Laid off from tannery job.
February 1947	Joins U.S. Army, serves with occupation forces in Germany.
December 1948	Discharged from Army for failure to adapt to military life.
1949	Sentenced to 90 days in Los Angeles for stealing a typewriter.
May 6, 1952	Charged with robbing a Chicago cab driver of $11. Shot by police. Sentenced to two years in jail. Released March 12, 1954.
March 1955	Convicted of stealing money orders in Hannibal, Missouri, and forging them to take a trip to Florida. Sentenced to Leavenworth Penitentiary. Released early in 1958.
1959	Convicted of robbing Kroger's supermarket in St. Louis of $120. Sentenced to 20 years in Missouri State Penitentiary, Jefferson City.
December 15, 1959	Unsuccessful attempt to escape from St. Louis courthouse during robbery trial.
1961	Unsuccessful attempt to escape prison.

1966	Unsuccessful escape attempt.
April 23, 1967	Escapes from Missouri State Penitentiary by hiding in a bread truck.
July 1967	Arrives in Montreal, Canada, and rents an apartment under the name Eric Starvo Galt.
August 28, 1967	Purchases white Mustang automobile in Birmingham, Alabama, using the name Eric S. Galt.
Oct. 7–Nov. 8, 1967	Drives to Mexico.
November 19, 1967	Arrives in Los Angeles.
December 1, 1967	Enrolls in dance course in Los Angeles, pays $364.
December 15–22, 1967	Drives to New Orleans and back to L.A., using the name Eric S. Galt.
January 19, 1968	Enrolls in bartenders school, Los Angeles. Graduates March 2.
March 17, 1968	Leaves Los Angeles, indicating on a postal change-of-address form that his address will be general delivery, Atlanta.
March 29, 1968	Purchases rifle in Birmingham, Alabama.
April 3, 1968	Arrives in Memphis and checks into the New Rebel Motel under the name Eric S. Galt.
April 4, 1968	Takes a room in Bessie Brewer's boarding house across from the Lorraine Motel, using the name John Willard. Martin Luther King, Jr. is assassinated.
April 6, 1968	Abandons the Mustang in Atlanta.
April 8, 1968	Rents a room on Ossington Street in Toronto, under the name Paul Bridgeman.
April 11, 1968	As Bridgeman, Ray has three passport photos taken at Arcade Photo Studio, Toronto.
April 16, 1968	Applies for a Canadian passport at Kennedy Travel Agency under the name of Ramon George Sneyd.
April 18, 1968	Pays his first rent to Mrs. Yee Sun Loo for a room at 962 Dundas Street.
April 19, 1968	FBI issues pictures of Ray, after discovering that it is James Earl Ray that the Bureau is hunting, not Eric S. Galt.

April 25, 1968	The "slight man" appears at 102 Ossington St. and asks for "Bridgeman," but Ray has moved to Dundas Street.
April 27, 1968	Ray/Sneyd gets a phone call at Dundas Street from an unidentified man. Ray is not in at the time.
April 30–May 2,1968	Ray is seen in the Silver Dollar Tavern in Toronto each night, accompanied on two occasions by an unidentified man.
May 2, 1968	"Fat man" visits Ray at Dundas Street. Ray pays $345 for an airplane ticket to London.
May 6, 1968	Departs Toronto for London.
May 7, 1968	Arrives in London.
May 8, 1968	Arrives in Lisbon, Portugal.
May 18, 1968	Arrives in London.
June 8, 1968	Arrested at Heathrow Airport in London as he attempts to board a plane for Brussels.
May 3, 1971	Unsuccessful escape attempt, Brushy Mountain Prison, Tennessee. Ray tried to escape through a steam tunnel.
February 7, 1972	Unsuccessful attempt to escape through gymnasium ceiling, Brushy Mountain Prison.
June 10, 1977	Ray and six others escape from Brushy Mountain by going over the wall while guards are distracted. Ray is captured 54 hours later in the woods eight miles from the prison.
1978	Ray marries Anna Sandhu, an artist for a local Tennessee TV station who covered his trial (for his escape).
June 4, 1981	Ray is stabbed 22 times by four black inmates as he sits reading law books in the prison library. He recovers.

Appendix C: Congressional Secrecy and the King Assassination

The pursuit of historical truth in the King assassination is, to some degree, impeded by the cloak of secrecy that shrouds the work of the House Select Committee on Assassinations. The committee's final report, covering the assassinations of both Martin Luther King, Jr., and President John F. Kennedy, was released in 1979, along with 13 volumes of testimony and exhibits relating to the King case. After the report was released, Committee Chairman Louis Stokes (Dem. Ohio) and Chief Counsel G. Robert Blakey arranged to have all of the committee's backup records, documents, unpublished transcripts, and investigative data locked up for 50 years.[1].

Chairman Stokes also requested that the FBI and CIA treat their relevant documents as "congressional materials" rather than as agency materials. FBI and CIA were very enthusiastic about complying with Stokes's request. By doing so, these agencies could place their JFK and MLK documents beyond the reach of the Freedom of Information Act (FOIA), which Congress had the political foresight to exempt itself from. Thus, by classifying FBI and CIA records as "congressional materials," they too can be locked away for 50 years and cannot be subject to Freedom of Information Act requests or litigation. This applies to some FBI and CIA documents which were sought by assassination researchers under FOIA long before HSCA came into existence.

At the start of its investigation, HSCA had proclaimed: "It is essential not only that persons be able to judge the performance of executive agencies, but that they be able to judge the committee's performance as well. Such is the essence of representative democracy."[2] But Stokes and Blakey and some other committee members evidently decided that full disclosure was not essential in a representative democracy. Instead, HSCA embraced Earl Warren's notion of deferring the public right to know for nearly a generation. The Warren Commission had planned to seal its files for 75 years; HSCA was more modest, sealing its records for only 50 years.

Chief Counsel Blakey bravely announced: "I'll rest on the historians' judgement 50 years from now, when everything becomes available. I'll rest on the historical judgement that is made on us in 50 years."[3] One cannot help but envision Blakey as a feisty centenarian answering the pointed questions posed by historians in the year 2038.

By sealing its records, the committee avoids the questioning and criticism that would inevitably follow a full, substantive analysis of its work by interested journalists, scholars, and lawyers.

Not everyone is as pleased with HSCA's secrecy policy as are Blakey and Stokes. Harold Weisberg, who has battled governmental secrecy in assassination cases for the last 20 years, charged that: "What Stokes has done is arrange it so that the mechanism by which people can correct the errors of government don't apply to Congress. He's arranged his own private cover-up."[4]

To which charge G. Robert Blakey, now an academician at Notre Dame, replied thoughtfully: "He [Weisberg] can kiss my ass. And you can quote me on that."[5]

A group called ACCESS (Association of Concerned Citizens for Ending Senseless Secrecy), composed of 70 members from the U.S., Canada, and England, has worked intensively for passage of a congressional bill that would place the HSCA records under the same disclosure process used for Warren Commission records.[6] That is, HSCA records would be subject to FOIA request, review, and processing. They could still be withheld on the grounds of national security, rights of privacy, or protection of investigation sources or intelligence methods; but the blanket 50-year secrecy policy would be abolished in favor of a legal-administrative process of disclosure. The legislation which sought this disclosure was introduced in April 1983 by Congressmen Stewart B. McKinney, Robert W. Edgar, Harold S. Sawyer, Walter E. Fauntroy, and Harold E. Ford, all former members of HSCA. During each of several attempts at passage, the bill became mired in the committee process.

Blakey wrote a letter to the House of Representatives strongly opposing the bill. In a November 1983 interview with assassinologist Paul Hoch, Blakey cited numerous grounds for his opposition.[7] He contended that the HSCA's King investigation involved promises of confidentiality to witnesses and sources and that there were "intense privacy interests" that rendered disclosure both inappropriate and impossible. What Blakey implies by the word impossible is that he doubts whether the sensitive material relating to privacy and confidentiality could be disentangled from the nonsensitive material. This ignores the fact that several hundred thousand pages of released documents dealing with the JFK assassination—documents from FBI, CIA, Secret Service, and the Warren Commission—have been sufficiently disentangled from rights to privacy, national security, and the methods and procedures of presidential protection.

In a statement supporting passage of the bill, Congressman Robert W. Edgar, a former HSCA member, indirectly disputed Blakey's claim.

We can affirm a policy of full disclosure of the proceedings in a manner consistent with the protection of classified information and the protection of innocent victims. The release of the Committee's work would be governed by the guidelines used in making the Warren Commission documents available, and I certainly believe the House proceedings are comparable documents.[8]

Edgar also cited other reasons for disclosure: the need for an "informed citizenry," the "aura of mistrust and skepticism" created by Congress's "standing alone in the witholding of its files," the historical "national interest" that would be served by releasing the data.

In contrast, Blakey argued: "Of course, history should judge what we do; but in the normal course of events, when it doesn't touch so much on [innocent] individuals."[9] It would appear that in Blakey's view, extraordinary, 50-year secrecy constitutes the "normal course of events," and the procedures used successfully to protect privacy while disclosing Warren Commission records have no relevance to HSCA materials. Blakey also opined that disclosure is "not worth the money it would take to do it . . . the gain would be marginal, marginal to nothing."[10]

Knowing how shoddy HSCA's King investigation was, the author will grant that there are probably no major revelations or case-breaking data hidden in HSCA files. But there may well be crucial information that appeared inconsequential to HSCA because the committee did not understand its significance or did not follow it up. HSCA has given the American public a provocative conclusion of "probable conspiracy." Having proclaimed and defended this conclusion on the basis of its investigative records, the committee owes it to the American polity to disclose, as fully as possible, the material upon which this conclusion is supposedly based, without a 50-year waiting period.

The U.S. Congress no longer blithely accepts the condescending argument from CIA that, "We have data that proves our position beyond any doubt, but it is too secret and sensitive to reveal, so you'll just have to believe us." The American public should not accept such an argument from HSCA.

Notes

INTRODUCTION

1. Frank Donner, "Why Isn't the Truth Bad Enough?" *Civil Liberties Review*, Jan.-Feb. 1978, pp. 68–72.

2. See David J. Garrow, *The FBI and Martin Luther King, Jr.* (New York: Penguin Books, 1983), ch. 3.

3. "Probe by Justice Concludes James Earl Ray Acted Alone," *Washington Post*, February 2, 1977, p. 3.

4. Select Committee on Assassinations, U.S. House of Representatives, *The Final Assassinations Report* (New York: Bantam, 1979), Contents page.

5. Ibid., pp. 470–86.

CHAPTER 1

1. The following description of the assassination is based upon *The Final Assassinations Report, U.S. House of Representatives* (New York: Bantam, 1979), pp. 364–69, hereafter referred to as HSCA *Report*. The author checked the basic accuracy of the committee's summary description by referring to FBI statements made by witnesses in 1968 and/or the full text of testimony before the House Assassinations Committee of those witnesses whom the committee used for its summary description.

2. Ibid., p. 519.

3. David J. Garrow, *The FBI and Martin Luther King, Jr.* (New York: Penguin Books, 1983), p. 101.

4. Ibid. pp. 124–29; 133–34. According to Garrow, most of the tape came from a bug planted in King's room at the Willard Hotel in Washington, D.C., Jan. 5–7, 1964 (Garrow, p. 104). In a 1968 monograph distributed by the FBI as part of its attempt to discredit King, the Willard Hotel happenings were described as a "two day drunken sex orgy" (Garrow, pp. 185–86).

5. Ibid., pp. 125–26.

6. HSCA *Report*, pp. 363–64. A detailed description of King's mood appears in David J. Garrow, *Bearing the Cross: Martin Luther King, Jr. and the Southern Christian Leadership Conference* (New York: Wm. Morrow & Co., 1986), pp. 621–23.

7. HSCA *Report*, p. 364.

8. Ibid., p. 365.

9. Ibid., p. 366.

10. Ibid., p. 368.

11. Ibid.

12. Ibid., p. 369.

13. Author's interview with Rev. Samuel Kyles, Memphis, Tenn., Jan. 10, 1986.

14. "U.S. Attorney General Confident King's Murderer Will Be Found," *Memphis Press Scimitar*, April 5, 1968, p. 13.

CHAPTER 2

1. James W. Clarke, *American Assassins: The Darker Side of Politics* (Princeton, N.J.: Princeton University Press, 1982), pp. 141–46.

2. *Hearings on the Investigation of the Assassination of Dr. Martin Luther King, Jr.*, vols. 1–13 (Washington, D.C.: U.S. Govt. Printing Office, 1979), at vol. 3, p. 174. Hereafter referred to as HSCA volumes.

3. Telephone conversation with Harold Weisberg, Sept. 5, 1984.

4. Ibid.

5. Ray's uses of aliases: HSCA, vol. 3, pp. 46–47, 136, 143, 246–51, 174–75; vol. 9, pp. 283–89, 291, 332–34, 343–45, 421, 425, 475; vol. 10, pp. 80, 373; vol. 11, pp. 23–28, 413–14, 417–27.

6. Ray wrote the Canadian veterans' administration under the name of Galt (HSCA, vol. 9, p. 421). Other uses: HSCA *Report* (New York: Bantam, 1979), p. 379.

7. FBI documents pertaining to Lohmeyer: April 13, 1968, teletype from Springfield, Ill. to headquarters (document number 44–38861–865); April 19, 1968, San Francisco to headquarters (44–38861–1788); April 23, 1968, San Francisco to headquarters (44–38861-[unintelligible]).

8. In 1968 the press tended to exaggerate the proximity of the residences. Jay Walz of the *New York Times* wrote that the aliases "all live within a few blocks of each other" ("Police in Canada Investigate Whether Ray Had Assistance," June 13, 1968, p. 3). Ray Biggart, *Washington Post*, June 11, 1968, p. A–1: "Galt Lives Within a Half Mile of the Two Other Men [Bridgeman and Sneyd]."

In HSCA Exhibit F–232, "James Earl Ray and His Use of Aliases" (vol. 5, p. 13), Ramon George Sneyd's address (1741 Victoria Park Avenue) was incorrectly marked on the map—2.8 miles south of its actual location on the same street.

9. Jay Walz, "3 Whose Names Ray Used Resemble Him," *New York Times*, June 12, 1968, p. 1; Cameron Smith and Loren Lind, "How Did Ray Get Names

of 3 Whose Description Fit His?" *Toronto Globe and Mail*, June 11, 1968, p. 5; HSCA, vol. 11, pp. 39–40 (on Sneyd and Bridgeman).

10. Walz, ibid., citing FBI description of Ray based upon Ray's prison files.

11. Pat McNenly, "Ray Couldn't Have Picked a Cleaner Name for His Alias," *Toronto Star*, June 10, 1968, p. 1; "False Birth Papers Easy to Get: Registrar," *Toronto Globe and Mail*, June 10, 1968, p. 1.

12. McNenly, "Ray Couldn't Have Picked a Cleaner Name."

13. Ibid.

14. "False Passport Papers Easy to Get."

15. Ibid.

16. Telephone interview with Bernard Simmonds, August 8, 1984.

17. "Mounties Found First Passport Clue," *Toronto Star*, June 8, 1963, p. 3.

18. Ibid.

19 "Sneyd: I'm Baffled," *Toronto Telegram*, June 10, 1968, p. 11.

20. Ibid. The misquote appeared on June 8 on p. 1 of the *Telegram*.

21. "RCMP Praise for Public," *Toronto Telegram*, June 8, 1984, p. 4.

22. "Ray's Alias a Metro Man," *Toronto Telegram*, June 8, 1968, p. 4.

23. Walz, "3 Whose Names Ray Used"; Smith and Lind, "How Did Ray Get Names?"; HSCA, vol. 11, pp. 39–40.

24. HSCA, vol. 4, p. 198; vol. 1, pp. 318–19.

25. HSCA, vol. 5, p. 10.

26. Interview with John Willard, Sept. 12, 1984.

27. Telephone interview with John Willard, August 28, 1984.

28. Interview with John Willard, Sept. 11, 1984.

29. Telephone conversation with Mrs. Willard, March 25, 1984.

30. Willard contacts: interviews of Sept. 11 and 12, 1984; telephone interviews: August 28, 1984, Sept. 10, 1984.

31. HSCA *Report*, p. 379.

32. HSCA vol. 10, pp. 373–74; renting room: HSCA *Report*, p. 379.

33. Walz, "3 Whose Names Ray Used"; Smith and Lind, "How Did Ray Get Names?"; "Ray's Alias Was Metro Man," *Toronto Telegram*.

34. Estimates of Galt's weight put forth by the press in 1968 varied from 170 to 190 pounds, with the American papers falling somewhere in between. Galt's own estimate is 180 pounds (telephone interview June 27, 1984).

35. Galt's scars are still visible (interview of Sept. 11, 1984). Ray's scars: HSCA, vol. 9, pp. 283–86.

36. Douglas Stuebing, "3 Aliases All from One Area," *Toronto Telegram*, June 10, 1968, p. 11 (confirmed by Galt interview, Sept. 11, 1984).

37. Smith and Lind, "How Did Ray Get Names?"

38. Interview with Eric S. Galt, Sept. 11, 1984.

39. Jay Walz, "Real Galt Calm About Publicity Over Ray," *New York Times*, June 13, 1968, p. 28.

40. Telephone interview with Jay Walz, June 6, 1984.

41. "Ray's Alias Was Metro Man," *Toronto Telegram*.

42. Interview with Eric Galt, Sept. 11, 1984.

43. HSCA, vol. 5, p. 11.

44. Willard contacts Galt: interview of Sept. 11, 1984; telephone interviews during 1984—March 26, April 8, May 8, June 27, Sept. 10.

CHAPTER 3

1. HSCA *Report* (New York: Bantam, 1979), pp. 470–90.
2. Ibid., p. 472.
3. Ibid., pp. 480–85.
4. Ibid., p. 485.
5. Ibid., p. 644.
6. Ibid., p. 533.
7. Ibid., p. 538.
8. Ibid., p. 542.
9. Ibid., pp. 540–41.
10. David J. Garrow, *The FBI and Martin Luther King, Jr.* (New York: Penguin Books, 1983), pp. 10–11.
11. Ibid., pp. 198–99.
12. HSCA, vol. 5, p. 10.
13. Ibid., p. 12.
14. Ibid.
15. Ibid., p. 14.
16. Ibid., p. 11.
17. Ibid., p. 14.
18. Ibid.
19. Ibid., p. 12.
20. Telephone conversation with G. Robert Blakey, May 14, 1984.
21. HSCA, vol. 5, p. 14.
22. Blakey Conversation.
23. HSCA, vol. 5, pp. 9–10. The restrictions were that:

• no Canadian citizen would be interviewed without permission
• permission to interview would be sought only by the RCMP
• an RCMP representative would be present for all interviews
• there would be no independent investigation without RCMP permission.

24. Blakey conversation.
25. HSCA, vol. 5, p. 10.
26. Ibid.
27. Blakey conversation.
28. Gregory Jaynes, "Canadians Checking Ray Say He Had 'Help of Some Kind.' " *Memphis Commercial Appeal*, June 11, 1968, p. 1.
29. Blakey conversation.
30. HSCA, vol. 5, p. 12.
31. After the HSCA had finished its work, Blakey coauthored a book which contended that President John F. Kennedy was assassinated as the result of a Mafia conspiracy. See G. Robert Blakey and Richard N. Billings, *The Plot to Kill the President* (New York: New York Times Books, 1981).

CHAPTER 4

1. Frank Howett, "Was James Earl Ray Gunman—Or Was He Decoy?" *Memphis Press Scimitar*, July 15, 1968,p. 1.

2. Jay Walz, "Real Galt Calm About Publicity Over Ray's Use of His Name,"*New York Times*, June 13, 1968, p. 28.

3. Telephone call to RCMP Public Affairs Officer John Lehman, Ottawa, March 13, 1984.

4. May 6, 1984, telephone call to RCMP National Crime Reporting Center, Ottawa.

5. P.E.J. Banning letter of May 5, 1984; telephone call of May 15, 1984.

6. May 15, 1984, telephone call to Banning.

7. Banning letter of June 1, 1984.

8. Telephone interview with Eric Galt, March 26, 1984.

9. Telephone conversation with Inspector George Timko, RCMP Federal Policy Branch, Ottawa, Sept. 17, 1984.

10. Telephone call to Banning, Sept. 17, 1984.

11. Simmonds letter to the author, April 19, 1984.

12. Telephone interview with Bernard Simmonds, Aug. 8, 1984.

13. Tyrrell letter to the author, April 30, 1984.

14. Telephone interview with Jay Walz, May 16, 1984.

15. Telephone interview with Jay Walz, June 6, 1984.

16. Jay Walz letter to the author, June 5, 1984.

17. Cameron Smith letter to the author, May 29, 1984; telephone interview with Earl McRae, July 23, 1983; telephone interview with Andy Salwyn, Sept. 12, 1984.

18. Interview with Earl McRae, Toronto, Sept. 12, 1984.

19. Discussion with Harold Weisberg (Frederick, Maryland), May 25, 1984.

20. HSCA, vol. 9, pp. 281–82.

21. Ibid., p. 282.

22. HSCA, vol. 10, p. 358.

23. HSCA, vol. 9, p. 334.

24. HSCA, vol. 11, p. 421.

25. HSCA, vol. 9, p. 284.

26. Ibid., pp. 284–85.

27. "Fat Man May Have Helped Ray," *Toronto Star*, June 10, 1964, p. 4.

28. HSCA, vol. 9, p. 335.

29. HSCA, vol. 11, p. 424.

30. HSCA, vol. 5, p. 12.

31. HSCA, vol. 11, pp. 24–25.

32. Ibid., pp. 39–40.

33. Ibid., p. 24.

34. HSCA, vol. 10, pp. 355–56.

CHAPTER 5

1. Telephone interview with Eric Galt, June 27, 1984.

2. Ibid.; interview with background source in U.S. military R&D, an air force colonel.

3. Telephone interview with Eric Galt, May 8, 1984.

4. Letter to the author from Deputy Under Secretary of Defense Edith W. Martin, May 4, 1984.

5. Telephone interview with Eric Galt, March 26, 1984.

6. Ibid.

7. Telephone interview with Malcolm Greenhall, public affairs office, Union Carbide of Canada Ltd., Toronto, April 2, 1984.

8. Martin letter to the author.

9. Letter to the author from Marian K. Singleton, Public Affairs Officer, Dept. of the Army, July 27, 1984.

10. Ibid.

11. Letter to the author from Edward D. Aebisher, Associate Director of Public Relations, Oak Ridge Laboratory, Jan. 28, 1985.

12. Telephone interview with Eric Galt, June 27, 1984.

13. HSCA, vol. 9, p. 421.

14. Telephone interview with Eric Galt, June 27, 1984.

15. Ibid.

16. Ibid.

17. Telephone interview with Eric Galt, March 26, 1984.

18. HSCA, vol. 3, p. 174.

19. HSCA, vol. 9, p. 284.

20. Ibid.

21. HSCA *Report*, p. 379.

22. HSCA, vol. 13, pp. 161–63.

23. Martin Waldron, "Alabamian Named in Dr. King Inquiry," *New York Times*, April 12, 1968, p. 1. The error of citing "Eric Starvo Galt" as the alias generally used by Ray continued well into June. See Cameron Smith, "Ray's Ties with Toronto May Go Back Some Time, " *Toronto Globe and Mail*, June 11, 1968, p. 1.

24. On Galt's change from Starvo to S., June 27, 1984, telephone interview with Galt.

25. Galt asserted that Carbide provided its own security (telephone interview of March 26, 1984). Carbide refused to confirm or deny this (telephone interview with Malcolm Greenhall, May 6, 1984).

26. David C. Martin, *Wilderness of Mirrors* (New York: Ballantine Books, 1983), pp. 165–66.

27. Ibid., pp. 205–6.

28. George O'Toole, *The Private Sector* (New York: W. W. Norton, 1978), p. 127.

29. Ibid., p. xiii.

30. Ibid., p. 146.

31. Ibid., pp. 131–32.

32. Ibid., p. 144 (note); Jerry Richmond, "Spies in Dallas?—Police Alert," *Dallas Times Herald*, Aug. 5, 1963.

CHAPTER 6

1. John Egerton, "The Enduring Mystery of James Earl Ray," *The Progressive*, Nov. 1986, p. 19.

2. See Lawrence Z. Freedman, "The Assassination Syndrome," *Saturday Evening Post*, July/August 1981, pp. 66–68; James B. Kirkham et al., eds., *Assassination and Political Violence* (New York: Bantam, 1970), pp. 77–81. Freedman has served as a consultant to the Secret Service. The Kirkham book is an edited version of the Kerner Commission final report. In the view of the U.S. Secret Service, there has been only one assassination attempt, whether successful or unsuccessful, that was not the work of a lone individual—the 1950 attempt on President Truman perpetrated by two Puerto Rican nationalists. See Philip H. Melanson, *The Politics of Protection: The U.S. Secret Service in the Terrorist Age* (New York: Praeger, 1984), pp. 74–75.

3. Philip H. Melanson, *The Politics of Protection: The U.S. Secret Service in the Terrorist Age* (New York: Praeger, 1984), pp. 78–82.

4. Freedman, "The Assassination Syndrome."

5. The notion that a KGB plot had been behind the attempted assassination of Pope John Paul II was the subject of two books in 1983: Claire Sterling, *The Time of the Assassin* (New York: Holt, Rinehart and Winston); Paul Henze, *The Plot to Kill the Pope* (New York: Charles Scribners & Sons). Sterling's book received a good deal of attention from both print and electronic media. Aquino assassination in the Philippines, see: Lewis M. Simons, "Aquino Probe Accuses General," *Chicago Tribune*, Oct. 11, 1984, p. 1.

6. Melanson, *The Politics of Protection*, p. 79.

7. HSCA vol.10, p. 80; James Kilpatrick, "5,000 Pages of State Evidence Convinced Ray to Plead Guilty," *Memphis Commercial Appeal*, March 16, 1969, p. 1.

8. HSCA, vol. 10, p. 80.

9. Ibid., pp. 79–80.

10. HSCA *Report*, p. 378.

11. Discussion with Bernard Fensterwald, Jr., Arlington, Va., July 31, 1984.

12. "Suspect: Police After Two Men Seen with Him," *Toronto Telegram*, June 10, 1968, p. 11; Homer Bigart, "Mounties Hunt 'Fat Man' in Ray Case," *New York Times*, June 10, 1968, p. 2.

13. "Police Believe Ray Had Girl Friend," *Toronto Star*, June 11, 1968, p. 2.

14. Ibid.

15. James Kilpatrick, "5,000 Pages of State Evidence."

16. Homer Bigart, "Ray Received Two Mystery Phone Calls in London," *Toronto Globe and Mail*, June 12, 1968, p. 5.

17. "Ray on the Run Had a Terrible Time," *Washington Daily News*, June 13, 1968, p. 1.

18. Ibid.; "Ray Had Tough Time in Europe," *Washington Evening Star*, June 13, 1968, p. 1.

19. Ray's tavern companion: Homer Bigart, "Galt Alias Taken in Toronto," *Washington Post*, June 11, 1968, p. A–1; "Suspect: Police After Two Men Seen with Him."

20. "Suspect: Police After Two Men Seen With Him."

21. Bigart, "Galt Alias Taken in Toronto."

22. "Suspect: Police After Two Men Seen with Him"; Bigart, "Galt Alias Taken in Toronto."

23. Ray's "Raoul" story: HSCA *Report*, pp. 394–96.

24. Ibid., p. 395. The following account of Ray's descriptions of Raoul comes from HSCA *Report*, pp. 394–96.

25. HSCA *Report*, pp. 456–70.

26. Ibid., p. 467.

27. Ibid., pp. 445–56.

28. Ibid., p. 470.

29. In both the U.S. Government Printing Office and Bantam editions of the final HSCA *Report*, endnotes 37–289 of section IIB, which includes the discussion of Ray's brothers, are missing.

30. Discussion with Harold Weisberg (Frederick, Maryland), May 25, 1984.

31. This account of Salwyn's investigation of "Raoul" comes from the author's interview with Salwyn, Toronto, Sept. 12, 1984, and from two follow-up telephone interviews, Sept. 16 and 17, 1984. Salwyn's account was corroborated by Earl McRae (interviewed in Toronto, Sept. 12, 1984).

32. Salwyn and McRae interviews.

33. Telephone interview with Sgt. Mike Power, RCMP, Ottawa, Sept. 17, 1984.

34. Telephone interview with Inspector George Timko, Federal Policy Branch, RCMP, Ottawa, Sept. 17, 1984.

35. Telephone conversation with G. Robert Blakey, Sept. 20, 1984.

36. Ray's letter to author, Dec. 3, 1984.

37. HSCA *Report*, pp. 514–15, "Jules Ricco Kimble." Unless otherwise specified, all references to HSCA's analysis of the Kimble matter refer to these two pages.

38. Citations to "Jules Ricco Kimble" section appear on pp. 762–63 of HSCA's final report. The specific cite is; #215, p. 762.

39. HSCA *Report*, p. 515.

40. Telephone interview with Andy Salwyn, Oct. 5, 1985.

41. Ibid.

42. HSCA *Report*, p. 515.

43. Oster data: author's telephone interviews with Joseph Oster, October 5, 8; Nov. 13, 18, 1985.

44. HSCA *Report*, p. 458.

45. Ibid., note #215, p. 762.

46. Telephone interviews with Oster, Nov. 18, 1985.

47. Ibid.

48. Telephone conversation with Harold Weisberg, Dec. 6, 1984.

49. Letter to the author from Harold Weisberg, Sept. 28, 1984.

50. Interview with James Earl Ray, Dec. 1, 1984, Nashville State Penitentiary, Nashville, Tenn.

51. Ray letter to the author, Dec. 3, 1984.

52. Ray letter to the author, Dec. 11, 1984.

53. HSCA *Report*, pp. 387–91.

54. HSCA, vol. 5, p. 10.

55. HSCA *Report*, p. 338 (note); "Suspect: Police After Two Men Seen with Him."

56. HSCA, vol. 5, p. 10.

CHAPTER 7

1. Mrs. Loo's account is derived primarily from Earl McRae's interview with her, as described in his article ("Who's the Fat Man?", *Toronto Star*, June 10, 1968, p. 1) and in his interview with the author (Toronto, Sept. 12, 1984). Also from: Homer Bigart "Mounties Hunt 'Fat Man' in Ray Case," *New York Times*, June 10, 1968, p. 1; "Suspect: Police After Two Men Seen with Him," *Toronto Telegram*, June 10, 1968, p. 11; Cameron Smith and Loren Lind, "Fat Man Visits Ray, Landlady Recalls," *Toronto Globe and Mail*, June 10, 1968, p. 1.

2. "Suspect: Police After Two Men Seen with Him."

3. Interview with Earl McRae, Toronto, Sept. 12, 1984.

4. "Cabby: I Picked up 'Fat Man' in King Killer Case, *Toronto Star*, June 12, 1968, p. 1.

5. Ibid.

6. This account is derived from " 'Fat Man' Cleared in King Killer Case," *Toronto Star*, June 13, 1968, p. 2; " 'Fat Man' Cleared in Ray Case Probe," Ward Just, *Washington Post*, June 14, 1968, p. A–5.

7. "Suspect: Police After Two Men Seen with Him."

8. McRae interview with author, Sept. 12, 1984.

9. Telephone conversation with Mrs. Yee Sun Loo and her son, Sept. 15, 1984.

10. HSCA, vol. 1, p. 135.

11. HSCA, vol. 3, p. 97.

12. HSCA, vol. 10, p. 359.

13. Earl McRae, "Who's the Fat Man?"

14. Ibid.

15. "Suspect: Police After Two Men Seen with Him."

16. Ibid.

17. Ibid.

18. "Life as a Fugitive: Cold Snacks in Locked Room," *Toronto Globe and Mail*, June 11, 1968, p. 3.

19. Earl McRae, "Who's the Fat Man?"

20. Slight man incident: Earl McRae, "Who's the Fat Man?"; "Suspect: Police After Two Men Seen with Him"; Ward Just, " 'Fat Man' Cleared"; Jay Walz, "3 Men Whose Names Ray Used Resemble Him," *New York Times*, June 12, 1968, p. 31.

21. Walz, "3 Men Whose Names Ray Used."

22. "Fat Man Cleared in King Killer Case, " *Toronto Star*; "Cabbie: I Picked up Fat Man."

23. Bolton interview: 1984, Canada.

CHAPTER 8

1. HSCA, vol. 4, p. 423.

2. HSCA *Report*, p. 558.

3. Ibid., p. 533.

4. Ibid., p. 559.

5. Ibid., p. 560; transcript of TACT 10 and dispatcher, HSCA vol. 4, pp. 290–317.

6. TACT 10 transcript, pp. 290–95.

7. Transcript, HSCA, vol. 4, p. 292.

8. TACT 10 transcript, p. 293.

9. HSCA vol. 4, p. 287, affidavit of MPD Lt. Frank Kallaher.

10. Ibid., pp. 287–89.

11. HSCA *Report*, p. 560.

12. HSCA, vol. 4, p. 326.

13. Ibid., p. 322.

14. Ibid., p. 326.

15. Ibid., p. 288.

16. Ibid., p. 292.

17. Ibid., pp. 288–89.

18. Ibid., p. 289.

19. Ibid.

20. HSCA *Report*, p. 592.

21. FBI memo, April 2, 1968, Memphis field office to Washington, one page. Reprinted in HSCA, vol. 6, p. 547 and entitled "Threat to American Airlines and Dr. Martin Luther King, Jr., April 1, 1968."

22. MPD memo "Civil Disorders Memphis Tennessee February 12 through April 16, 1968." The origin and nature of the memo are discussed later in this chapter.

23. The account of the movements of the security detail is taken from HSCA *Report*, pp. 547–49 and the statement of Inspector Donald Smith (HSCA, vol. 4, pp. 259–61), who headed the detail.

24. Author's interview with Rev. Samuel Kyles, Memphis, Jan. 10, 1986.

25. HSCA *Report*, p. 547.

26. Ibid., p. 548.

27. For a description of Secret Service methods and procedures see Philip H. Melanson, *The Politics of Protection: The U.S. Secret Service in the Terrorist Age* (Praeger, 1984), ch. 6.

28. HSCA, vol. 4, p. 235.

29. HSCA, vol. 6, p. 593. FBI report of March 29, 1985, Memphis to Director.

30. HSCA *Report*, p. 552.

31. Ibid., pp. 549–55, "The Removal of Detective Redditt."

32. Ibid., p. 550.

33. Ibid., p. 552.

34. Ibid., p. 552.

35. Ibid., p. 555.

36. Ibid., p. 553.

37. HSCA, vol. 4, p. 267.

38. Ibid.

39. Author's interview with E. H. Arkin, Memphis, Jan. 10, 1986.

40. HSCA's conclusion: *Report*, p. 533; MPD memo: Tines to McDonald, April 4, 1968, one page, "Information Concerning Assassination Plot of Possibly Det. Redditt,"reprinted in HSCA, vol. 4, p. 268.

41. HSCA *Report*, p. 554.

42. HSCA *Report*, p. 553; MPD memo: "Tines to McDonald."

43. HSCA, vol. 4, p. 269, MPD memo from Arkin to Tines "Threat on Negro Lt. Memphis Police Department," April 4, 1968, one page.

44. Ibid.

45. HSCA, vol. 4, p. 271.

46. Ibid., p. 273.

47. Ibid., p. 272.

48. Memphis, Jan. 10, 1986.

49. HSCA *Report*, p. 554.

50. HSCA *Report*, p. 558; testimony of Public Safety Director Frank Holloman, HSCA, vol. 4, p. 278.

51. Holloman, ibid.

52. HSCA, vol. 4, p. 282.

53. Affidavit of Officer William O. Crumby, HSCA, vol. 4, p. 279.

54. Crumby affidavit, pp. 279–80.

55. HSCA, vol. 4, p. 282.

56. Interview with Rev. Samuel Kyles, Memphis, Jan. 10, 1986. Also, Holloman testimony, HSCA, vol. 4, p. 278.

57. Ibid., p. 279.

58. Crumby affidavit. HSCA, vol. 4, p. 279.

59. Telephone interview with Sam Evans, Nov. 4, 1985.

60. See Harold Weisberg, *Frame-Up* (New York: Outerbridge and Dienstfrey, 1971), p. 166.

61. Telephone interview with TACT 10 Officer Barney G. Wright, Nov. 18, 1985.

62. Ibid.

63. Telephone interview with George W. Leonneke, May 15, 1985.

64. HSCA *Report*, pp. 533–65.

65. HSCA, vol. 4, pp. 233, 236, 243, 325.

66. Ibid., p. 243.

67. FBI memo March 29, 1968 (157–944–45) "Sanitation Workers Strike Memphis, Tennessee, Racial Matters," 13 pp. Reprinted in HSCA, vol. 6, pp. 472–78.

68. Author's interview of Arkin.

69 David J. Garrow, *The FBI and Martin Luther King, Jr.* (New York: Penguin Books, 1981), p. 11.

70. Ibid., p. 175.

71. Ibid., p. 198.

72. HSCA *Report*, pp. 534–37; FBI claims no surveillance: HSCA vol. 6, p. 412. For an in-depth description of FBI sources and methods of intelligence gathering, spying, and provocateuring see Gerald D. McKnight, "Harvest of Hate: The FBI's War Against Black Youth—Domestic Intelligence in Memphis, Tennessee," *South Atlantic Quarterly*, Winter 1987, pp. 1–21.

73. See Philip H. Melanson, "The CIA's Secret Ties to Local Police,"*The Nation*, March 26, 1983.

74. HSCA *Report*, pp. 540–41.

75. HSCA, vol. 6, p. 428.

76. McKnight provided key documents to the author. He described the Bu-

reau's file on McCullough as containing "over a thousand documents." Letter to the author, April 16, 1985.

77. April 3, 1968 FBI memo (157–1092–232) William H. Lawrence to SAC, "Cominfil of SNCC," pp. 1–2. This memo bears the file number of the file on "Memphis Sanitation Workers Strike." The main body of the McCullough File resides within the file entitled "Invaders," (157–8490).

78. Ibid.,p. 4.

79. HSCA, vol. 6, pp. 546–47.

80. April 3, 1968 FBI memo (157–1092–232), p. 2.

81. HSCA, vol. 6, p. 442.

82. Ibid., pp. 442–43.

83. Ibid., p. 433.

84. Orange: HSCA *Report* p. 366; Garrow, *The FBI and Martin Luther King, Jr.*, p. 198. Bevel: HSCA *Report*, p. 366.

85. HSCA, vol. 6, pp. 433–44, 442.

86. Ibid., p. 441.

87. FBI document 157–1092–326, William H. Lawrence to SAC, "Sanitation Workers Strike Memphis Tennessee," 7 pp., at p. 2 (Orange) and p. 7 (Bevel).

88. HSCA, vol. 6, p. 442.

89. Author's interview with Samuel Kyles; Kyles FBI statement, April 26, 1968 (44–1987 Sub–D–91), p. 3.

90. While standing on the balcony, King specifically invited Jesse Jackson, of SCLC's Chicago office, to come along to dinner (HSCA *Report*, p. 366). King had told Ralph Abernathy that "all" the staff were invited to the dinner (HSCA *Report*, p. 365).

91. HSCA, vol. 6, p. 434.

92. HSCA, vol. 6, p. 418.

93. HSCA *Report*, p. 364; author's interview with Kyles.

94. HSCA, vol. 4, pp. 246–52.

CHAPTER 9

1. For a description of the crime scene, see HSCA, vol. 13, pp. 32–34.

2. HSCA *Report*, pp. 374–75.

3. Ibid, p. 375.

4. Autopsy: HSCA, vol. 13, pp. 4–5, 16–19, 30–31.

5. HSCA, vol. 13, p. 4.

6. Ibid., p. 17.

7. Ibid., p. 30.

8. HSCA *Report*, p. 374; HSCA, vol. 13, p. 31.

9. Solomon Jones interview, FBI, April 13, 1968 (ME44–1987 Sub D–76), 4 pp., at p. 3.

10 HSCA *Report*, p. 373.

11. HSCA, vol. 13, p. 4; Bessie Brewer: FBI interview, April 13, 1968 (44–1987–Sub–D–74), 7 pp.

12. Landers: FBI interview, May 15, 1968 (ME–1987 Sub D–77), 2 pp.

13. Howard Teten: FBI interview, April 4, 1968 (44–1987 Sub D) [unintelligible], 2 pp. at p. 1.

14. HSCA *Report*, p. 375.

15. Ibid.

16. George W. Loenneke: FBI interview April 15, 1968 (44–1987 Sub D–53), 3 pp. at p. 1.

17. HSCA *Report*, p. 375.

18. HSCA, vol. 13, pp. 4–5.

19. HSCA *Report*, p. 378.

20. Ibid.

21. The following description of the evidence is taken from HSCA *Report*, pp. 386–87.

22. Bessie Brewer: FBI interview April 13, 1968 (44–1987 Sub D–74), 7 pp. at pp. 1–2.

23. HSCA *Report*, p. 376.

24. Ibid., p. 381.

25. Ibid.

26. Ibid., p. 380.

27. Ibid., pp. 380–81.

28. Vernon Dollahite: FBI interview April 13, 1968 (44–1987 Sub D–75).

29. HSCA *Report*, p. 29.

30. Ibid, pp. 388–89.

31. Ibid., pp. 393–94.

32. Ibid., p. 392.

33. Ibid.

34. Ibid.

35. Ibid., pp. 392–93.

36. HSCA, vol. 13, pp. 145–51.

37. Ibid., pp. 149–50.

38. Ibid., p. 151.

39. Ibid.

40. HSCA *Report*, p. 380.

41. Bessie Brewer: FBI interview April 13, 1968 (44–1987 Sub D–74) 7 pp. at p. 2.

42. Ibid., pp. 2–3.

43. Ibid., p. 2.

44. Ibid.

45. Even HSCA admitted this point (pp. 386–87 of its final report), but not when it described the renting of the room as part of the crime scene evidence (p. 380).

46. HSCA *Report*, p. 387.

47. Brewer: FBI interview April 8, 1968 (44–1987 Sub D [unintelligible], 4 pp. at p. 1.

48. McCullough: FBI interview April 12, 1968 (44–1987 Sub D–3) 7 pp. at p. 3.

49. Laue: FBI interview April 4, 1968 (44–1987–537A).

50. Wright: FBI interview April 5, 1968 (ME–44–1987–Sub D–50) 3 pp. at p. 1.

51. Reeves: FBI interview April, 1968 (DC 44–1989–Sub D–20), 2 pp.

52. Bessie Brewer: FBI interview April 8, 1968 (14–1987–Sub D) 3 pp. at p. 2; Frank Brewer FBI interview April 7, 1968 (14–1987–Sub D–7), 2 pp.

53. Grace Stephens: FBI interview April 6, 1968 (14–1987–Sub–D4) 1 p.

54. HSCA *Report*, pp. 402–4.

55. Ibid., p. 408.

56. Anshutz: FBI interview April 7, 1968 (14–1987–Sub D11), 2 pp.; FBI interview April 9, 1968 (document no. unintelligible), 2 pp.

57. Charles Stephens, FBI interviews: April 10, 1968 (44–1987–Sub D78), 5 pp; April 7, 1968 (44–1987–Sub D–16), 2 pp.

58. Stephens, FBI April 7, 1968, p. 2.

59. Stephens, FBI April 10, 1968.

60. Ibid.

61. Stephens, two FBI statements of April 7 and 10, 1968.

62. Anshutz, FBI interview April 17, 1968, p. 1.

63. Anshutz, ibid.; Stephens: FBI interview April 10, 1968.

64. HSCA *Report*, p. 375.

65. Ibid., p. 376.

66. Ibid.

67. Stephens's affidavit is partially reprinted in Harold Weisberg, *Frame-Up* (New York: Outerbridge and Dienstfrey, 1971), appendix.

68. Tom Jones, "Man Claims He's Entitled to Rewards in King Slaying," *Memphis Press Scimitar*, Jan. 21, 1974, p. 15; James Cole, "Witness Says He Hoped to Collect King Reward," *Memphis Commercial Appeal*, Jan. 22, 1974, p. 15.

69. Ibid.

70. Jones, "Man Claims He's Entitled to Rewards."

71. Stephens affidavit in Weisberg, *Frame-Up*.

72. Stephens FBI interview of April 10, 1968, p. 4.

73. HSCA, vol. 13, p. 287.

74. This biographical data comes from Weisberg, *Frame-Up*, p. 156.

75. HSCA, vol. 13, pp. 285–87, at p. 286.

76. Ibid.

77. Ibid.

78. Ibid.

79. HSCA *Report*, p. 381.

80. HSCA, vol. 13, p. 113.

81. Ibid.

82. Ibid., pp. 114–15.

83. Ibid., p. 117.

84. HSCA *Report*, p. 381.

85. HSCA, vol. 13, p. 114.

86. Ibid.

87. Weisberg, *Frame-Up*, p. 209.

88. HSCA, vol. 13, p. 112.

89. Ibid.

90. Ibid.

91. Ibid.

92. HSCA *Report*, pp. 382–83.

93. HSCA, vol. 13, p. 63.

94. HSCA Report, p. 382.

95. HSCA, vol. 13, p. 64.

96. Ibid., p. 67.

97. Ibid., pp. 66–67.

98. Ibid.

99. Ibid.,p. 67.

100. Ibid., p. 65.

101. Weisberg. *Frame-up*, p. 173.

102. Charles E. O'Hara, *Fundamentals of Criminal Investigation* (Springfield, Mass.: Thomas Pub. Co., 1980), pp. 754–56; see also David S. Lifton, *Best Evidence* (New York: Macmillan, 1980), pp. 556–57; Michael Kurtz, *Crime of the Century* (Knoxville: Univ. of Tennessee Press, 1982), pp. 104–5. Kurtz and Lifton discuss neutron activation tests relating to similar problems of bullet identification in assassination of President Kennedy.

103. HSCA, vol. 13, p. 56.

104. Ibid., p. 59.

105. Kurtz, *Crime of the Century*, pp. 104–6.

CHAPTER 10

1. Stephens: FBI interview April 10, 1968 (ME 44–1987 Sub D–70), pp. 2–3; Anschutz: FBI interview April 5, 1968 (ME 44–1987 Sub D–11), p. 1.

2. Harold Weisberg, *Frame-Up* (New York: Outerbridge and Dienstfrey, 1971), p. 168.

3. HSCA *Report*, p. 387.

4. Carpenter: FBI interview April 15, 1968 (ME 44–1987 Sub D–64), 3 pp.

5. HSCA, vol. 13, p. 35.

6. Abernathy: FBI interview April 8, 1968 (ME 44–1987 Sub D–61), 2 pp. at p. 1; Solomon Jones, FBI interview April 13, 1968 (ME 44–1987 Sub D–76), 4 pp. at p. 2; David J. Garrow, *Bearing the Cross* (New York: William Morrow, 1986), pp. 622–23.

7. Jones FBI interview, p. 2.

8. See FBI interview of Samuel Kyles, April 26, 1968 (ME 44–1987 Sub D–91) 7 pp., at p. 4. Kyles had already started walking toward the stairs and King was going with him.

9. HSCA *Report*, pp. 366–67.

10. Kyles FBI interview, p. 3.

11. Eskridge: FBI interview April 8, 1968, (ME 44–1987 Sub D–65) p. 1.

12. Carpenter: FBI interview, p. 1.

13. Ghormley: FBI interview April 16, 1968, (ME 44–1987 Sub D–56), 3 pp.

14. Ibid., p. 3.

15. Finley: FBI interview April 10, 1968 (ME 44–1987 Sub D [illegible]), p. 1.

16. Wright: FBI interview April 15, 1968 (ME 44–1987 Sub D–581), 3 pp. at p. 2.

17. Dollahite: FBI interview April 13, 1968 (ME 44–1987 Sub D–75), 4 pp. at p. 1.

18. Martin: FBI interview April 7, 1968 (ME 44–1987 Sub D–20), 2 pp. at p. 1.

19. HSCA *Report*, p. 560.

20. Ibid., p. 381.

21. Finley FBI interview.

22. Graham: FBI interview April 10, 1968 (ME 44–1987 Sub D [illegible]), 3 pp.

23. HSCA *Report*, p. 381.

24. Canipe: FBI interview April 10, 1968 (ME 44–1987 Sub D–6), 4 pp. at p. 1.

25. Ghormley FBI interview, p. 2.

26. Canipe FBI interview, pp. 3–4.

27. HSCA *Report*, p. 81.

28. Ibid.,p. 429.

29. Ibid., pp. 429–30.

30. Gross: FBI interview April 15, 1968 (ME 44–1987 Sub D–51), 4 pp. at p. 4.

31. HSCA *Report*, p. 560.

32. Wright, FBI interview April 15, 1968 (ME 44–1987 Sub D–50), 3 pp. at p. 1.

33. Telephone interview with George W. Loenneke, May 18, 1985.

34. Graham FBI interview, p. 2.

35. Anschutz FBI interview April 7, 1968, p. 1.

36. Weisberg, *Frame-Up*, p. 181.

37. Ibid., p. 183.

38. HSCA, vol. 4, p. 284.

39. HSCA *Report*, p. 561.

40. Weisberg, *Frame-Up*, p. 181.

41. Jowers: FBI interview April 7, 1968 (ME 44–1987 Sub D–92), 2 pp. at p. 1.

42. Weisberg, *Frame-Up*, p. 184; " 'Sing It Real Pretty' Was Last Request of Civil Rights Leader," *Memphis Commercial Appeal*, April 6, 1968, p. 1.

43. Cupples: FBI interview April 15, 1968 (ME 44–1987 Sub D–93), 2 pp. at p. 1.

44. Reed: FBI interview May 15, 1968 (ME 44–1987 Sub D–102), 2 pp.Hendrix: FBI interview April 25, 1968 (Sub D–103), 2 pp.

45. Parker: FBI interview April 15, 1968 (ME 44–1968 Sub D–54), 2 pp.

46. Copeland: FBI interview April 17, 1968 (ME 44–1987 Sub D–14), 1 p.

47. Thompson: FBI interview April 17, 1968 (ME 44–1987 Sub D–15), 1 p.

48. Ibid.

49. April 11, 1968 article in *Memphis Commercial Appeal*, quoted in Weisberg, *Frame-Up*, p. 182.

50. Copeland FBI interview.

51. Carpenter FBI interview, p. 1.

52. Reed FBI interview, p. 2; Hendrix FBI interview, p. 1.

53. Reed FBI interview, p. 2.

54. Ibid.

55. Jowers FBI interview, pp. 1–2.

56. Ibid., p. 1.

57. Wynne: FBI interview April 10, 1968 (ME 44–1987 Sub D–69), 2 pp.

58. Ibid., pp. 1–2.

59. FBI interview April 10, 1968 (ME 44–1987 Sub D–113), 8 pp.

60. Ibid., p. 2.

61. Ibid., p. 2.

62. Ibid., pp. 3–4.

63. Ibid., p. 8.

64. FBI memo June 24, 1968 (44–1987 Sub–234), 1 p.

65. FBI document (44–1987 Sub B–69C), memo from Agent Franklin L. Johnson, April 10, 1968, Special Agent in Charge (SAC) Memphis, 2 pp.

66. Ibid., p. 1.

67. Ibid.

68. Ibid., p. 2.

69. Andrews FBI interview, p. 5.

70. Telephone interviews with Mrs. Ellen Andrews, June 5, 1985, and July 6, 1985.

71. HSCA *Report*, p. 369.

72. James W. Clarke, *American Assassins: The Darker Side of Politics* (Princeton, N.J.: Princeton University Press, 1982), pp. 253, 257.

73. Ibid.,p. 243.

74. FBI document 44–1987 Sub D–107, April 24, 1968, 2 pp. The inmate, whose name is deleted, was with Ray in Missouri State Penitentiary for four months in 1962 and, as the FBI described it, "became friendly with him."

75. HSCA *Report*, p. 58.

76. Clarke, *American Assassins*, p. 243.

77. HSCA *Report*, pp. 428–33.

78. FBI document 44–1987 Sub D–1, April 5, 1968, memo written by Agent Orville B. Johnson, 2 pp. at p. 1.

79. Hoover memorandum, June 20, 1968, 7 pp. at page 5, entitled "Memorandum for Messrs. Tolson, DeLoach, Rosen, Bishop."

CHAPTER 11

1. "U.S. Government Killed King: Jackson," *San Francisco Chronicle*, Feb. 10, 1976, p. 5.

2. David J. Garrow, *The FBI and Martin Luther King, Jr.* (New York: Penguin Books, 1981), pp. 22, 24–25, 40–45, 51–53, 57.

3. "Memorandum for the Record," May 11, 1965, CIA Office of Security.

4. Garrow, *The FBI and Martin Luther King, Jr.*, p. 139–44. Garrow's description of Kennedy's role as a CIA source comes from CIA documents and from interviews or "conversations" with Kennedy.

5. "Memorandum for the Record."

6. Ibid.

7. Garrow, *The FBI and Martin Luther King, Jr.*, pp. 143–44.

8. Memorandum for Chief, CIA Security Research Staff, June 9, 1965.

9. Garrow, *The FBI and Martin Luther King, Jr.*, p. 144.

10. "CIA Infiltrated Black Groups Here in the 1960's,"*Washington Post*, March 30, 1978, p. A1.

11. Ibid.

12. Memorandum for [deleted]. Subject: "Martin Luther King, Jr." November 28, 1975.

13. CIA internal memorandum of November 28, 1975, subject: "Martin Luther King, Jr." This memo, which characterizes the substance of the Agency's King File, claims that "one dissemination was made to the FBI on a possible activity of King while in Rome." But the author found a memo concerning King's activities in Chicago (Oct. 5, 1967) which CIA passed on to the FBI.

The CIA's November 28, 1975, memo on its King file concludes: "While there is a large number of documents available which mention King, the vast majority are dated after his death and are in some way related to world reaction to his assassination." Although this is literally true, it downplays the fact that 40 of the 134 pages released to the author involve domestic surveillance of King prior to his death, and they reveal an active interest in King's domestic political activities.

The Agency by no means provided all of the documents that should have been surfaced by my FOIA request. Several documents released to David J. Garrow were not provided to me, even though they pertained directly to King (This was apparent from Garrow's book and was confirmed by Garrow in a conversation with the author). On January 27, 1984, I wrote CIA Information and Privacy Coordinator Larry R. Strawderman and inquired about the discrepancy, citing no fewer than seven specific CIA documents on King which Garrow had received but I had not. In a letter of March 23, 1984, Strawderman responded: "Upon receipt of your recent letter, we immediately queried our system again, but were not able to locate the missing documents." Unable to find the documents "by retrieving the original FOIA cases on which the releases were based," the Agency then initiated what it described as "new documents searches." Seven months later, the CIA's glacial FOIA process succeeded in finding the seven missing documents. In a letter of Oct. 25, 1984, Strawderman's successor, John H. Wright, explained that there had been an error in the CIA's microfilming system.

The extreme deletion of released documents coupled with their conspicuously small quantity (134 pages) in comparison to King's prominence and to CIA concerns about his Communist ties and his opposition to the Vietnam War, would seem to indicate that the actual extent of CIA surveillance of King remains an open question.

14. Philip H. Melanson, "The CIA's Secret Ties to Local Police," *The Nation,* March 26, 1983.

15. Garrow, *The FBI and Martin Luther King, Jr.*, pp. 177–78.

16. Ibid., p. 178.

17. Garrow, *The FBI and Martin Luther King, Jr.*, p. 180.

18. *Life,* April 21, 1967, p. 4.

19. Garrow, *The FBI and Martin Luther King, Jr.*, p. 182.

20. Ibid.

21. A CIA memo dated February 8, 1968, "Memorandum for Chief, Security Research Staff," subject deleted, refers to having obtained a report that King was receiving funds from the "Chicoms" (Chinese communists).

22. This is taken from an FBI transcript of a tape recording of the speech and is not possible to determine whether grammatical errors originated in the speech or the transcription.

23. "Memorandum for the Attorney General," Jan. 2, 1968, subject: "Communists Infiltration of Southern Christian Leadership Conference," 1 p.

24. Dec. 29, 1967, memo on "Communist Infiltration of Southern Christian Leadership Conference," William Sullivan to G. C. Moore, 2 pp. at p. 1.

25. "Memorandum for the Attorney General," April 2, 1968, subject: "Communist Infiltration of Southern Christian Leadership Conference," 2 pp. at p. 2.

26. Lewis Chester, Godfrey Hodgson, and Bruce Page, *An American Melodrama: The Presidential Campaign of 1968* (New York: The Viking Press, 1969), pp. 16–17.

CHAPTER 12

1. "The Gentlemen Killers of the CIA," *Penthouse*, May 1975, p. 53.

2. HSCA *Report*, p. 430.

3. Telephone interview with Peter Dale Scott, June 21, 1984.

4. J. O. O'Leary, "Greatest Manhunt in History," *Readers Digest*, August 1968, pp. 63–69.

5. John Means, "Intensive Manhunt Is Quickly Mounted," *Memphis Commercial Appeal*, April 5, 1968, p. 1.

6. As described in Chapter 2, the Lowmeyer alias is an exception to the pattern in that it is the name of a prison associate of Ray's brothers rather than a Toronto man. Thus it is the only assassination-related alias to fit Ray's previous criminal pattern of selecting as aliases family names or the names of prison associates or criminals. Ray could not possibly have gotten the Galt and Willard aliases himself, but Lowmeyer was surely selected by Ray.

HSCA stated (p. 464, *Report*) that Ray's use of the name of a prison associate of his brother's indicated that one or both brothers gave Ray "the idea for" this alias; and, since Ray did not "stockpile" aliases, this further indicated contact with one or both brothers during the rifle purchase. But the actual name was Lo*h*meyer, not Lo*w*meyer, suggesting that Ray was appropriating the name phonetically, probably from recall. It is not clear why his brothers would encourage him to use an alias that could be linked to them, any more than they would encourage James to call himself "John Larry," his brother's name, or "Raines," their father's original name.

Ray admits that he purchased the rifle but insists that he did so at the direction of Raoul in connection with a gunrunning deal. Perhaps the conspirators who selected the Galt alias and provided it to Ray were hesitant to instruct him to purchase a rifle under that name, for fear of spooking him. Ray may have been instructed to purchase a rifle but left to his own devices, in order not to make him skittish about the real purpose of the Galt alias and of the crime being planned.

Until the FBI finally realized that it was chasing Ray instead of "Galt," the fact that there was a real Harvey Lohmeyer who knew Ray's brothers would have had no relevance to the Bureau's investigation and thus could not have helped to exculpate the real Galt in the eyes of the authorities.

7. Telephone interview with Eric S. Galt, March 26, 1984.

8. Cameron Smith and Loren Lind, "Fat Man Visits Ray, Landlady Recalls," *Toronto Globe and Mail*, June 10, 1968, p. 1.

9. HSCA *Report*, p. 485.

10. CIA document 201–0–832732, April 18, 1968. Most of the substance on page one of this three-page cable from headquarters to stations is deleted.

11. FBI document 44–38861–1448, "urgent" teletype from Kansas City to FBI headquarters. Subject: "MURKIN."

12. Telephone interview with Eric Galt, August 8, 1984.

13. Ibid.

14. "Ray's Alias Was Metro Man,"*Toronto Telegram*, June 8, 1968, p. 4.

15. Homer Bigart, "Galt Alias Taken in Toronto," *Washington Post*, June 13, 1968, p. 1A. The confusion manifested by law enforcement agencies concerning Ray versus Galt is sometimes difficult to imagine when viewing the case from historical retrospect. On the day Ray was finally arrested in London (June 8), CIA headquarters sent a cable to its London field office requesting more information on "James Earl Galt who sought in connection Assassination Dr. Martin Luther King and who arrested London today."

16. Telephone interview with Galt, June 27, 1984.

17. Interview with Galt, Toronto, Sept. 11, 1984.

18. HSCA, vol. 13, p. 123.

19. Ibid., p. 119.

20. Ray's letter to the author, April 9, 1986.

21. "Police Believe Ray Was Headed for Africa When Captured in U.K.," *Toronto Star*, June 11, 1968, p. 1.

22. Ibid.

23. Ibid.

24. Ibid.

25. Ibid.

26. Frank Howett, "Was James Earl Ray Gunman or Decoy?" *Memphis Press Scimitar*, July 15, 1968, p. 1.

27. Ibid.

28. Letter to the author from Cameron Smith, August 13, 1984.

29. Howett, "Was Ray Gunman or Decoy?"

30. Ibid.

31. HSCA, vol. 13: handwriting, pp. 123–24; fingerprint, pp. 116–17.

32. Homer Bigart, "Ray Received Two Mystery Calls in London," *Toronto Globe and Mail*, June 12, 1968, p. 5.

33. Howett, "Was Ray Gunman or Decoy?"

34. This description of CIA assassination plots against Castro is taken from the hearings conducted by Senator Frank Church's Committee in 1975: *Interim Report of the Select Committee to Study Government Operations with Respect to Intelligence*, "Alleged Assassination Plots Involving Foreign Leaders," Washington, D.C.: U.S. Gov. Printing Office.

35. Ibid., pp. 37, 43, 45–48, 182, 260. The account of QJ/WINN's activities against Lamumba is taken from these pages of "Alleged Assassination Plots Involving Foreign Leaders."

36. CIA cable, 1962, quoted by Church Committee.

37. Church Committee Report, p. 47.

38. David C. Martin, *Wilderness of Mirrors* (New York: Ballantine, 1983), p. 217. Harvey's allegedly unauthorized activities during the Cuban missile crisis are described by Robert F. Kennedy in a recorded interview with J. B. Martin, April 30, 1964, transcribed in vol. 3, pp. 22–25, JFK Oral History Program, JFK Library, Boston, Mass.

CHAPTER 13

1. The scar on Ray's forehead is still clearly visible. At least he did not try to pretend that he had no visible scars at all, as he had done during an HSCA interview in which he was questioned about the matching scars.

2. In a post-interview letter to the author (April 9, 1986) Ray appeared to deny using Starvo. "As for Starvo, I never use a middle name, although in the south middle names are used frequently." Ray did not deny using Starvo during my interview or during his HSCA interviews.

3. HSCA, vol. 10, p. 358.

4. HSCA, vol. 9, pp. 284–85.

5. HSCA, vol. 10, pp. 79–80.

6. Conversation with Bernard Fensterwald, Jr., Arlington, Va., July 30, 1984.

7. Letter to the author from Harold Weisberg, October 11, 1984.

CHAPTER 14

1. Jim Hougan, *Spooks: The Haunting of America* (New York: Bantam, 1979).

2. Telephone conversation with Harold Weisberg, Dec. 6, 1984.

3. "Ray's Breakout," *Time*, June 20, 1977, p. 18.

APPENDIX C

1. George Lardner, Jr., "Secrecy Shrouds Assassination Data," *Boston Globe*, May 27, 1981, p. 28.

2. Ibid.

3. Ibid.

4. Ibid.

5. Ibid.

6. ACCESS letter to members, May 31, 1983, written by Director Mark Allen and Legislative Coordination Kevin Walsh.

7. *Echoes of Conspiracy*, vol. 5, no. 4 (Nov. 16, 1983), pp. 1–2. (Paul Hoch, ed., Berkeley, California). Hoch interview with Blakey.

8. Statement of Rep. Robert W. Edgar (Dem. Penn.), April 12, 1983.

9. Hoch, *Echoes of Conspiracy*.

10. Ibid.

Selected Bibliography

BOOKS

Clarke, James W. *American Assassins: The Darker Side of Politics.* Princeton, N.J.: Princeton University Press, 1982.

Crotty, William J., ed. *Assassinations and the Political Order.* New York: Harper & Row, 1971.

Garrow, David J. *Bearing the Cross: Martin Luther King, Jr. and the Southern Christian Leadership Conference.* New York: William Morrow & Co., 1986.

——. *The FBI and Martin Luther King, Jr.* New York: Penguin Books, 1983.

Halpern, Morton et al. *The Lawless State: The Crimes of U.S. Intelligence Agencies.* New York: Penguin Books, 1976.

Hougan, Jim. *Spooks: The Haunting of America—the Private Use of Secret Agents.* New York: Bantam, 1979.

Huie, William Bradford. *He Slew the Dreamer.* New York: Delacorte Press, 1970.

Kirkham, James B. et al. eds. *Assassination and Political Violence.* New York: Bantam, 1970.

Lane, Mark, and Dick Gregory. *Code Name "Zorro": The Murder of Martin Luther King, Jr.* Englewood Cliffs, N.J.: Prentice Hall, 1977.

Marchetti, Victor, and John D. Marks. *The CIA and the Cult of Intelligence.* New York: Dell, 1974.

Martin, David C. *Wilderness of Mirrors.* New York: Ballantine Books, 1983.

McKinley, James. *Assassinations in America.* New York: Harper & Row, 1977.

McMillan, George. *The Making of an Assassin.* Boston: Little, Brown, 1976.

Melanson, Philip H. *The Politics of Protection: The U.S. Secret Service in the Terrorist Age.* New York: Praeger, 1984.

O'Toole, George. *The Private Sector.* New York: W. W. Norton, 1978.

Select Committee on Assassinations, U.S. House of Representatives. *The Final Assassinations Report.* New York: Bantam, 1979.

Summers, Anthony. *Conspiracy.* New York: McGraw-Hill, 1980.

Weisberg, Harold. *Frame-Up*. New York: Outerbridge and Dienstfrey, 1971.
Wise, David. *American Police State—The Government Against the People*. New York: Vintage Books, 1976.

ARTICLES

Bigart, Homer. "Mounties Hunt 'Fat Man' in Ray Case." *New York Times*, June 10, 1968, p. 2.
———."Ray Received Two Mystery Phone Calls in London." *Toronto Globe and Mail*, June 12, 1968, p. 5.
"Cabby: I Picked up 'Fat Man' in King Killer Case." *Toronto Star*, June 12, 1968, p. 1.
"CIA Infiltrated Black Groups Here in the 1960s." *Washington Post*, March 30, 1978, p. A–1.
Donner, Frank. "Why Isn't the Truth Bad Enough?" *Civil Liberties Review*. Jan.–Feb. 1978, pp. 68–72.
Freedman, Lawrence Z."The Assassination Syndrome." *Saturday Evening Post*, July/August 1981, pp. 77–81.
Howett, Frank. "Was James Earl Ray Gunman—Or Was He Decoy?" *Memphis Press Scimitar*, July 15, 1968, p. 1.
Jaynes, Gregory. "Canadians Checking Ray Say He Had 'Help of Some Kind'." *Memphis Commercial Appeal*, June 11, 1968, p. 1.
Just, Ward. " 'Fat Man' Cleared in Ray Case Probe." *Washington Post*, June 14, 1968, p. A-5.
Kilpatrick, James. "5000 Pages of State Evidence Convinced Ray to Plead Guilty." *Memphis Commercial Appeal*, March 16, 1969, p. 1.
Lardner, George, Jr. "Secrecy Shrouds Assassination Data." *Boston Globe*, May 27, 1981, p. 28.
"Life as a Fugitive: Cold Snacks in Locked Room." *Toronto Globe and Mail*, June 11, 1968, p. 3.
McKnight, Gerald D. "Harvest of Hate: The FBI's War Against Black Youth—Domestic Intelligence in Memphis, Tennessee." *South Atlantic Quarterly*, Winter 1987, pp. 1–21.
McRae, Earl. "Who's the Fat Man?" *Toronto Star*, June 10, 1968, p. 1.
Means, John. "Intensive Manhunt is Quickly Mounted." *Memphis Commercial Appeal*, April 5, 1968, p. 1.
Melanson, Philip H. "The CIA's Secret Ties to Local Police." *The Nation*, March 26, 1983.
"Police Believe Ray was Headed for Africa When Captured in U.K." *Toronto Star*, June 11, 1968, p. 1.
"Probe by Justice Concludes James Earl Ray Acted Alone." *Washington Post*, Feb. 2, 1977, p. 3.
"Ray's Breakout."*Time*, June 20, 1977, p. 18.
Smith, Cameron. "Ray's Ties with Toronto May Go Back Some Time." *Toronto Globe and Mail*, June 11, 1968, p. 1.
Smith, Cameron and Loren Lind. "Fat Man Visits Ray, Landlady Recalls." *Toronto Globe and Mail*, June 10, 1968, p. 1.

———. "How Did Ray Get Names of 3 Whose Description Fit Him?" *Toronto Globe and Mail*, June 11, 1968, p. 5.

"Suspect: Police after Two Men Seen with Him." *Toronto Telegram*, June 10, 1968, p. 11.

"U.S. Attorney General Confident King's Murderer Will be Found." *Memphis Press Scimitar*, April 5, 1968, p. 13.

"U.S. Government Killed King: Jackson." *San Francisco Chronicle*, Feb. 10, 1976, p. 5.

Walz, Jay. "Police in Canada Investigate Whether Ray Had Assistance." *New York Times*, June 13, 1968, p. 3.

———. "Real Galt Calm about Publicity Over Ray." *New York Times*, June 13, 1968, p. 28.

———. "3 Whose Names Ray Used Resemble Him." *New York Times*, June 12, 1968, p. 1.

PUBLIC DOCUMENTS

Federal Bureau of Investigation. *MURKIN File* (Martin Luther King, Jr. Assassination Investigation). FBI Reading Room, Washington, D.C. (approximately 50,000 pages).

U.S. Congress, House. *Hearings on the Investigation of the Assassination of Martin Luther King, Jr.*, vols. 1–13. Washington, D.C.: U.S. Govt. Printing Office, 1979.

U.S. Congress, Senate. *Interim Report of the Select Committee to Study Government Operations with Respect to Intelligence*. Washington, D.C.: U.S. Govt. Printing Office, 1975.

U.S. Department of Justice. *Report of the Department of Justice Task Force to Review the FBI Martin Luther King, Jr. Security and Assassination Investigation*. Washington, D.C.: U.S. Dept. of Justice, Jan. 11, 1977.

Index

ABOUT THE AUTHOR

PHILIP H. MELANSON is Professor of Political Science at Southeastern Massachusetts University, where he is chair of the Robert F. Kennedy Assassination Archives.

Dr. Melanson has published widely in the area of political science. His articles and reviews have appeared in the *American Political Science Review, Comparative Political Studies, Political Methodology, Politics and Society, Polity, Public Policy, Transaction/Society*, as well as in *The Nation* and in various newspapers and magazines. He is the author of *Political Science and Political Knowledge, The Politics of Protection: The U.S. Secret Service in the Terrorist Age* (Praeger, 1984), and the editor of *Knowledge, Politics and Public Policy*.

Dr. Melanson holds a B.A., M.A., and Ph.D. from the University of Connecticut.